CAREERS
IN THE ENVIRONMENT

MICHAEL FASULO
PAUL WALKER

SECOND EDITION

VGM Career Horizons
NTC/Contemporary Publishing Group

Library of Congress Cataloging-in-Publication Data

Fasulo, Michael.
    Careers in the environment / Michael Fasulo, Paul Walker. — 2nd
ed.
       p.   cm. — (VGM professional careers series)
    ISBN 0-658-00223-6 — ISBN 0-658-00224-4 (pbk.)
    1. Environmental sciences—Vocational guidance.
    2. Environmental engineering—Vocational guidance. I. Walker, Paul,
1963– II. Title. III. Series.
    GE60.F37   2000
    363.7′0023′73—dc21   99-056366
                                       CIP

Cover photograph copyright © PhotoDisc

Published by VGM Career Horizons
A division of NTC/Contemporary Publishing Group, Inc.
4255 West Touhy Avenue, Lincolnwood (Chicago), Illinois 60712-1975 U.S.A.
International Standard Book Number: 0-658-00223-6 (cloth)
                                           0-658-00224-4 (paper)

00 01 02 03 04 05 HP 19 18 17 16 15 14 13 12 11 10 9 8 7 6 5 4 3 2 1

DEDICATION

This book is dedicated to the loving memory of Michael Fasulo's dad, Mario A. Fasulo, and to our friend Norman Roettgen.

CONTENTS

PART THREE   PLANNING AND DESIGN
Overview. A closer look at planning and design. Projected growth and
employment trends. The planning profession. Planning-related professions.
The design professional. Design-related professions.

PART FOUR   FORESTRY AND OUTDOOR RECREATION
Overview. Introduction. Professions related to forestry and outdoor
recreation. Background and recent history of U.S. conservation work.
Major employers. Projected trends and employment growth. Sources of
further information.

ABOUT THE AUTHORS

Michael Fasulo is a writer, college instructor, and environmental activist. He teaches geography and environmental studies at Truckee Meadows Community College in the Lake Tahoe basin of California. An ardent environmental preservationist, Mike is a volunteer interpretive naturalist and a member of several environmental action organizations. He is also the author of VGM's *Careers for Environmental Types and Others Who Respect the Earth.* Mike earned his Bachelor of Arts degree in Sociology from the University of Wisconsin, Madison, and his Master of Arts degree in Sociology from Pennsylvania State University.

Paul Walker is a principal of Walker Associates in San Francisco, California. His firm specializes in commercial appraisal, asset management, and real estate consulting. Paul has worked with government agencies on several redevelopment projects, assisted in preparing an environmental impact report for a proposed landfill, and worked with nonprofit and government agencies to value natural resources such as old-growth redwood trees. He is an outdoor enthusiast who enjoys camping, rafting, and skiing in the mountains of California. Paul holds a Bachelor of Science degree in Business Administration with a major in Real Estate and Urban Land Economics and a Master of Science degree in Business with a major in Real Estate Appraisal and Investment Analysis from the University of Wisconsin, Madison.

This edition has been revised by Julie Rigby, a writer and editor living in Vermont.

INTRODUCTION

VGM's *Careers in the Environment* was written to provide up-to-date information on scientific and technical careers for people who want to contribute to protecting and restoring the environment. Within these pages you will find descriptions of many scientific, professional, and technical careers in well-established as well as new environmental fields. For each highlighted career we supply information on the type of work performed, typical setting, education requirements, advancement potential, and salary levels. In addition, we provide cross-references to related careers that may better fit with your personal interests. The book includes chapters on tips for finding a job and a comprehensive guide to environmental education. In each part and chapter you will find numerous listings of books and organizations that can give you more detailed information for each job and career area. The appendices include hundreds of additional resource listings. Contact addresses are also provided for hundreds of professional organizations, government agencies, and nonprofit groups to help you collect additional career information and make important career contacts.

OUTLINE OF THE BOOK

Chapter 2 provides detailed information on how to organize your job search, resources for finding a job, a discussion of the major government agencies employing environmentalists, and information about finding an organization or company that meets your career objectives.

Chapter 3 provides an overview of both technical education and college programs; information on how to select a college or technical school or pursue an advanced degree; and sources of financial aid.

The rest of the book is divided into seven parts providing detailed information on the following fields:

Part One—Air and Water Quality Management

Part Two—Energy and Resource Engineering

Part Three—Planning and Design

Part Four—Forestry and Outdoor Recreation

Part Five—Biological and Life Sciences

Part Six—Agricultural and Animal Sciences

Part Seven—Waste Management and Environmental Assessment

OUTLINE OF EACH PART

Introduction to the Field Each of the seven parts begins with a general introduction to the job category and discusses important environmental issues being addressed in the field. The *Overview* presents employment statistics, graphs of employment by job sector and of projected growth, and a bar graph of salary ranges.

This is followed by discussions of the history of the field, major employers, projected growth and trends, issues of concern to the field, and sources of further information.

Job Descriptions Following the introduction you will find chapters with job descriptions for the field. Each chapter describes the type of work performed, working conditions, responsibilities, and advancement potential. Each chapter also provides the following:

Educational Requirements describes the level of education needed for each job and the various educational programs available. Two-year associate degrees, college and university degrees, and special training programs are discussed in detail.

Special Certifications describes mandatory state and federal licenses as well as voluntary certificates provided by professional and trade associations.

Setting provides a description of the work environment, the locations of major employers, safety issues, and typical work hours, schedules, and special benefits.

Employment Statistics and Major Employers provides a detailed description of major employers, government agencies, and projected employment demand.

Salary Statistics includes data on starting salaries and average salaries, broken down by levels of education. In addition, comparisons of salaries for the public, private, and nonprofit sectors and average salaries for college and university faculty are provided.

Sources of Additional Information provides the addresses of professional organizations and publications that can assist you in choosing a career and finding a job.

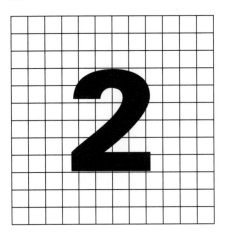

TIPS FOR JOB HUNTERS

Do you want to find a career that will provide you with challenges and opportunities in the twenty-first century? Are you committed to finding a position working in one environment? If you answered *yes* to both of these questions, then this is the book for you. It contains a wealth of information on careers in the public and private sectors.

For most jobs discussed in this book, there are career opportunities in all levels of government—federal, state, and local—as well as in the private sector. While job functions, pay, benefits, and other characteristics of the jobs themselves may be similar among the public and private sectors, the methods of securing employment differ greatly. In the next few pages we will give you a thumbnail sketch of how to approach employment opportunities in government and the private sector. Several federal departments, agencies, and commissions employ sizable environmental science workforces, and these are discussed in detail. In the private sector, perhaps the most important aspect of the job hunt is knowing how to leave a good impression of yourself with potential employers. Some strategies will be discussed for resumes, application forms, cover letters, and interviews. There are numerous other resources and books that are very useful for finding and landing your ideal job. Some of the most popular and best works are included in the *Sources of Further Information* sections of this chapter. This book and the numerous additional sources listed will provide you with powerful tools to use in your job search.

GOVERNMENT EMPLOYMENT OPPORTUNITIES

The federal, state, and local governments are major employers of environmental scientists and technicians. The process of landing a job in government is very different from that in the private sector. In the public sector scores of standardized forms must be completed and volumes of hiring guidelines must be followed before just one person can be hired. In the private sector the process is much less bureaucratic, and hiring decisions are often made on an individual basis, such as in response to a well-placed recommendation, a successful interview, or an immediate job need. Next, the process of securing a federal job will be outlined. While the individual state and local government agencies may have slightly different hiring practices, the federal model is most often followed.

Applying for a Government Job

By federal law anyone applying for a nonpolitical civil servant position in the federal government must submit standard form (SF) 171 for employment. This is a long application form, spanning five pages, that requires you to submit your employment history for the past ten years. Because each agency receives thousands of these forms annually, it is beneficial for you to somehow make your application stand out from the others. Along with each job description or announcement number, in the government's terms, is a quality ranking factor (QRF). This is a short list of qualifications or areas of specific substantive knowledge that the agency is seeking in an applicant. Mary Louise Uhlig, assistant administrator for Pesticides and Toxic Substances in the Environmental Protection Agency, suggests that applicants write a short paragraph for each QRF point in which they describe their knowledge and/or experience. This should then be used as a cover letter to the SF 171. This method will not only make your application stand out from the rest, but also provide a more specific profile of your qualifications and, more importantly, an edge over other equally qualified applicants.

Each state and local government agency has its own standard application form. These forms are no doubt easier to complete than the SF 171. The same cover letter strategy presented is suggested for use with other levels of government because they too receive a large number of applications per year.

Pay and Job Benefits for Government Workers

Government employees generally earn lower wages than their counterparts in private industry, but they usually receive better benefits, like vacation time, medical plans, flexible work hours, and greater job security. Federal employees receive the highest average pay and are followed, in order, by state, county, and local civil servants. All levels of government have strict hiring and salary regulations. While you will rarely be in a position to negotiate salary or job responsibilities, you can be confident that you'll be treated fairly and equally. The old anecdote "It's not what you know but who you know" is much more applicable in the private sector.

In the federal government, the pay schedule or General Schedule (GS) is divided into fifteen pay steps. Within each GS step, there are ten pay levels. The actual pay difference between the lowest and highest levels within each GS step differs by about 30 percent. The following was the GS pay schedule (steps 5 through 11) as of January 1999:

U.S. Federal Government General Schedule

Step	Lowest Pay	Highest Pay
GS-5	$20,588	$26,762
GS-6	$22,948	$29,833
GS-7	$25,501	$33,151
GS-8	$28,242	$36,711
GS-9	$31,195	$40,555
GS-10	$34,353	$44,658
GS-11	$37,744	$49,066

The starting level of pay depends on an applicant's level of education and relative professional experience. In general, you can expect to start at the lowest level of each GS pay step. With a high school or equivalent diploma, you can expect to receive GS-5 wages. A bachelor's degree will earn you a GS-7 rating, while a master's degree will secure you a GS-9 rate. Those who have gone the extra mile and have earned a Ph.D. will be rewarded with the GS-11 pay rate. In order to jump up one full GS step, you first have to go through a complete yearly performance evaluation. Periodic pay raises within each GS step are usually a routine matter. State hiring practices and salaries are structured similarly.

ENVIRONMENTAL SCIENCE JOBS IN FEDERAL AGENCIES

The U.S. Department of Agriculture (USDA)

The USDA houses a large number of services that focus on environmental activities. The USDA has more than 120,000 employees, which makes it the largest single employer of environmental professionals in the federal government. Its major functions include agricultural research, financial and technical support to farmers, and management of the national forest system. Within the USDA are four services that hire a large number of conservation scientists. These are the Forest Service, Agricultural Research Service, Extension Service, and Soil Conservation Service.

Employment inquiries for all of the following services can be made to

> Staffing and Personnel Information Systems Staff
> Office of Personnel
> 14th and Independence Ave.
> U.S. Department of Agriculture
> Washington, DC 20250

The Forest Service. The Forest Service manages 144 million acres of public land, mostly in 156 national forests in forty-four states, the Virgin Islands, and Puerto Rico, and employs thirty thousand civil servants. A guiding principle of the service is its formula for mixed land use between economic and recreational interests. The service has been criticized, especially in the West, for inadequately managing the clear-cutting of timber by logging companies. Recently the service adopted an innovative program for tree harvesting that focuses on maintaining species biodiversity. The ongoing Spotted Owl controversy in the Northwest has ensured that the Forest Service will be at the center of the battle between environmentalists and lumber interests for quite some time.

The Forest Service employs a wide range of career-minded environmentalists, including biologists, foresters, ecologists, soil scientists, forest rangers, range managers, and planners. The service also employs a number of seasonal summer workers and has a limited number of paid intern programs in the Job Corps and the Senior Community Service Employment Program.

The Agricultural Research Service. This is the research branch of the USDA. Some of its recent activities are research on plant and animal production and protection; tackling problems in the distribution of farm products; human nutritional studies; and air, water, and soil conservation practices. The Agricultural Research Service has more than eight thousand employees, and a large number of these people hold advanced degrees in the agricultural and biological sciences. Most of the service's activities are conducted in cooperation with state and local agencies. A large share of its research is conducted at state and private universities and at field experimental stations.

The Extension Service. This service is the educational arm of the USDA and works with state and local partners to form the national Cooperative Extension System. The Extension Service maintains a small staff in Washington, D.C., that provides leadership in developing educational programs for rural American farmers. In addition, state and local cooperative members hire a number of professionals to administer these programs. The focus is on providing scientific knowledge to improve the quality and yields of rural farms. Current Extension Service concerns include sustainable agriculture, the revival of small terms, food safety and quality, and waste management.

The Extension Service hires people with backgrounds in the agricultural sciences—agronomy, biology and animal sciences; agricultural economics; the food sciences; and natural resources. Most Extension Service professionals have a master's or bachelor's degree with some substantive training and are hired through the individual state land grant universities (each state has at least one).

The Extension Service publishes a booklet entitled *Commitment to Change* that lists addresses for all state and U.S. territory land grant universities. To get a free copy of this brochure, write to

> USDA Extension Service
> 14th and Independence Ave.
> Washington, DC 20250-0900

The Soil Conservation Service (SCS). The SCS is responsible for developing and carrying out a national soil and water conservation program in cooperation with landowners, land users and developers, community planning agencies, regional resource groups, and other federal, state, and local government agencies.

The SCS oversees about three thousand conservation districts nationwide, which cover more than two billion acres in all fifty states, Guam, Puerto Rico, and the Virgin Islands. Assistance includes providing soil maps and other resource data and suggesting ecologically sensitive alternatives to farming, pesticide treatment, and land development.

One of the SCS's most important functions is watershed planning and flood protection. This program is intended to curtail the erosion of topsoil in multiple-use areas. In particular, the Great Plains Conservation Program gives farmers in the nation's breadbasket technical and financial assistance with agricultural practices. The SCS works closely with the Agricultural Stabilization and Conservation Service, which administers various volunteer land-use programs to protect, expand, and conserve farmland, wetlands, and forests.

The SCS employs a large number of professionals with degrees in soil science, agronomy, hydrology, agricultural science, fish and wildlife biology, geology, chemistry, and ecology. For further information contact

> Public Information Division
> Natural Resources Conservation Service
> Department of Agriculture
> P.O. Box 2890
> Washington, DC 20013

The Department of the Interior

The Department of the Interior has the most far-reaching jurisdiction over national environmental issues, and its responsibilities include the protection and management of more than 549 million acres of public land—about 28 percent of the land area in the United States—the protection and preservation of wildlife, the management and conservation of wetlands, and the enforcement of federal surface mining regulations. The Department of the Interior employs about 120,000 people. The department has always been at the center of the battle between conservation and development, and it has historically sided with the latter. In recent years, however, the department has softened its bond with industry and is tending to side more with mainstream environmentalists.

The National Park Service. This service runs the nation's 361 national parks, historic sites, monuments, and recreation areas and employs more than thirteen thousand full-time environmental professionals and workers. In addition, it hires a large number of summer workers. Environmental professionals from a wide variety of backgrounds work to formulate and administer Park Service policies, maintain park lands, and educate the public. Backgrounds in forestry, business administration, geography, parks and recreation, ecology, and biology are well represented in this service. Park rangers, who function as conservation specialists, environmental educators, and law enforcement officials, play an important role in the service. There are also many openings for summer seasonal employment. Applications for seasonal employment must be received between September 1 and January 15.

For more employment information, contact

Division of Personnel Management
Department of the Interior
Interior Bldg.
1849 C St. NW
Washington, DC 20240

The U.S. Fish and Wildlife Service. This service is responsible for the management of more than 500 national wildlife refuges, encompassing more than ninety million acres of lands and waters. In addition, the National Wildlife Refuge System provides resting and feeding areas for waterfowl migrating along the four major "flyways." The jurisdiction of the service also includes areas in the National Park system that are reserved for hunting and fishing. Its mission is to "preserve and enhance fish and wildlife and their habitats for the continuing benefit of the American people." Other responsibilities include the enforcement of wildlife laws, surveillance of pesticides, and listing of endangered species. The service employs professionals with specific training in fields like fish and wildlife biology, wildlife management, limnology, ornithology, toxicology, and taxonomy as well as engineers and chemists.

Employment inquiries should be made to

Division of Personnel Management
U.S. Fish and Wildlife Service
Department of the Interior
1849 C St. NW
Room 3012
Washington, DC 20240

The U.S. Geological Survey (USGS). The USGS was established in 1879 to provide for "the classification of public lands and the examination of geological structure, mineral resources, and products of the national domain." Its original project was to map the entire nation and make this information available to the public. Its present concerns are investigating natural hazards like earthquakes, volcanoes, landslides, floods, and droughts and examining the nation's mineral and water resources.

In the summer of 1993, Secretary of the Interior Bruce Babbit proposed a mapping of the nation's ecosystems akin to the highly detailed topographic mapping of the country by the U.S. Geological Survey. This is a long-term project that aims to provide a greater understanding of natural biological systems and evaluate the impact that humans have when manipulating these systems through logging, development, or habitat restoration. The underlying assumption of this project is that traditional methods of natural resource management may need to be changed, and the USGS hopes to be the innovator in this area.

The USGS is one of the government's most productive services in terms of the number of scientific studies that it publishes. Employees include geographers, cartographers, geologists, meteorologists, ecologists, soil scientists, and engineers. All employment inquiries can be made to

U.S. Geological Survey
Recruitment and Placement
12201 Sunrise Valley Dr.
Reston, VA 22092

The Bureau of Land Management (BLM). The BLM oversees 270 million acres of public land, which makes it the single largest federal manager of public property. Most of this land is public grazing land located in the western states and Alaska. While the BLM manages a vast expanse of land, it employs only nine thousand workers. Its central responsibility is to manage energy and mineral exploration by private companies and oversee livestock grazing on public lands. The bureau maintains a policy of multiple-use and sustainable yield practices for its three principal interests: forestry, mining, and recreation. Its "coziness" with industry and particularly with Western ranchers has earned it the reputation of being prodevelopment and quite unsympathetic to environmental concerns. However, Secretary of the Interior Bruce Babbit is making sweeping changes in the agency that will restore it as a force for sensible land stewardship. The BLM primarily recruits people with backgrounds in civil engineering, mineral and petroleum engineering, range management, chemistry, cartography, and biology.

The BLM publishes a booklet entitled *Career Opportunities in the BLM.* Questions about employment should be directed to

Personnel Officer
Bureau of Land Management
Department of the Interior
1849 C St. NW
Washington, DC 20240

The Bureau of Reclamation. These folks are considered the "busy beavers" of the federal government because they have overseen the construction of most major dams in the West. In addition, the bureau provides water to towns, farms, and industry; oversees the generation of hydroelectric power; and provides river regulation and water control measures. The administration of water rights is no small chore because the semiarid West has grown tremendously in population and in acres used for farming and livestock in the last twenty years. The bureau has had a stormy relationship with environmental groups and has fought some historic battles with John Muir and David Brower of the Sierra Club over the building of dams like Hetch Hetchy and Hoover and the proposed dam at the head of the Grand Canyon.

The bureau primarily hires people with degrees in civil and mechanical engineering, geology, hydrology, and the soil sciences. Employment inquiries should be directed to

Personnel Office
Engineering and Research Center
P.O. Box 25007
Denver, CO 80225
Attn: D-7750

The Environmental Protection Agency (EPA)

The EPA was created in 1970 as an independent body to consolidate the environmental activities of five executive departments and various other agencies. Its basic purpose is to carry out federal laws to protect the environment, especially air and water. The EPA is responsible for the enforcement of most federal environmental laws, which gives it a full agenda. The EPA has grown tremendously since its inception, and it now has seventeen thousand employees and a budget of more than $6 billion. There are 5,700 people working at the EPA's headquarters in Washington, D.C., which serves as its administrative center, and there are an additional 11,000 environmental professionals employed at the EPA's ten regional offices in Boston, New York, Philadelphia, Atlanta, Chicago, Dallas, Kansas City, Denver, San Francisco, and Seattle. The regional offices are responsible for carrying out and enforcing all federal environmental law and regulations. The regional personnel work directly with state and local agencies, industry, environmental organizations, and private citizens.

The EPA is organized into nine divisions; each deals with specific environmental areas. These programs are administration and resource management, enforcement and compliance, policy planning and evaluation, air and radiation, water, pesticides and toxic substances, solid waste and emergency response, international activities, and research and development. Global concerns like ozone depletion, global warming, and sustainable development are becoming a top priority of the EPA. There are twenty-five EPA scientific research facilities located throughout the nation.

The EPA hires about one thousand new employees annually. Most of these openings are at entry-level positions (GS 5, 7, and 9). A little more than half of all new employees have training in the environmental sciences. The most frequently advertised job opening is for environmental engineers. The majority of the remaining job openings are for environmental protection specialists, who often have backgrounds in the conservation sciences.

Other Federal Agencies with Environmental Regulatory Responsibilities

Some agencies and commissions share environmental regulatory responsibilities in areas of transportation, health, and commerce. In the Department of Transportation there are environmental jobs in the Federal Aviation Administration, the Federal Highway Administration, the Materials Transportation Bureau, and the

National Transportation Safety Board. There are also environmental jobs in the following commissions: Consumer Product Safety Board, Federal Energy Regulatory Commission, Federal Maritime Commission, National Bureau of Standards, and Federal Trade Commission.

SOURCES OF FURTHER INFORMATION ON JOB HUNTING

The Book of U.S. Government Jobs (1995), by Dennis V. Damp and Michelle Marie, published by Eden Jack Gardener Catalog.

Careers for Environmentalists and Others Who Respect the Earth (1993), by Michael Fasulo and Jane Kinney, published by VGM Career Horizons, NTC/Contemporary Publishing Group. Included is an excellent strategy called "Navigating the Federal Job Maze" for landing a government job and a description and diagram of all federal environmental activities.

Careers for Nature Lovers and Other Outdoor Types (1993), by Louise Miller, published by VGM Career Horizons, NTC/Contemporary Publishing Group. Included are chapters on careers in the biological sciences, agricultural sciences, and forestry and resource management.

Conservation Directory (annual), by the National Wildlife Federation. Included is a listing of all federal agencies, committees, and departments that have an environmental focus. To order, write to

> National Wildlife Federation
> 8925 Leesburg Pike
> Vienna, VA 22184-0001

Federal Jobs: The Ultimate Guide (1997), by Dana Morgan, published by IDG Books Worldwide.

Career Profiles in Forestry, Conservation, Ecology, and Environmental Management, published and distributed free by the U.S. Department of Agriculture. To order, write to

> USDA
> P.O. Box 2417
> Washington, DC 20013

RESUMES, APPLICATION FORMS, COVER LETTERS, AND INTERVIEWS

Employers look for people with the proper qualifications for a given job. To learn who these people are, they request resumes and they use application forms, written tests, performance medical examinations, and interviews. You can use each of these different evaluation procedures to your advantage.

Creating Effective Resumes and Application Forms

Resumes and application forms are two ways to achieve the same goal: to give the employer written evidence of your qualifications. When creating a resume or completing an application form, you need two different kinds of information: facts about yourself and facts about the job you want. With this information in hand, you can present the facts about yourself in terms of the job. You have more freedom with a resume—you can put your best points first and avoid blanks. But even on application forms you can describe your qualifications in terms of a job's duties.

Know Yourself. Begin by assembling information about yourself. Some items, including the following, appear on virtually every resume or application form:

- Current address and phone number. If you are rarely at home during business hours, try to give the phone number of a friend or relative who will take messages for you.

- Job sought or career goal.

- Experience (paid and volunteer). Include date of employment, name and full address of the employer, job title, starting and finishing salary, and reason for leaving (moving, returning to school, and seeking a better position are among the readily accepted reasons).

- Education. Include the school's name, the city in which it is located, the years you attended it, the diploma or certificate you earned, and the course of studies you pursued.

- Other qualifications. Include hobbies, organizations you belong to, honors you have received, and leadership positions you have held.

- Office machines, tools, equipment you have used and skills that you possess.

Other information, such as your Social Security number is often requested on application forms but is rarely presented on resumes. Application forms might also ask for a record of past addresses and for information that you would rather not reveal, such as a record of convictions. If asked for such information, you must be honest. Honesty does not, however, require that you reveal disabilities that do not affect your overall qualifications for a job.

Know the Job. Next, gather specific information about the job you are applying for. You need to know the pay range (so you can make the employer's top your bottom), education and experience usually required, and hours and shifts usually worked. Most importantly, you need to know the job duties (so that you can describe your experience in terms of those duties). Study the job description. Some job announcements, especially those issued by government, even have checklists that assign a numerical weight to different qualifications so that you can be certain which is the most important; such announcements will give you an idea of what employers look for even if you are not applying for a government job. If the announcement or ad is vague, call the employer to learn what is sought. Once you have the information you need, you can prepare a resume. You may need to prepare more than one master resume if you are going to look for different kinds of jobs. Otherwise, your resume will not fit each job you seek.

Two Kinds of Resumes. The way you arrange your resume depends on how well your experience seems to have prepared you for the position you want. You can either describe your most recent job first and work backward (reverse chronology) or group similar skills together. No matter which format you use, the following advice applies generally:

- Use specifics. A vague description of your duties will make only a vague impression.

- Identify accomplishments. If you headed a project improved productivity, reduced costs, increased membership, or achieved some other goal, say so.

- Type your resume, using a standard typeface. (Printed resumes are becoming more common, but employers do not indicate a preference for them.)

- Keep the length down to two pages at the most.

- Remember your mother's advice not to say anything if you cannot say something nice. Leave all embarrassing or negative information off the resume but be ready to deal with it in a positive fashion at the interview.

- Proofread the master copy carefully.

- Have someone else proofread the master copy carefully.

- Have a third person proofread the master copy carefully.

- Use the best-quality photocopying machine and good white or off-white paper.

The following information appears on almost every resume:

- Name.

- Phone number at which you can be reached or receive messages.

- Address.

- Job or career sought.

- References. Often just a statement that references are available suffices. If your references are likely to be known by the person who reads the resume, however, their names are worth listing.

- Experience.

- Education.

- Special talents.

- Personal information such as height, weight, marital status, and physical condition. Although this information appears on virtually every sample resume I have ever seen, it is not important according to recruiters. In fact, employers are prohibited by law from asking for some of it. If some of this information is directly job related—the height and weight of a bouncer is important to a disco owner, for example—list it. Otherwise, save space and put in more information about your skills.

Reverse chronology is the easiest method to use. It is also the least effective because it makes when you did something more important than what you can do. It is an especially poor format if you have gaps in your work history, if the job you seek is very different from the job you currently hold, or if you are just entering the job market. About the only time you would want to use such a resume is when you have progressed up a clearly defined career ladder and want to move up another rung.

Resumes that are not chronological may be called *functional, analytical, skill oriented, creative,* or some other name. All of these names stress ability. The advantage of this type of resume to a potential employer—and, therefore, to your job campaign—should be obvious. The employer can see immediately how you will fit the job. This format also offers advantages to many job hunters because it camouflages gaps in paid employment and avoids giving prominence to irrelevant jobs.

You begin writing a functional resume by determining the skills the employer is looking for. Again, study the job description for this information. Next, review your experience and education to see when you demonstrated the ability sought. Then prepare the resume, putting first the information that relates most obviously to the job. The result will be a resume with headings such as *Engineering, Computer Languages, Communications Skills,* or *Design Experience*. These headings will have much more impact than would the dates that you would use on a chronological resume.

Fit Yourself to a Form. Some large employers, such as fast-food restaurants and government agencies, make more use of application forms than of resumes. The forms suit the style of large organizations because it is possible to find information more quickly if it always appears in the same place. However, creating a resume before filling out an application form will benefit you. You can use the resume when you send a letter inquiring about a position. You can submit a resume even if an application is required; it will spotlight your qualifications. And the information on the resume will serve as a handy reference if you must fill out an application form quickly. Application forms are really just resumes in disguise anyway. No matter how rigid the form appears to be, you can still use it to show why you are the person for the job.

Remember that the attitude of the person reading the form is not, "Let's find out why this person is unqualified," but, "Maybe this is the person we want." Use all the parts of the form—experience blocks, education blocks, and others—to show that person is you.

Here is some general advice on completing application forms:

- Request two copies of the form. If only one is provided, photocopy it before you make a mark on it. You'll need more than one copy to prepare rough drafts.

- Read the whole form before you start completing it.

- Prepare a master copy if the same form is used by several divisions within the same company or organization. In this case, do not put the specific job applied for, date, and signature on the master copy. Fill in that information on the photocopies as you submit them.

- Type the form if possible. If it has many little lines that are hard to type within, type the information on a piece of blank paper that will fit in the space, paste the paper over the form, and photocopy the finished product. Such a procedure results in a much neater, easier to read page.

- Leave no blanks. Enter *n/a* (for "not applicable") when the information requested does not apply to you; this tells people checking the form that you did not simply skip the question.

- Carry a resume and a copy of other frequently asked information (such as previous addresses) with you when visiting potential employers in case you must fill out an application on the spot. Whenever possible, however, fill the form out at home and mail it in with a resume and a cover letter that point up your strengths.

Writing Intriguing Cover Letters

You will need a cover letter whenever you send a resume or application form to a potential employer. The letter should capture the employer's attention, show why you are writing, indicate why your employment will benefit the company, and ask for an interview. The kind of specific information that must be included in a letter means that you must write a new letter for each employer. Each letter must also be typed perfectly, which may present a problem. Word-processing equipment helps. Frequently only the address, first paragraph, and specifics concerning an interview will vary. These items are easily changed on word-processing equipment and memory typewriters. If you do not have access to such equipment, you might be able to rent it. Or you might be able to have your letters typed by a resume or employment services company listed in the Yellow Pages. Be sure you know the full cost of such a service before agreeing to use one.

Let's go through a letter point by point.

Salutation. Each letter should be addressed by name to the person you want to talk with. That person is the one who can hire you. This is almost certainly not someone in the personnel department and probably not a department head either. Most likely this is the person who will actually supervise you after you start work. Call the company to make sure you have the right name, and spell it correctly.

Opening. The opening should appeal to the reader. Cover letters are sales letters. Sales are made after you capture a person's attention. You capture the reader's attention most easily by talking about the company rather than yourself. Mention projects under development, recent awards, or favorable comments recently published about the company. You can find such information in the business press, including the business section of local newspapers and the many magazines that are devoted to particular industries. It you are answering an ad, you may mention it. If someone suggested that you write, use his or her name (with permission, of course).

Body. The body of the letter gives a brief description of your qualifications and refers to the resume, where your sales campaign can continue.

Closing. You cannot have what you do not ask for. At the end of the letter, request an interview, and say that you will call in the next week to set one up at the reader's convenience. Use a standard complimentary close, such as "Sincerely yours," leave three or four lines for your signature, and type your name. You might type your phone number under your name; this recommendation is not usually made, although phone numbers are found on most letterheads. The alternative is to place the phone number in the body of the letter, but it will be more difficult to find there should the reader wish to call you.

Triumphing on Tests and at Interviews

A man with a violin case stood on a subway platform in the Bronx. He asked a conductor, "How do you get to Carnegie Hall?" The conductor replied, "Practice! Practice! Practice!"

Tests. That old joke holds good advice for people preparing for employment tests or interviews. The tests given to job applicants fall into four categories: general aptitude tests, practical tests, tests of physical agility, and medical examinations. You can practice for the first three. If the fourth is required, learn as soon as possible what the disqualifying conditions are and then have your physician examine you for them so that you do not spend years training for a job that you will not be allowed to hold.

To practice for a test, you must learn what the test is. Once again, you must know what job you want to apply for and for whom you want to work in order to find out what tests, if any, are required. Government agencies, which frequently rely on tests, will often provide a sample of the test they use. These samples can be helpful even if an employer administers a different test. Copies of standard government tests are usually available at the library.

If you practice beforehand, you'll be better prepared and less nervous on the day of the test. That will put you ahead of the competition. You will also improve your performance by following this advice

- Make a list of what you will need at the test center including a pencil; check it before leaving the house.

- Get a good night's sleep.

- Be at the test center early—at least fifteen minutes early.

- Read the instructions carefully; make sure they do not differ from the samples you practiced with.

- Generally, speed counts; do not linger over difficult questions.

- Find out if guessing is penalized. Most tests are scored by counting up the right answers; guessing is all to the good. Some tests are scored by counting the right answers and deducting credit for wrong answers; in this case, blind guessing may lose you points, but if you can eliminate two wrong choices, a guess might still pay off.

Interviews. For many of us, interviews are the most fearsome part of finding a job. But they are also our best chance to show an employer our qualifications. Interviews are far more flexible than application forms or tests. Use that flexibility to your advantage. As with tests, you can reduce your anxiety and improve your performance by preparing for your interviews ahead of time.

Begin by considering what interviewers want to know. You represent a risk to the employer. A hiring mistake is expensive in terms of lost productivity, wasted training money, and the cost of finding a replacement. To lessen the risk, interviewers try to select people who are highly motivated, understand what the job entails, and show that their background has prepared them for it.

You show that you are highly motivated by learning about the company before the interview, by dressing appropriately, and by being well mannered—which means that you greet the interviewer by name, you do not chew gum or smoke, you listen attentively, and you thank the interviewer at the end of the session. You also show motivation by expressing interest in the job at the end of the interview. You show that you understand what the job entails and that you can perform it when you explain how your qualifications have prepared you for specific duties as described in the company's job listing and when you ask intelligent questions about the nature of the work and the training provided new workers.

One of the best ways to prepare for an interview is to have some practice sessions with a friend or two. Here is a list of some of the most commonly asked questions to get you started:

- Why did you apply for this job?

- What do you know about this job or company?

- Why should I hire you?

- What would you do if . . . ? (The question usually asks about a work-related crisis.)

- How would you describe yourself?

- What would you like to tell me about yourself?

- What are your major strengths?

- What are your major weaknesses?

- What type of work do you like to do most?

- What are your interests outside work?

- What type of work do you like to do least?

- What accomplishment gave you the greatest satisfaction?

- What was your worst mistake?

- What would you change in your past life?

- What courses did you like most or least in school?

- What did you like most or least about your last job?

- Why did you leave your last job?

- Why were you fired?

- How does your education or experience relate to this job?

- What are your goals?

- How do you plan to reach them?

- What do you hope to be doing in five years? in ten years?

- What salary do you expect?

Many job-hunting books available at libraries discuss ways to answer these questions. Essentially, your strategy should be to concentrate on the job and your ability to do it no matter what the question seems to be asking. If asked for a strength, mention something job related. If asked for a weakness, mention a job-related strength (you work too hard, you worry too much about details, you always have to see the big picture). If asked about a disability or a specific negative factor in your past—a criminal record, a failure in school, a job termination—be prepared to stress what you learned from the experience, how you have overcome the shortcoming, and how you are now in a position to do a better job.

So far, only the interviewer's questions have been discussed. But an interview will be a two-way conversation. You need to learn more about the position to find out if you want the job. Given how frustrating it is to look for a job, you do not want to take just any position only to learn after two weeks that you cannot stand the place and have to look for another job right away. Here are some questions for you to ask the interviewer:

- What would a day on this job be like?

- Whom would I report to? May I meet this person?

- Would I supervise anyone? May I meet them?

- How important is this job to the company?

- What training programs are offered?

- What advancement opportunities are offered?

- Why did the last person leave this job?

- What is that person doing now?

- What is the greatest challenge of this position?

- What plans does the company have with regard to . . . ? (Mention some development about which you have read or heard.)

- Is the company growing?

After you ask such questions, listen to the interviewer's answers and then, if at all possible, point to something in your education or experience that is related. You might notice that questions about salary and fringe benefits are not included in the list. Your focus at a first interview should be on the company and what you will do for it, not on what it will pay you. The salary range will often be given in the ad or position announcement, and information on the usual fringe benefits will be available from the personnel department. After you have been offered a position, you can negotiate the salary. The job-hunting guides available in bookstores and at the library give many more hints on this subject.

At the end of the interview, you should know what the next step will be: whether you should contact the interviewer again, whether you should provide more information, whether more interviews must be conducted, and when a final decision will be reached. Try to end on a positive note by reaffirming your interest in the position and pointing out why you will be a good choice to fill it.

Immediately after the interview, make notes of what went well and what you would like to improve. To show your interest in the position, send a follow-up letter to the interviewer, providing further information on some point raised in the interview and thanking the interviewer again. Remember, someone is going to hire you; it might be the person you just talked to.

SOURCES OF FURTHER INFORMATION ON RESUMES

Damn Good Resume Guide (1996), by Yana Parker, published by Ten Speed Press.

The Complete Guide to Environmental Careers in the 21st Century (1993), by the Environmental Careers Organization, published by Island Press. Included is a chapter entitled "Breaking into the Environmental Field," which describes formal and informal approaches to the job search.

Occupational Outlook Handbook (annual), compiled by the U.S. Department of Labor, published by VGM Career Horizons, NTC/Contemporary Publishing Group. There is some very good job search information in the section entitled "Leads to More Information."

Resumes for College Graduates and Recent Graduates (1998), published by VGM Career Horizons, NTC/Contemporary Publishing Group. This book includes nearly 100 sample resumes and cover letters and is a helpful guide to creating a strong resume.

What Color Is Your Parachute? (annual), by Richard Nelson Bolles, published by Ten Speed Press. This classic career planning book, which has been thoroughly updated, should occupy a prominent place on every job searcher's bookshelf.

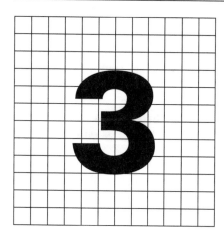

ENVIRONMENTAL EDUCATION

A PRIMER FOR CAREERS IN THE ENVIRONMENTAL SCIENCES

In the formula for a successful and rewarding file component stands high above the rest—a solid education. For those working in the environmental sciences, a solid education and the willingness to keep on learning are the tickets to a rewarding career. A solid understanding of scientific principles and technical skills are important assets for all environmental scientists. The attainment of these skills will open the door to many rewarding environmental science careers.

A scant ten years ago, there were only a handful of environmental businesses, while today the U.S. Department of Commerce estimates that more than 70,000 companies, organizations, and governmental agencies have environmental agendas. Career opportunities in the environmental sciences are at an all-time high, but the number of college graduates with training in the sciences has not kept pace. According to the National Science Foundation, by the mid-1990s more than 5 percent of the college-age population had completed a bachelor's degree in a field of science or engineering. This represented an icrease from 307,000 in 1981 to 378,000 in 1985. However, it still fell far short of the national need for scientists and engineers. A 1998 NSF study revealed that, between 1996 and 2006, employment in science and engineering is expected to increase by more than three times the rate for all other occupations.

Environmental Science Trends

The vast majority of environmental jobs require some kind of science background. A study by *Hazmat World* magazine found that most companies searching for environmental managers list a technical background, particularly in the field of engineering, as their major hiring criterion. Yet, of all the job openings in the environmental sciences each year, thousands go unfilled because applicants do not possess the necessary training or education. The complaint most often heard by companies and government officials in environmental fields is the lack of qualified applicants to fill their science and technical positions. This gap is the direct result of dwindling student involvement in the sciences. Since the early 1970s, student interest and aptitude in mathematics and the basic sciences have steadily declined. While this trend seems to be somewhat reversing itself, the serious shortage of qualified environmental science professionals will continue for some time to come.

Today there is an immediate need for thousands of new engineers, chemists, geologists, biologists, and environmental planners, but the pool of college graduates from which to choose is small. For the past few years, the majority of college graduates have had to reckon with a grim job market in which the workforce in many traditionally strong sectors of the economy is remaining stagnant or shrinking. Graduating college students with business and humanity degrees have found themselves without jobs or even interviews for many months. This is not the case for students interested in the environmental sciences. The U.S. Department of Labor estimates that, by the end of the decade, the U.S. economy could absorb four times the number of science graduates presently employed. In fact, the U.S. Government Accounting Office (GAO) estimates that the federal government will employ 90 percent of all new environmental engineering graduates and 20 percent of environmental science majors in the next ten years, leaving a huge employment gap for the private sector to fill with only a handful of graduates. The environmental field is one of the fastest growing sectors of the economy, and the continuing shortage of qualified people will guarantee those with the proper training lucrative job offers and commensurate salaries in the coming years.

Recent Trends in Environmental Education

Some recent trends in the environmental job sector deserve particular attention. First, a college degree is becoming a standard criterion for employment. This is a solid requirement for young entry-level applicants and a definite edge for those with established job experience. A four-year bachelor of science degree is becoming the norm for most professional job candidates, while a two-year associate's degree or certificate of training from a community college or vocational institute is the prerequisite for most technical positions. Employers are typically requiring their workers to have higher levels of education than their predecessors in the same positions. Further, it is also not unusual for employers to hire a large number of candidates with some form of graduate training. Increasingly, private companies and government agencies are requiring, as a condition of employment, their employees to take continuing environmental education courses. These classes, partially or fully paid for by employers, often lead to technical certificates or even graduate degrees. The reason for these rigorous educational standards is quite simple: The complexity of environmental problems and level of technological and organizational sophistication necessary to solve our most pressing environmental problems make those with postsecondary educations and a willingness to keep on learning the most attractive job candidates.

There is presently a large career advantage for those trained in the basic sciences, and a majority of environmental job descriptions stress some type of specific technical training. The complexity of design and maintenance of mechanical systems and the technical know-how needed to operate these systems have made job functions highly specialized. The advantage is that a person can seek training at a college or technical institute that prepares him or her for a specific job. Thus, for example, someone interested in water pollution control systems can seek training as a pollution control technician or as a water quality engineer.

While this deployment of human resources will continue for environmental technicians and specialists, it is in a state of change for environmental professionals. The ability to manage projects that transcend science disciplines and the skills necessary to make sound business decisions are becoming essential. Many environmental professionals lack this type of training because they have been boxed in to narrow scientific disciplines. In the *Complete Guide to Environmental Careers in the 21st Century,* a frustrated state Department of Environmental Protection supervisor commented on this problem: "Our wildlife biologists know wildlife, but they can't talk to our foresters. How, then, can they possibly perform the integrated natural resources management that is being called for?" Also, according to a recruiter for a nationwide environmental recruiting agency, environmental professionals now need a broader base of knowledge because many companies are seeking professionals with a combination of technical and business skills. In response to this trend, it is becoming more common to find fresh college graduates with both engineering and master's of business administration (MBA) degrees. A combination of broad scientific knowledge and administrative skills is beginning to define the ideal environmental professional.

Finally, increasing attention is being paid to prospective professional environmental scientists with solid decision-making and communication skills. These are liberal arts tools, like analytical thinking, writing, speaking, and cooperative abilities. While these are the strengths of most students interested in the humanities, they have historically been weaknesses for those trained in the physical sciences. Increasingly, employers are looking for people who have a substantive understanding of technical issues and who can develop creative solutions and, most importantly, relate their thinking to others. The vice president of a large timber firm pointedly addressed this issue: "What separates the forest managers from the technicians is not their knowledge of forestry but their liberal arts skills: They can work with people, they can communicate, and they can see and solve problems." There is a definite trend toward seeking professionals with more well-rounded educations, and those able to master these communication and cognitive skills will surely trace the brightest job market.

SOURCES OF FURTHER INFORMATION ON THE ENVIRONMENTAL SCIENCES

Careers for Environmental Types and Who Respect the Earth (1993), by
   Michael Fasulo and Jane Kinney, published by VGM Career Horizons,
   NTC/Contemporary Publishing Group. Describes environmental careers in
   government, the nonprofit sector, the media, and the greening of the
   corporate sector.

The Complete Guide to Environmental Careers in the 21st Century (1998), by the Environmental Careers Organization, published by Island Press. An excellent resource for scientific and technical careers. Included is a discussion of both formal and informal educational information.

Careers for Nature Lovers and Other Outdoor Types (1992), by Louise Miller, published by VGM Career Horizons, NTC/Contemporary Publishing Group. Includes information on careers in the biological sciences, agricultural sciences, land planning, forestry and conservation science, geology, and pollution control and waste management.

100 Jobs in the Environment (1997), by Debra Quintana, published by IDG Books Worldwide. Contains detailed information on jobs, salaries, and education needed for a wide range of positions.

EDUCATIONAL PATHWAYS TO AN ENVIRONMENTAL SCIENCE CAREER

High School Preparation   In the environmental sciences, people make daily use of the skills they learned in high school. A mechanical engineer uses calculus formulas to design a drinking water delivery system; a chemist refers back to basic biology when analyzing enzyme mutations; an air quality specialist uses computer skills when monitoring smokestack discharges; and a forester recalls the fundamentals of ecology when describing the effects of a proposed land-use plan on a local ecosystem. There is simply no substitute for the educational basics of a public or private high school education. Further, a firm grasp of the basic subjects taught in junior high and high school will make your college experience easier and more rewarding. Success in later life is directly related to a successful high school education. Those with the best postsecondary educational experiences, in terms of not only grades but also the development of healthy self-esteem and intellectual curiosity, will surely stand out among the job-seeking crowd.

The three Rs—reading, writing and arithmetic—together create the key that opens the door to the power of learning. First, a solid grasp of math and science is an absolute necessity for a career in the environmental sciences. Mathematics is the foundation of all the sciences and is an indispensable skill for any career-minded environmentalist. You should take a full four years of high school math with two years of algebra, one year of geometry and trigonometry, and at least one year of calculus. Next, you should take the full complement of science classes. Courses in biology, the earth sciences, physics, and chemistry are a good start. Besides helping you understand complex issues like hazardous waste problems, global warming, and ozone depletion, these courses will prepare you for similar but much more challenging college classes. Computer science and programming classes are also a must for anyone interested in the sciences. In most jobs you will be required to enter, analyze, and manipulate information using a computer. In careers like engineering, architecture, and geology, professionals often design their own custom software programs for specific tasks.

English skills, particularly writing and communication, are equally important. No matter what you later choose as a field of study or occupation, it cannot be overstressed that English skills are an essential part of the formula for professional success. The principal of an environmental services firm summarized a recent trend in hiring new engineers with strong technical communication skills: "We look for fresh graduates who not only have demonstrated academic excellence, but who also possess the ability to share and explain their information to colleagues and nonscientists alike. One bright and well-spoken engineer is worth three who know their stuff but lack the verbal skills."

Your College Education: Toward a Technical or Professional Career

The two distinct career paths in the environmental sciences can be most easily classified by two criteria: educational training and the nature of the work. *Environmental science professionals* are those who have completed at least a bachelor of science (B.S.) degree in majors like engineering, biology, chemistry, forestry, geology, physics, or meteorology. Entry-level professionals are usually asked to perform work that is directly related to their scientific training and do administrative or managerial tasks as well. As they gain seniority, these professionals tend to perform less technical work and take on greater managerial responsibilities. *Environmental science specialists* or *technicians* possess a certificate of training or a two-year degree from a technical school or community college and sometimes a four-year bachelor of science degree. They are heavily oriented to hands-on work, especially field or laboratory work. For every one environmental science professional, there are four specialists or technicians. These are the people who bridge the gap between the theoretical knowledge of an engineer and the skill of a precision mechanic. This path is for those who like to work with their hands and spend time outdoors.

School Accreditation

National professional and technical associations accredit academic programs that meet their educational standards. Most land-grant colleges and universities, for example, offer bachelor's or higher degrees in forestry; forty-eight have been accredited by the Society of American Foresters. An accredited program is not necessarily superior to a nonaccredited program, but depending on the reputation of the accrediting association, it may later be a slight career advantage to attend a program that has been accredited. When researching potential schools, find out if the program you're interested in has some type of accreditation and, more importantly, how well recent graduates have fared in finding jobs.

ASSOCIATE'S DEGREE PROGRAMS AND TECHNICAL CERTIFICATES

Two-Year Schools: A Technical Environmental Education

Two-year colleges are a convenient, affordable, and rewarding way to continue your education and are often a direct conduit to an environmental job. The term *two-year school* is an umbrella term for junior and community colleges, private occupational schools, area vocational schools, adult education centers, and correspondence schools. These schools enroll more than six million students per year, or 40 percent of all college students. The reason for this high enrollment rate is quite simple: Our technological society demands a large number of highly skilled workers to keep it functioning. For every one professional job in the environmental sciences, for example, four technicians are employed.

These schools differ from four-year liberal arts colleges primarily in that they are oriented to teach students specific skills that are directly related to employment opportunities. Two-year schools are also a good choice for those who don't feel that an academic program at a four-year college is quite right for them. For example, high school students who are absorbed in one subject like science, mechanics, or the arts; returning students who are seeking further training or a certification for a specific job; or people looking to be retrained in order to change careers are all well suited for this type of education.

Tuition at two-year public schools is less than half the tuition at four-year public colleges and one-eighth the cost of private colleges. Further, many two-year schools have open-door admission policies that make them accessible to everyone. Also, these colleges are community based, which makes them convenient for students who need to maintain a close link with family or employers. You may have to move a great distance to attend a particular program offered by a four-year college; two-year schools are much more numerous and the chances of finding just the right program close to home are quite good. Most community colleges also offer liberal arts transfer curricula that prepare students with the first two years of courses, after which they can transfer to four-year schools and receive baccalaureate degrees.

In the environmental field, workers with many forms of technical training are in high demand. The areas of solid waste management, hazardous waste management, air and water quality, and land and water conservation, just to name a few, presently have a shortage of qualified technicians. The cleanup work generated by the closing of military bases across the country and the federal and state Superfund hazardous and toxic waste cleanup programs alone will employ hundreds of thousands of new workers well into the next century. In fact, the projected demand for hazardous waste management technicians alone in the 1990s was between 300,000 and 1.5 million. Environmental technicians and specialists are the backbone of plant operations and testing facilities. There literally would be no environmental job field without these individuals.

Some community colleges that have developed strong programs for hazardous materials training are Truckee Meadows Community College, Nevada; Eastern Iowa Community College; South Seattle Community College; Front Range Community College, Colorado; and Stark Technical College, Ohio.

SOURCES OF FURTHER INFORMATION ON ASSOCIATE'S DEGREE PROGRAMS

Peterson's Guide to Two-Year Colleges (annual), published by Peterson's Guides. Lists more than thirty majors related to the environment and includes a two-page description of most schools.

The Blue Book of Occupational Education (1997), published by MacMillan Library Reference. Lists schools both by state and type of occupational education program.

The Career College Association is a good place to write for additional information on vocational and technical schools. Write to

> Career College Association
> 10 G St. NE
> Suite 750
> Washington, DC 20002-4241

Technical Certificate Programs: Specialized Environmental Training

One valuable asset for career growth is a certificate of training from an educational institution or a certificate of qualification from a national technical society. Many community colleges, technical schools, and continuing education departments of universities offer short-term certificate classes that teach environmental science specialists or technicians how to use particular technologies or systems. Employers often pay the tuition costs, and classes are taught during off-working hours and are of short duration, ranging from one-day seminars to several classes over an eight-week period. Many of these programs are viewed by employers as criteria for advancement, such as from technician to plant operator. Some common certificate programs are in hazardous waste management, water quality management, air pollution control, and biotechnology.

Many national technical societies offer certificates of qualification to their members. To attain a certificate members usually must take a written test and prove that they have the required amount of work experience. While these certificates do not carry the same weight with employers as do program certificates, they give society members access to national and regional job listings and an established network to other technicians. In addition, membership in a national technical society is a resume builder. Technical societies normally charge nominal annual dues.

SOURCES OF FURTHER INFORMATION

The Junior Engineering Technical Society publishes information on technical societies for many technical fields. Write to

> The Junior Engineering Technical Society (JETS)
> 1420 King St.
> Suite 405
> Alexandria, VA 22314-2794

BACHELOR'S DEGREE PROGRAMS

Four-Year Schools: Professional Career Preparation

Almost all environmental professionals need to complete at least a four-year bachelor of science degree (B.S.). There are two related but substantively different routes to an environmental career. *Environmental studies* is a broad field that encompasses not only the basic sciences but also the life sciences, social sciences, and humanities. The term *interdisciplinary* is often used when describing this field because students are exposed to environmental issues from the perspectives of several academic disciplines. Course requirements include, along with the basic science courses, environmental ethics, environmental policy, human ecology, and economics. *Environmental Science* is a much narrower approach to the study of the environment. Students study specific environmental issues using the scientific tools of their chosen discipline. Some of the more popular majors like chemistry, engineering, soil science, biology, ecology, geology, industrial hygiene, and forestry are considered environmental science majors. Students finish their degree with a specialized research or field project applying the methods of analysis of their major discipline.

Environmental Science Programs

In the agricultural sciences, which focus on the study of plants and animals, environmentally focused majors include fish and game management, forestry, animal and food science, natural resource management, range management, and soil science.

The biological sciences, which concentrate on the study of all living organisms from humans to microbes, their life processes, and their evolutionary development, offer focused programs in biochemistry, micro and molecular biology, ecology, zoology, marine biology, and botany.

In the earth sciences, in which the processes that created, sustain, and change the earth are the focus, there are such degree offerings as chemistry, geology, geography, physics, meteorology, and oceanography.

In engineering, the focus is on the application of mechanical principles to practical situations by the use of tools and machines. Some majors in the environmental field are agricultural engineering, architectural engineering, civil engineering, health engineering, and materials engineering. There are more than two dozen undergraduate degree programs in environmental engineering, a large number of which are certified by the Accreditation Board for Engineering Technology (ABET). Programs in environmental engineering can be found at a wide range of public and private institutions, including California Polytechnic State University—San Luis Obispo, Clemson University, the University of Florida, Massachusetts Institute of Technology, Michigan Technology University, University of Massachusetts—Amherst, Northwestern University, the Pennsylvania State University, and Rensselaer Polytechnic Institute.

The planning discipline, which includes environmental architects and designers, urban, regional, state, and federal planners, architects, and landscapers, deals primarily with land and space use issues. For the planning professions, there are few, if any, employment opportunities for those without undergraduate degrees and many jobs require a master's degree. Generally, planners are required to take courses in planning theory, economics, public policy, economic development, environmental issues, and planning law, among other subjects. Graduates design and implement environmental projects and work to maintain a balance between functional and aesthetic properties. There are numerous programs in general planning, and fifteen colleges offer a specific degree program in environmental design.

There are also concentrations in the health sciences that provide evidence of the medical effects of environmental modification. Health scientists mainly monitor and enforce the complex set of environmental health and safety regulations. Some of the medical concentrations are public health specialists, occupational and industrial hygienists, safety engineers, emergency/disaster scientists, and toxicologists.

SOURCES OF FURTHER INFORMATION ON BACHELOR'S DEGREE PROGRAMS

Education for the Earth (1994), published by Peterson's Guides, Princeton, New Jersey. A school-by-school profile of programs in environmental engineering, health, and science; natural resource management; and environmental studies.

Peterson's Guide to Four-Year Colleges (annual), published by Peterson's Guides, Princeton, New Jersey.

Barron's Profiles of American Colleges (annual), published by Barron Educational Service Inc.

Index of Majors and Graduate Degrees (annual), published by the College Entrance Examination Board.

Environmental Studies Programs

Many schools have brought together faculty from different departments to form interdisciplinary environmental programs. The purpose of these programs is to integrate the teachings of various disciplines and present the student with a more complete understanding of environmental issues. According to the College Entrance examination Board, presently 317 four-year schools offer an undergraduate major in environmental studies.

Because the definition of *ecology* emphasizes the interrelation of humans and their environment, it is logical to study the social and physical sciences simultaneously. It makes little sense to study solutions to air pollution exclusively from an engineering standpoint. To do so would disregard the importance of the economic, social, and political factors, all of which influence the outcome of any program designed to abate air pollution. It may be technically feasible to place scrubber devices on all smokestacks and drastically curtail the amount of toxins released into the air, but it may be difficult, if not impossible, to get companies to actually install them without government regulations. What appears to be a simple task from an engineering standpoint is actually a quite challenging objective when considered in the economic and political realms.

The intent of interdisciplinary programs is to overcome the shortfalls of unidimensional classroom learning. A course that considers the subject of air pollution control would have economists, sociologists, and political scientists as well as engineers explaining their various approaches to the problem and would give the student a more realistic conception of how environmental problems are approached and solved. This combination of technical, social, political, and economic teachings is becoming the core of many environmental programs.

One large university that has developed solid interdisciplinary environmental curricula is Pennsylvania State University, which, through the cooperation of the departments of meteorology, geology, and geography, operates the Earth Systems Science Center. At the State University of New York at Syracuse, the College of Forestry and Environmental Science has built a good reputation. The University of North Carolina at Chapel Hill has built its Department of Environmental Science and Engineering into one of the finest programs in the country. Indiana University at Bloomington offers environmental studies in both the College of Liberal Arts and the School of Public and Environmental Affairs, and Illinois State University at Normal has an environmental health program that integrates medical and public policy issues. Also, the University of California at Santa Barbara has a fine environmental studies curriculum in its School of Liberal Arts.

Alternative Environmental Study Programs

Many small environmental colleges established in the 1960s and 1970s have developed outstanding environmental studies programs. Most of these schools offer alternative educational experiences that encourage students to be independent and creative thinkers. These schools have shed the rigid classroom structure of larger colleges and universities in favor of a more individual and hands-on approach to environmental issues.

Students in these programs are motivated by curiosity rather than grades, and a good number of these schools have done away with the rigid grading system altogether in favor of faculty and peer review of students' progress. Learning is demonstrated through small group interactions, individual projects, fieldwork, and internships. The major advantage of these small and focused schools is the faculties' deep commitment to teaching. Descriptions of two of the better-known alternative schools follow.

The College of the Atlantic is a four-year, independent college located on Mount Desert Island in Bar Harbor, Maine. The campus consists of twenty-six shorefront acres adjacent to Acadia National Park and overlooking Frenchman Bay. The school offers both bachelor of arts and master of arts degrees in ecology. Teaching the interconnection of humans and their physical surroundings is a central mission of the college. The curriculum is split into three areas of concentration: environmental science, arts and design, and human studies. The college has a strong concentration of classes in marine biology, environmental design, environmental media, and education. Undergraduate requirements include at least two courses in each area of concentration, a human ecology essay, an internship, a senior project, and community service. The master's program is a more intensive extension of the undergraduate program, and many students who enter the program continue their undergraduate focus.

The college and Acadia National Park have a cooperative agreement, and students conduct much of their fieldwork in the park. The college also maintains the Island Research Center where, according to the college bulletin, "students monitor populations of endangered or threatened bird species, develop censoring techniques for bird populations, and observe the impact of changes in island vegetation on animal species." For more information write to

> College of the Atlantic
> 105 Eden St.
> Bar Harbor, ME 04609

Evergreen State College is a four-year public school tucked away in the forested mountains of Olympia, Washington. This is one of the few state schools that has both an alternative curriculum and an environmental focus. Evergreen offers both a bachelor of arts and a bachelor of science degree as well as a master's degree in environmental studies. The environmental studies program stresses the interaction of human societies with nature. This program is also linked with the political economy and social change and science, technology, and health programs. The master's program combines public policy and environmental science so that graduates have a combination of management and technical skills.

A student's academic pathway is at first structured, with a number of core program requirements, but later becomes more independent and specialized. Instead of giving grades, faculty members write a narrative evaluation of each student's work, and students prepare both self-evaluations and evaluations of instructors. Thus, Evergreen stresses learning through an open and honest two-way communication system between faculty and students. Further information can be obtained by writing

> The Evergreen State College
> 2700 Evergreen Parkway NW
> Olympia, WA 98505

Other notable, small, environmentally focused alternative colleges are Hampshire College in Amherst, Massachusetts; Williams College in Williamstown, Massachusetts; Colorado Mountain College in Leadville, Colorado; and the Huxley College of Environmental Studies, a unit of Western Washington University in Bellingham, Washington.

SOURCES OF FURTHER INFORMATION ON ENVIRONMENTAL STUDY PROGRAMS

The Right College (1994), published by Arco Press. A reference guide that lists interdisciplinary environmental study programs.

Opportunities in Environmental Careers (1995), by Odom Fanning, published by VGM Career Horizons, NTC/Contemporary Publishing Group. This book has an in-depth chapter on educational opportunities focusing on alternative schools.

Graduate School

The environmental field is ripe for professionals with advanced educational training. Most companies and government agencies are looking for people with both advanced scientific training and modern management skills. A recent salary survey by *Hazmat World* magazine found that 20 percent of all new environmental professionals have a master's degree. The most popular graduate training today is a master's of business administration (M.B.A.) degree combined with an undergraduate engineering degree.

Graduate school can be a wonderful learning experience and very helpful for your career, but you should think long and hard about your motivations for wanting a graduate degree and the type of degree and training you hope to receive. Unlike most undergraduate programs, which have their core subject matter and offer a general learning experience, graduate programs are intensive and specific.

If you have just finished your undergraduate education and are torn between going directly to graduate school or first getting some work experience, most college faculty find that returning students are generally more focused and successful because their studies are tied directly to their careers. This doesn't mean that you should not go directly from undergraduate to graduate school, but today many students enter graduate school as if it were an extension of their undergraduate training, with little if any idea of what they would like to do after finishing their degree.

SOURCES OF FURTHER INFORMATION ON GRADUATE SCHOOL

Peterson's Annual Guide to Graduate Study, published by Peterson's Guides, Princeton, New Jersey. The most complete and detailed information source on graduate programs. Comes in five volumes and gives a detailed description of schools, programs, departments and faculty, and present academic focus. Volume 1: Graduate and Professional Programs, Overview; Volume 2: Humanities and Social Sciences; Volume 3: Biological, Agricultural, and Health; Volume 4: Physical Sciences and Mathematics; Volume 5: Engineering and Applied Sciences.

EXTRACURRICULAR ENVIRONMENTAL EXPERIENCE

Summer Work Programs, and Volunteer and Internship Organizations

Students majoring in the environmental sciences are often encouraged by their advisors to seek practical field experience through summer work programs or internships. In many college programs, practical work experience is part of the curriculum requirements. Through working with professionals in their field, students can see firsthand the daily job duties and facets of the job that are not covered in the classroom. These programs give students the opportunity to decide beforehand if a career in their major is what they really want.

Many students find paid summer jobs with federal, state, and local government agencies. The U.S. Forest Service, Soil Conservation Service, National Park Service, and many other federal agencies offer a limited number of summer employment opportunities. State and local agencies offer an even greater number of summer jobs. Students can find employment in water conservation, planning, parks, and health agencies, just to name a few. Agencies of interest should be contacted directly. In most cases, the deadline for submission of an application is several months before the job begins.

There are also a large number of nonprofit conservation organizations like the Sierra Club and Friends of the Earth that have volunteer programs. These organizations maintain offices or chapters in many local communities. Volunteer work is a great way for students to be exposed to ongoing conservation work projects. Students are usually assigned to support office staff members or fieldwork crews, enabling them to meet professionals in the conservation field with diverse work backgrounds. Check the *Conservation Directory,* published by the National Wildlife Federation, for volunteer opportunities around the country.

Some conservation organizations have staff that place students in paid or volunteer jobs throughout the country. The following two organizations have excellent reputations and have been very successful in placing students in good environmental positions.

The Environmental Careers Organization (formerly the CEIP Fund) or ECO is a highly respected organization that places college students (both undergraduate and graduate) with at least three years of credit in paid intern positions. These jobs last from three months to two years, and in many cases lead to employment. The ECO estimates that 80 percent of its interns are hired after their initial job period. The majority of jobs are in private companies and government organizations. Intern positions are highly competitive, and only one in eight applicants is placed in a job. ECO has five regional offices and an alumni network of more than six thousand people. In addition, the ECO distributes all types of information on environmental organizations, job search strategies, and resources. It publishes *The New Complete Guide to Environmental Careers*, which is a valuable book for anyone interested in an environmental career, and *Beyond the Green*. For an application and more information contact

> The Environmental Careers Organization, Inc.
> 179 South St.
> Third floor
> Boston, MA 02111

The Student Conservation Association (SCA) offers internships to high school and college students, teachers, senior citizens, and anyone else interested in helping manage public lands in the United States. The SCA is active on many college campuses. It has two management programs: the High School World Group and the Resource Assistance Program. When writing for information, please specify which program you are interested in.

The SCA also publishes *Earth Work,* a monthly listing of environmental and natural resource management jobs including information on internships and volunteer positions. For more information contact

> The Student Conservation Association, Inc.
> P.O. Box 550
> Charlestown, NH 03603

SOURCES OF FURTHER INFORMATION ON EXTRACURRICULAR ENVIRONMENTAL EXPERIENCE

Directory of Natural Science Centers, published by National Science for Youth Foundation, 130 Azalea Dr., Roswell, GA 30075. Gives detailed information on more than 1,350 nature centers throughout the country.

Jobs You Can Live with: Working at the Crossroads of Science and Technology, published by Student Pugwash USA, 815 15th St. NW, Suite 815, Washington, DC, 20005, www.spusa.org. Profiles more than 200 organizations and provides information on careers in energy, environment, food and agriculture, global security, information technology, and health care and biomedical research.

Summer Employment Directory of the United States (annual), by Peterson's Guides, P.O. Box 2123, Princeton, NJ 08543-2123. More than 75,000 summer jobs at resorts, camps, national parks, and government offices, many with an environmental bent.

The National Directory of Internships (1999), by Gita Gulati, published by Ginn Press. This guide describes how to find an intern program that is right for you and how to develop that experience into a career.

Volunteer!: The Comprehensive Guide to Voluntary Services in the U.S. and Abroad, by the Council on International Exchange Services, Campus Services, 205 E. 42nd St., New York, NY 10017.

Helping Out in the Outdoors: A Directory of Volunteer Jobs in State and National Forests, published by Northwest Trails Association, 16812 36th Ave. West, Lynwood, WA 90836.

Conservation Directory (annual), by the National Wildlife Federation. Includes a state-by-state listing of nonprofit volunteer organizations including full descriptions and contact numbers, addresses, and names.

The Yale Daily News Guide to Internships (annual), by the staff of the *Yale Daily News*, published by Kaplan. Describes how to secure an internship in a wide range of organizations and businesses.

Professional Society Membership and Certifications

Many professional societies and organizations were created to tie the work of individual or related academic fields to the career world. Some of these societies are the American Geophysical Union, the Association of Energy Engineers, the Ecological Society of America, and the National Association of Environmental Professionals. Members pay a yearly fee, and students can join while in school or after graduation. Societies keep members informed of advances in their field by distributing periodic newsletters and journals, sponsoring conferences, and maintaining job banks and professional consulting services. Society membership is an excellent career network with other professionals in the field.

Many societies offer certifications to people who meet the required qualifications. In some fields, like health, these certifications or designations are mandatory, such as for medical doctors (M.D.). In most fields, certifications are voluntary, but members must pass some type of exam and have the necessary work experience. In the environmental field, some common certifications are Professional Engineer (P.E.), Professional Hydrologist (P.H.), Certified Environmental Professional (C.E.P.), and Registered Hazardous Substance Professional (R.H.S.P.). In most cases, these designations indicate a high level of professionalism and are a definite career advantage.

FUNDING YOUR EDUCATION

The cost of a college education has more than doubled in the last ten years and is expected to rise at an even faster rate in the coming decade. Not long ago only students interested in private schools or specialized programs like law and medicine had to factor in cost as a deciding factor because the vast network of public schools offered high-quality educations at affordable costs. This simply is no longer the case. According to the College Board, in 1999 most of the top colleges crossed the $28,000 a year barrier, and prices are expected to rise about 5 percent a year. Public universities and colleges averaged around $8,000 a year in 1999, although tuition of one of the "public Ivies," such as the University of Michigan, will cost an out-of-state resident more than $23,000 a year.

Student Loans

Loans and scholarships are the two main sources of financial aid available to all students. Student loans are relatively straightforward and easy to secure. Almost every school has a financial aid office or representative that can give information on the amounts and terms of loans as well as help with filling out the required forms. The majority of students seeking money for school use these loans as their main sources of financial aid. The largest loan programs in the country are the Stafford Loan Program (formerly the Guaranteed Student Loan Program) and the Perkins Loan Program (formerly the National Direct Student Loan Program). In addition, the Clinton Administration developed the National Service Program through which students are forgiven a percent of their Stafford or Perkins Loan in exchange for government service after graduation.

Parent Loans for Undergraduate Students (PLUS) and Supplemental Loans for Students (SLS) are also available. These loans provide additional funds to cover the difference between the financial aid provided by the federal government and/or student/parent contributions. A parent or student may borrow $4,000 per year to a maximum of $20,000. In addition, many states offer financial assistance. Information on state financial aid programs can be obtained from the school you plan to attend.

Student loan programs once had the reputation of being sources of easy money because many students simply did not repay their loans. The government and banks are now much more strict with their lending policies. The Internal Revenue Service is stepping up the freezing of offenders' bank accounts and forcing them to repay their defaulted loans. Some offenders have even been brought to court and been fined and given community service time in lieu of loan repayment.

Scholarships and Grants Scholarships and grants are money given, not lent, to students. Money is granted to those who, on the basis of need or merit, meet the requirements of the granting body. There are literally thousands of organizations with scholarship funds throughout the United States, and every year thousands of individual scholarships, worth millions of dollars, go unused simply because no one bothers to apply for them. Many students are under the incorrect impression that scholarships are only for the poor and academically or physically gifted. You can receive a scholarship because of particular interests like writing or reading, hobbies, the geographic area in which you were raised, special skills, language abilities, mechanical inclinations, and more. Thousands of grants have been created specifically for the study of environmental problems.

There are no universal standards for scholarships; the amount of financial award depends solely upon the granting organization. In general, most scholarships range from $50 to $1,000, while some even pay full tuition costs. There is no single listing of scholarships or their sources, and, consequently, the most difficult part of receiving a scholarship is just finding out about it. You can either do the research on your own or use a scholarship search service. These services, which typically charge $50 to $100 per search, have the advantage of being able to narrow the scholarship search specifically to awards that highlight your personal strengths and to specific sources of environmental funding. The best services are offered through on-line databases at college libraries.

Two types of grants are offered by the federal government: the Pell Grant, with a maximum award of $2,300 based on need, and the Federal SEOG, with a maximum award of $4,000 depending, in part, on the funds available from the school. Both Pell grants and SEOG programs are available to undergraduates only. In addition to offering grants, scholarships, and loans, the federal government offers student work-study programs that provide students with on-campus or off-campus jobs to offset the cost of college.

SOURCES OF FURTHER INFORMATION ON FUNDING YOUR EDUCATION

The African American Student's Guide to College (1998), published by the *Princeton Review*, Princeton, New Jersey.

Chronicle Financial Aid Guide (1999), published by Chronicle Guidance Publications, Inc., P.O. Box 1190, Moravia, NY 13118-1190. Publishes more than 1,600 programs for financial aid, including undergraduate awards, grants, and loans as well as information on federal and state programs. A word of caution: Some programs charge to help you find money and are often not very reliable

The College Blue Book: CD-ROM edition (1997), published by MacMillan & Company. An extensive listing of sources of student financial aid, arranged by inroad fields of interest, including a section on environmental studies.

The Complete Book of Colleges (annual), published by Random House Reference. Profiles more than 1,400 schools.

Paying for College Without Going Broke (1998), by Kalman Chany, published by Random House Reference.

The Scholarship Book 2000 (1999), published by Prentice Hall. A complete guide to private-sector scholarships, loans, and grants for undergraduates. Includes a section on funding for environmental studies. The chapter "Special Publications" lists career and scholarship guides for individual careers.

Scholarships, Fellowships and Loans 2000 (1999), published by Gale Research. An extensive listing of sources of financial aid with a detailed description of each source.

ADDITIONAL SOURCES OF INFORMATION

Conservation Directory (annual), by the National Wildlife Federation Included in this potpourri of environmental information is a chapter on colleges and universities with environmental programs.

Educational Resource Information Center (ERIC). Sponsored by the U.S. Department of Education, ERIC is a database that provides computer access to information about education. This system includes more than 10,000 documents on environmental education. Check local colleges and high schools for access to ERIC.

Opportunities in Environmental Careers (1995), by Odom Fanning, published by VGM Career Horizons, NTC/Contemporary Publishing Group. Includes a chapter on educational opportunities.

World Environmental Directory (annual), by Business Publishers, Inc. A large reference manual including entries on environmental education programs, databases, and funding sources.

Part One
Air and Water Quality Management

OVERVIEW

**Total Employment
200,000**

Employment Breakdown by Job Sector

Air Quality Management

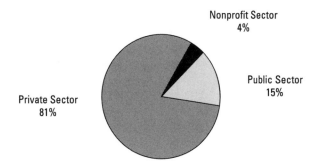

Nonprofit Sector
4%

Public Sector
15%

Private Sector
81%

Water Quality Management

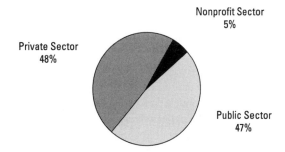

Nonprofit Sector
5%

Private Sector
48%

Public Sector
47%

Projected Growth

Employment in air and water quality management is expected to increase faster than the average for all occupations through the year 2006. Growth in air quality management jobs is expected to be brisk, with some estimates as high as 25 percent per year. Most of this growth is due to the sweeping Federal Clean Air Act amendments of 1990. Water pollution standards have also become more stringent, as more contaminants are regulated by statutes such as the 1996 Safe Drinking Water Act amendments. Job growth in water quality management is also expected to be strong, averaging nearly 7 percent per year.

HISTORY OF AIR AND WATER QUALITY MANAGEMENT

We are accustomed to believing that certain resources, such as air and water, are free and limitless. Up until the middle of the present century, there were virtually no federal or state regulations on air or water purity. Between the start of the industrial revolution in our nation, around 1800, and the implementation of most of our environmental regulations in the 1970s, a great amount of damage was done to these vital resources. Today, we are faced with the dual task of sharply

Salary Range

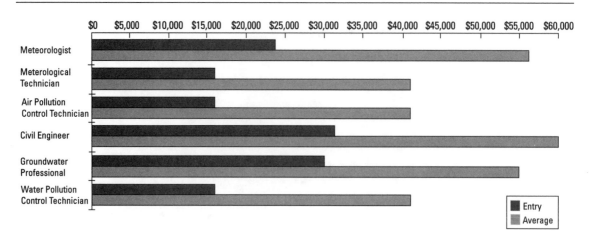

reducing the amount of pollutants discharged into the environment and cleaning up the environmental mess accumulated during the past two centuries.

Before the 1960s there was little public information about the dangers of chemicals and other compounds and only a handful of laws regulating air and water. In 1962 Rachel Carson published *Silent Spring,* a book that systematically described the dangers of the pesticide DDT. Only when people finally understood that the food that they were placing on their tables was literally poisoning their children was there a public outcry that led directly to many of the federal air and water pollution regulations of today. Within the span of just a few years after *Silent Spring*'s publication, several federal laws were created, including the Water Quality Act (1965), the Clean Water Restoration Act (1966), the Air Quality Act (1967), the National Environmental Policy Act (1969), the Water Quality Improvement Act (1970), and the Safe Drinking Water Act (1974). Today more than thirty-five federal and many hundred state laws govern air and water safety.

There are still vivid memories of contamination of cities like Pittsburgh, Pennsylvania; Love Canal, New York; and Newark, New Jersey. These people lived under toxic clouds of assorted airborne pollutants and on top of ground oozing with hazardous waste. In the summer of 1970, a passerby flicked a cigarette butt into an Ohio river, and it immediately caught fire and burned for several hours. Lake Erie, one of the majestic Great Lakes, was pronounced biologically dead in 1972. Today, the Ohio river has been cleaned up, commercial fishing has returned to Lake Erie, and the air above Pittsburgh is among the cleanest of major cities.

We have made great strides in cleaning up these and many other pollution problems, but the question that still haunts us is, "Are environmental conditions really much better today?" The answer is that we face a whole new set of pollution challenges but with a better understanding through experience of how to manage air and water quality through improved technology. Work in the air and water quality sciences is an evolutionary process, and the workers of today will help solve our past pollution problems and help prevent any future damage.

MAJOR EMPLOYERS

Air Quality

The majority of air quality personnel are employed in the private sector. Much of the work of private companies is tied directly to the 1990 amendments to the Clean Air Act. The areas of air pollution control that the government considers most important are improving air quality standards, reducing motor vehicle emissions, controlling airborne toxic emissions, preventing acid rain, and controlling the ozone hole.

Heavy manufacturers, such as refineries and chemical and plastics companies, are hiring air quality scientists and technicians to monitor their airborne outputs and devise methods of trapping more pollutants. Automobile manufacturers need more air quality engineers and scientists to upgrade emission standards. In the chemical industry, research on the effects of thousands of chemical compounds requires the services of thousands of air quality professionals. In particular, the search for alternatives to chlorofluorocarbons (CFCs), the major contributors to the destruction of the ozone layer, requires the work of many air quality personnel. The domestic market for the manufacture of air pollution control equipment is growing. While foreign companies have produced most of this equipment in the past, American companies have doubled their output, from $5 billion to $10 billion during the past few years, creating thousands of new jobs. Many consulting firms do contract work for the federal, state, and local governments. With the strengthening of most air quality standards, the employment outlook for air quality scientists and technicians in consulting firms is excellent.

In the public sector, air quality professionals work to establish, enforce, and conduct research on air quality standards. Most federal responsibility falls on the Environmental Protection Agency (EPA). The EPA's Air and Radiation Division employs most federal air quality personnel. State air control agencies are rapidly expanding their staffs to keep up with state-level regulatory reforms, many of which are more stringent than federal pollution standards. Local air pollution agencies hire a large number of air quality technicians as inspectors and field and laboratory technicians.

Water Quality

The breakdown of employment in water quality is almost evenly split between the private and public sectors. In the private sector, large and medium-sized manufacturing companies that have installed and maintain their own groundwater treatment plants employ groundwater professionals. Engineers, hydrologists, chemists, and technicians work at these facilities. Private companies also run drinking and wastewater facilities in communities around the country. In addition, consulting firms offer water quality professionals excellent employment opportunities. These firms design and construct water treatment facilities and run private laboratories that provide a range of water-testing services.

Water quality personnel are employed at all levels of government. The EPA is the largest employer of water quality personnel in the federal government, but employment opportunities are available at the National Park Service, the U.S. Fish and Wildlife Service, the Bureau of Land Management, the Soil Conservation Service, the U.S. Geological Survey, the National Oceanic and Atmospheric

Administration, and the Army Corps of Engineers. According to the amendments in the 1987 Clean Water Act, responsibility for water has shifted from the federal government to state and local governments. State governments are hiring many professionals in enforcement and testing, while local governments need personnel to run drinking and wastewater treatment facilities.

In the nonprofit sector an unusually large number of organizations are involved with clean water issues. A Ralph Nader brainchild, the Public Interest Research Group (PIRG), has a chapter in each state with members working specifically on clean water issues. A number of foundations fund groups concerned with water quality.

In both air and water quality, there are employment opportunities in higher education. Most state colleges, universities, and private institutions support geology, meteorology, chemistry, hydrology, civil engineering, and geophysics programs in which a large number of air and water quality faculty teach and conduct research.

PROJECTED TRENDS AND EMPLOYMENT GROWTH

Both air and water quality management fields are expected to experience higher than average employment growth well into the next decade. Presently, the air quality workforce stands at about 140,000, while there are about 60,000 water quality workers. According to the Environmental Careers Organization, employment growth in air quality management is expected to average 25 percent per year, while growth in water quality management will be around 7 percent through the opening years of the twenty-first century. Most of this growth is associated with new air and water standards mandated in the 1990 Clean Air Act, the Clean Water Act amendments of 1987, the Safe Drinking Water Act, and the numerous state environmental acts. The broad focus of the Clean Air Act amendments is expected to create fifty thousand new jobs in the private sector alone. In all levels of government, agencies responsible for air and water regulations will be hiring more people to enforce and monitor federal and state laws.

A number of concerns and issues will affect employment trends in the air and water quality fields:

- **Clean air.** The 1990 Clean Air Act amendments focus on seven topics (or titles) identified as major pollution concerns or regulatory guidelines aimed at keeping air pollution in check:

  Title I: *Improving Air Quality Standards*. More than one hundred million citizens live in urban areas where air pollution exceeds government standards. These areas now have a specified amount of time to bring their emissions down to acceptable levels.

  Title II: *Reducing Motor Vehicle Emissions*. Automobile emissions account for the largest share of urban pollution. Cleaner running vehicles and a greater dependence on public transportation are two goals.

  Title III: *Controlling Airborne Toxic Emissions*. Using pollution control technology, chemical manufacturers, refineries, dry-cleaning operations, and many others must reduce their output of toxic and dangerous airborne substances.

Title IV: *Preventing Acid Rain*. Using pollution control technology, energy utilities that discharge sulfur dioxide must cut their emissions in half by the year 2000.

Title V: *Creating Incentives*. Polluters will be charged $25 per ton of pollutants emitted. The aim is to create a monetary incentive to reduce emissions and a fund for cleanup programs.

Title VI: *Closing the Ozone Hole*. Calls are being issued for the phasing out of ozone depleting chlorofluorocarbons (CFCs) and HCFCs during 2000.

Title VII: *Increasing Enforcement*. Enforcement personnel will be hired, and fines will be raised. It is a felony to willfully violate any provision of the Clean Air Act.

- **Groundwater contamination.** As methods to measure groundwater quality improve, scientists are finding that much more of the nation's groundwater is contaminated than previously believed and that much of the existing groundwater data are incorrect. Because more than half of the nation's drinking water is derived from underground sources (as opposed to surface water, such as lakes and reservoirs), this contamination poses a serious threat to water supplies and public health. In addition, the number of hazardous waste sites such as the 10,000 EPA Superfund sites, former military bases, and solid waste landfills are all potential threats to groundwater drinking supplies. The monitoring and cleanup of these sites will create employment opportunities for thousands of air and waste scientists and technicians.

- **Wetland loss.** In spite of efforts to protect wetlands, the United States is losing from 200,000 to 300,000 acres of vital wetlands per year. These areas are important fish and bird breeding grounds and also act as natural pollution filters. There are increasing efforts by federal, state, and local governments as well as nonprofit organizations to purchase and protect wetlands, return former wetlands to their natural state, and construct artificial wetland areas. These efforts have created employment opportunities for water quality specialists.

SOURCES OF FURTHER INFORMATION

The Conservation Directory (annual), written and published by the National Wildlife Federation. Contains listings and descriptions of federal agencies and nonprofit and international organizations involved in air and water issues.

The Complete Guide to Environmental Careers in the 21st Century (1998), by the Environmental Careers Organization, published by Island Press.

Included are separate chapters on air and water quality management. This guide is an excellent companion to this book, because it concentrates on the effects of federal regulations on the job market, gives tips on getting started in a career, and gives profiles and case studies of companies and employees.

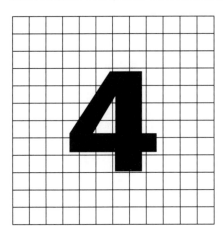

METEOROLOGIST

including
Operational Meteorologist
Physical Meteorologist
Climatologist

Meteorology is the study of the atmosphere—the blankets of air surrounding the earth. Meteorologists collect and examine scientific data to forecast the weather, measure air pollution, and study trends in the earth's climate, such as global warming or ozone depletion. They study the atmosphere's physical characteristics, motions, and processes and the way that these features affect the rest of the environment. They use modern technology, such as computers and satellites, to monitor and predict weather patterns and study the chemical composition of air. They create atmospheric models using powerful computer programs. They also investigate the upper atmosphere by satellite, rocket, radio, and optical methods; conduct field and laboratory research on the physics of clouds, rain, snow, and thunderstorms; and study the relationship between life on earth and the weather.

Atmospheric studies are highly complex because of the millions of factors that influence weather and wind patterns. The well-known example of this complexity in weather forecasting is that the flapping wings of a tropical butterfly in Brazil could have a substantial impact on the weather as far away as New York. While the best-known application of meteorology is the forecasting of the weather, research is also applied to such diverse and important considerations as air pollution, acid rain, ozone depletion, global warming, air and sea transportation, and agriculture. In fact, Chaos Theory, a widely accepted approach that helps explain the organization of all matter, was discovered by a meteorologist.

Because the atmosphere has many different and complex components, meteorologists specialize in one of three distinct areas. Operational or synoptic meteorologists are specialists in weather forecasting. They gather and interpret data to predict weather, usually in specific geographic areas. They use instruments and machines to measure temperature, humidity, wind speed, precipitation, and air quality. Increasingly, meteorologists are using photographs and satellite data to predict the weather. These data, combined with powerful computer weather modeling programs, provide meteorologists with weather and storm information for long-term, short-term, and local forecasts. In 1994, the Doppler weather radar system was completed. Doppler radar can detect air flow patterns in active storm systems and greatly increases a meteorologist's ability to forecast severe weather such as tornadoes, heavy rains causing flash flooding, and hurricanes in specific areas. By using a combination of radar and satellite observations, meteorologists are now better able to predict when and where a flash flood will occur.

Physical meteorologists are concerned with the chemical and physical properties of the atmosphere. They study the transmission of sound, radio, and light waves; the transfer of energy in the atmosphere; and the properties of geomagnetic fields. Using new sensors and other sophisticated equipment, physical meteorologists study the behavior of small particles and contaminants, much of which are released in the form of industrial pollution. These meteorologists are leaders in understanding the spread of acid rain and have determined the long-term consequences of ozone depletion by studying the release of chlorofluorocarbons (CFCs) and other ozone-destroying chemicals. They also study factors affecting the formation of clouds, rain, snow, and other atmospheric phenomena.

Climatologists collect, analyze, and interpret past records of wind, rainfall, temperature, and sunshine in specific global regions. They track past global atmospheric and weather patterns and create mathematical models to forecast future patterns. Climatologists track the movement, growth, and decline of glaciers; study the effects that shifting climate patterns have on landscape and vegetation; and first hypothesized the greenhouse effect by noticing a trend of rising temperatures. Much of their work is centered on improving medium-range and long-range weather forecasting, mainly through building better computer models. The work of climatologists is also used to help design buildings, plan heating and cooling systems, and improve agricultural practices.

RELATED PROFESSIONS

Oceanographer	Hydrologist
Geophysicist	Civil Engineer
Geologist	Environmental Engineer
Geographer	Petrologist

EDUCATIONAL REQUIREMENTS

The minimum educational requirement for a career in meteorology is a bachelor of science degree in meteorology or a closely related degree, such as mathematics, physics, geophysics, engineering, or geography. Only a handful of colleges offer a major in meteorology, but many schools combine their meteorology programs with other academic disciplines, such as agriculture, engineering, or physics. Prospective students should make sure that specific courses required by the main employers of meteorologists, including the National Weather Service and the National Oceanic and Atmospheric Administration, are offered by the colleges they are considering.

Although some positions are available for those with only a bachelor's degree, obtaining a graduate degree greatly enhances job and advancement potential. A master's degree is often required for conducting research, and a doctorate is required for college teaching.

There are specific educational requirements for meteorologists seeking government employment. Federal guidelines require entry-level meteorologists to hold a bachelor's degree in meteorology or one of the related sciences. Students must have twenty-four hours of meteorology coursework, including six hours in the analysis and prediction of weather systems and two hours of remote sensing in the atmosphere or instrumentation, six hours of differential and integral calculus, six hours of physics, six hours of physical science classes, such as statistics, physical oceanography, chemistry, or physical climatology, and three hours of computer science.

PROFESSIONAL CERTIFICATION

There are no federal or state licensing requirements for meteorologists, but the American Meteorological Society (AMS) offers the Certified Consulting Meteorologist (CCM) certificate. Candidates are certified only after meeting the following three requirements: knowledge, experience, and character. The experience criterion requires at least five years of work at the professional level, and three letters of reference are necessary to prove character. In order to receive the CCM designation, a written and oral examination must be passed and at least one report or professional publication must be presented and critiqued. Contact the AMS, listed at the end of this chapter, for further information.

SETTINGS

Meteorologists work in a variety of locations and situations. Some are employed in metropolitan areas, forecasting weather for commercial television, radio stations, or commercial airlines. In general, meteorologists working in small offices work independently, while in larger offices they work as part of teams. Others run weather stations around the nation and globe. The level of comfort and quality of equipment depend heavily upon the location. Most physical meteorologists and climatologists work in offices at public and private research centers.

Beginning meteorologists usually start off doing routine data collection, computation, and basic forecasting. Entry-level meteorologists in the federal government usually begin in intern positions, learning about the National Weather Service's equipment and procedures. After completing the initial training period they are assigned to permanent duty stations.

Meteorologists working as metropolitan weather forecasters or researchers generally work regular forty-hour weeks. Jobs in weather stations, some of which operate around the clock, seven days a week, often involve night work and rotating shifts. During storms or other severe conditions, meteorologists may be required to work overtime.

EMPLOYMENT STATISTICS AND MAJOR EMPLOYERS

Meteorologists held about 7,000 jobs in early 1996. The federal government is the single largest employer of civilian meteorologists employing about four of ten meteorologists. Most work for the National Oceanic and Atmospheric Administration (NOAA), which employs nearly 2,700 meteorologists. About 90 percent of NOAA's meteorologists work in the National Weather Service at stations in all parts of the United States. The rest of NOAA meteorologists work in research or program management in Washington, D.C. The Department of Defense is the other large federal employer of meteorologists, with about 280 civilian meteorologists on staff.

In private industry, meteorologists work for private weather consultants, such as Accuweather and WeatherData. Others work as weather forecasters and support personnel for commercial television and radio stations. Some work for computer processing and data centers.

Hundreds of people with doctorate degrees teach meteorology and related courses in college and university departments of meteorology or atmospheric science, physics, earth science, and geophysics. Other college faculty conduct research in college facilities and at locations around the globe. Civilian meteorologists and hundreds of members of the armed forces do forecasting and other meteorological work that could lead to jobs in any of the civilian job sectors.

Meteorologists may face strong competition in the coming years if the number of graduates in the field remains at current levels. The National Weather Service recently completed an intensive modernization of the weather forecasting equipment, which will also cut into the demand for meteorologists. While jobs in federal government will decrease, the private sector will create new jobs for meteorologists through the year 2006.

SALARY STATISTICS

The average salary for meteorologists working for the federal government was about $57,000 in 1997. Entry-level meteorologists working for the federal government with a bachelor's degree can expect to earn $19,500 to $24,200, depending on their grades. The holder of a master's degree will earn between $24,200 and $29,600, while those with a Ph.D. can expect a salary of $35,800 to $42,900. Starting salaries for those in private industry are generally about 20 percent higher for each degree.

According to the American Association of University Professors, the average starting salary for a meteorology professor is $37,012. The average salary for a tenured professor is $62,531, while part-time instructors earn about $27,000.

SOURCES OF FURTHER INFORMATION

American Geophysical Union
2000 Florida Ave. NW
Washington, DC 20009
Internet address: www.agu.org

American Meteorological Society
45 Beacon St.
Boston, MA 02108
Internet address: www.ametsoc.org

National Weather Service
Silver Spring Metro Center 2
1325 East-West Highway
Silver Spring, MD 20910
Internet address: www.nws.noaa.gov

National Oceanic and Atmospheric Administration
Department of Commerce
Herbert C. Hoover Building
Room 5128
14th and Constitution Ave. NW
Washington, DC 20230
Internet address: www.noaa.gov

Ozone Action
1636 Connecticut Ave. NW
Third floor
Washington, DC 20009
Internet address: www.ozone.org

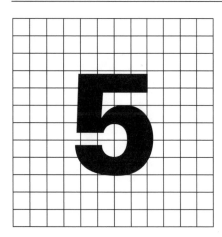

METEOROLOGICAL TECHNICIAN

In order for meteorologists to accurately forecast the weather, they must be provided with up-to-date information. The task of collecting this data is the job of a meteorological technician. Technicians work with meteorologists, geophysicists, air traffic controllers, and other atmospheric scientists to help forecast and observe atmospheric conditions. They are often involved in more than one task at a time and use computers, weather balloons, and measuring instruments to collect, record, and interpret information. They read instruments that measure air pressure, temperature, wind speed and direction, precipitation, and other conditions.

Many meteorological technicians use their technical skills and knowledge of computers to transmit data to and from the National Weather Service and supply information to other federal, state, and local agencies. Technicians are responsible for preparing and disseminating Weather Service information to the public. They issue severe weather watches and warnings for flood, tornado, high wind, and hurricane conditions and continually monitor weather conditions to report any sudden changes.

Technicians are responsible for plotting meteorological data on maps and charts, which atmospheric scientists use to study air pollution and predict climate trends. They also launch weather balloons several times a day. These balloons carry data-gathering instruments that can be monitored from the ground with computers. Overall, meteorological technicians combine the principles of the atmospheric sciences with their broad technical knowledge to keep scientists and civilians informed about weather and other atmospheric conditions.

RELATED OCCUPATIONS

Ocean Technician

Air Pollution Technician

Meteorologist

Geophysicist

Air Traffic Controller

Survey and Mapping Technician

Engineering Technician

Hydrologist

Geographer

Computer Programmer

EDUCATIONAL REQUIREMENTS

Meteorological technicians have completed either a bachelor of science degree in meteorology or a closely related degree, such as mathematics, physics, geophysics, engineering, or geography or they have received their training in the military. Some technicians attend two-year colleges or technical institutes, but more advanced training is usually required.

Before enrolling in a school program or enlisting in the military, students should contact potential future employers to check what courses and hands-on experience they require. In high school, students should acquire a strong background in mathematics and science. Courses in algebra, calculus, statistics, physics, chemistry, earth science, electronics, and computer science are very helpful.

Many employers prefer technicians with military backgrounds because they have received many hours of practical hands-on experience. In addition, enlistees in the Air Force and Navy may train specifically in the atmospheric sciences at the Technical Training School at Chanute Air Force Base in Illinois. Courses at the training school include weather forecasting, climatology, computer processing of weather maps and charts, atmospheric instrumentation use, and weather station operation.

SPECIAL CERTIFICATION

The American Meteorological Society (AMS) offers the Certified Consulting Meteorologist (CCM) certificate to all meteorologists and meteorological technicians, regardless of level of education. Candidates are certified only after meeting the following three requirements: knowledge, experience, and character. The experience criterion requires at least five years of work at the professional level, and three letters of reference are necessary to prove character. In order to receive the CCM designation, a written and oral examination must be passed and at least one report or professional publication must be presented and critiqued. Contact the AMS, listed at the end of this chapter, for further information.

SETTINGS

Meteorological technicians work in a variety of situations and locations. Many technicians are employed at about 300 weather stations throughout the United States. The climate and population characteristics at and near these stations are as diverse as those for the United States as a whole. Some stations are in isolated places in cold, temperate, or humid climates, while others are in metropolitan areas from Anchorage to Miami. Generally, technicians spend a substantial amount of working time indoors monitoring atmospheric conditions from computer stations and some time outside collecting data or informing the public about weather conditions.

Many technicians work alone in small weather stations, but there are a number of positions in large stations with many other people. The working hours tend to be regular forty-hour weeks, but most technicians work in stations that are operated twenty-four hours a day, seven days a week. They can work any daily shift and be required to work weekends. Overtime is required in times of prolonged severe weather conditions.

EMPLOYMENT STATISTICS AND MAJOR EMPLOYERS

Several thousand meteorological technicians work in the United States. Employment growth is expected to be slower than the average for all occupations. Presently there are more trained meteorological technicians than there are positions available. The armed forces, which train the majority of meteorological technicians, are downsizing; this will add to an already bloated employment market in the short term. Employment opportunities are expected to pick up soon after the last wave of military personnel are released from service.

The federal government is the single largest employer of civilian meteorological technicians, and most work for the National Oceanic and Atmospheric Administration (NOAA), in the National Weather Service, which runs about 300 weather stations throughout the country. Other federal agencies hiring meteorological technicians are the National Aeronautics and Space Administration, the Department of Agriculture, and the Department of the Interior.

In private industry, meteorological technicians work for private weather consultants, such as Accuweather and WeatherData. Some work for commercial television and radio stations and computer processing and data centers. Others are employed by commercial airlines or work in air traffic control.

SALARY STATISTICS

Salaries depend heavily upon education, experience, and type of work performed. In the federal government in 1997, entry-level technicians started at $15,500, $17,400, or $19,500, depending on education and experience. The average annual salary for meteorologic technicians employed by the federal government was $41,460 in 1997. Starting salaries in private industry are slightly higher.

SOURCES OF FURTHER INFORMATION

American Meteorological Society
45 Beacon St.
Boston, MA 02108
Internet address: www.ametsoc.org

National Weather Service
Silver Spring Metro Center 2
1325 East-West Highway
Silver Spring, MD 20910
Internet address: www.nws.noaa.gov

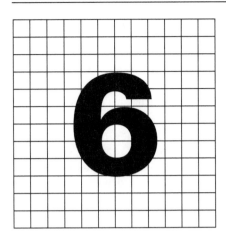

AIR POLLUTION CONTROL TECHNICIAN

including
Field Technician
Laboratory Technician
Air Pollution Inspector

Air pollution control technicians perform laboratory and field tests to monitor the level of air pollution near industrial sites, cities, towns, and isolated areas and indoors in commercial buildings and private homes. They collect samples for testing to determine the contaminants and sources of pollution. They are also often involved in working to abate or eliminate major sources of airborne contamination. More and more, they are also engaged in working to prevent pollution. The breadth of these tasks requires them to have a working knowledge of chemistry, electronics, and mathematics as well as a mechanical aptitude. Much of the information collected by these technicians is supplied to engineers and atmospheric scientists for use in monitoring air pollution and quality. During the past twenty-five years, strict air quality standards have been set by federal and state legislators, which has created a large number of job opportunities for air technicians. The rising incidences of indoor air pollution caused by poor ventilation systems in large buildings, toxic fumes from carpeting, passive smoke inhalation, and radon gas seeping into homes through cracks in their foundations are tested by air pollution control technicians.

Air pollution control technicians are involved in all aspects of monitoring and regulating air quality. There are several stages in the careers of air control technicians, and these jobs give technicians progressively more responsibility and independence. Most technicians start their careers as field technicians. These individuals set up, operate, and repair air-monitoring equipment. Most of this work is conducted in the field, sometimes in existing research buildings but most often from mobile trucks and vans. Field technicians use pumps, filters, canisters of gas, batteries and other equipment to collect air samples and are sometimes responsible for building structures to hold their equipment.

Laboratory technicians analyze the data and samples collected by field technicians to calculate air quality. They work in laboratories using complex instruments, such as gas chromatographs and atomic absorption spectrophotometers and standard laboratory equipment such as beakers, test tubes, and computers.

These technicians must have a solid understanding of chemistry and mathematics and possess solid communication skills. Laboratory technicians report their findings to air and atmospheric scientists mostly in written reports, but occasionally they must testify in court or to legislative bodies concerned with air pollution legislation.

After proving their technical competence, some technicians become air pollution inspectors. These people study the results of laboratory tests to determine if there are any pollution problems. When problems arise, they are responsible for finding the source, consulting with the owner, and making sure that the problem is corrected. Inspectors visit industrial plants to check that air pollution devices are installed according to federal and state regulations and to make sure that they are operating correctly. In some cases they may be required to close down a factory or levy a fine against operators for exceeding emission standards. Air inspectors also inspect private residences when public health issues such as the presence of radon gas, chemical leakage from nearby plants, or potentially dangerous airborne emissions from smokestacks are suspected. These people must have the technical know-how to interpret complex data and be knowledgeable about modifications and changes in laws that deal with air pollution.

RELATED OCCUPATIONS

Hazardous Waste Technician	Engineering Technician
Science Technician	Mine Safety and Health Inspector
Agricultural Technician	Consumer Safety Inspector
Chemical Technician	Soil Conservation Technician

EDUCATIONAL REQUIREMENTS

The minimal educational requirement for a career as an air pollution control technician is a high school diploma. Because the field is relatively new and expanding rapidly, people with a variety of educational backgrounds and levels of experience can find employment. Most employers, however, prefer applicants who have at least two years of specialized training. More and more technical schools and community colleges now offer one-year to three-year programs in pollution control technology. One-year programs typically award the graduate a certificate of completion, while two- and three-year courses lead to an associate degree. Some schools offer cooperative-education or internship programs, in which students work for a local company while completing their academic requirements. In addition, many employers hire people with associate degrees in the physical and biological sciences or chemistry. Practical work experience is also very important in this field; employers are willing to hire technicians who have minimal educational training but specific technical skills.

In a typical two-year college program, first-year courses may include introduction to atmospheric pollution, chemistry, air pollution management, physics, atmospheric sampling and analysis, and mathematics. During the second year, students may choose from courses such as meteorology, mathematics, inorganic chemistry, biology, statistics, air pollution instrumentation, and advanced sampling and analysis techniques. Because hands-on experience is as important as book learning, students must complete lab exercises and participate in field trips.

SPECIAL CERTIFICATION

There are no special certifications for this field.

SETTINGS

The places and conditions of work for air pollution control technicians depend heavily upon the nature of the job. Field technicians can work in urban or wilderness areas collecting samples and data and are sometimes stationed in very remote areas. They may work in clean and comfortable environments or in places that are hot or cold or where they may be exposed to hazardous chemicals or gases. They are usually required to operate trucks or vans to go to and from job sites. They often must lift heavy equipment and move it from place to place. In most cases, field technicians work a thirty-five– to forty-hour week.

Laboratory technicians also work a regular forty-hour week. They most often work in clean and comfortable laboratories that are well lit. The quality of laboratory equipment depends upon the place of employment. Many local and state laboratories have older and more worn equipment, while federal and private laboratories usually provide better facilities and equipment.

Inspectors work both in offices and in the field at industrial and commercial sites as well as private residences. They spend much of their time visiting various sites, writing reports, and meeting with business owners, lawmakers, and representatives. They most often work a regular forty-hour week but may be required to work some odd hours.

EMPLOYMENT STATISTICS AND MAJOR EMPLOYERS

Employment for air pollution control technicians is expected to grow about as fast as the average for all occupations through the year 2006. The recent strengthening of air pollution control regulations and continued public awareness and pressure on government and industry both contribute to employment strength in this field. However, job openings are not evenly distributed geographically. Technicians trained in one place must be willing to move to another location where job opportunities are more abundant. Jobs for technicians are clustered near urban areas, particularly in industrial states and in legislative centers such as county and state capitals. Those technicians who have above-average technical and communication skills should experience the brightest job prospects.

The greatest employment growth should occur in the private sector. An increasing number of field and laboratory technicians work for private research firms and for manufacturing companies. Consulting and research firms conduct air quality tests for private homeowners and businesses. In addition, more companies are hiring their own air pollution control specialists to ensure compliance with government air pollution standards.

The federal and state governments also employ a large number of air pollution control technicians. Employment opportunities in government depend heavily upon budgeting and issue priority. While we are in an era of belt-tightening in order to reduce the huge federal deficit, there is also a great interest in addressing the pollution issue; therefore, employment opportunities in government are expected to grow slightly. Each year, many enforcement agents retire or change jobs, providing many openings for entry-level technicians. Air control technicians work primarily in the U.S. Environmental Protection Agency, which has declared indoor air pollution one of its top priorities. Other agencies hiring these technicians are the Occupational Safety and Health Administration and the Department of Defense. In state governments check job openings at the departments of health, transportation, and environmental protection.

SALARY STATISTICS

Salaries depend heavily upon education, experience, and type of work performed. In general, pollution control technicians receive salaries roughly equivalent to those of other engineering and science technicians. In 1997, entry-level technicians earned between $15,500 and $19,500 per year. Technicians in supervisory or managerial positions can earn as much as $40,000 a year.

In the federal government, salaries are based on the General Schedule (GS). For entry-level technicians with a two-year degree, salaries range from around $15,000 to 20,000 per year. Starting technicians with a bachelor's degree can expect salaries to range between $25,000 and $27,000 per year. Starting salaries in private industry are slightly higher.

SOURCES OF FURTHER INFORMATION

Air and Waste Management Association
One Gateway Center
Third floor
Pittsburgh, PA 15222

State of California Air Resources Board
P.O. Box 2815
Sacramento, CA 95812
This organization publishes the bulletin *Employment Opportunities*, which describes employment opportunities at state and local air pollution agencies around the nation.

Environmental Protection Agency
Office of Air and Radiation
401 N. St. SW
Washington, DC 20460

State and Territorial Air Pollution Program Administrators
   (STAPPA), and the Association of Local Air Pollution Control
   Officials (ALAPCO)
444 N Capitol St. NW
Suite 307
Washington, DC 20001

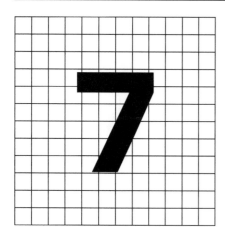

CIVIL ENGINEER

including
Environmental Engineer
Water Resources Engineer
Structural Engineer
Geotechnical Engineer
Public Works Engineer

Engineers use their knowledge of science and mathematics to research and develop ecomomical solutions to a wide range of technical problems. Most engineers specialize in a particular field of research and development. There are twenty-five major specialties of engineering and many subdivisions within each area that are recognized by professional societies.

Civil engineering is the oldest branch of the engineering profession. Civil engineers design and supervise the construction of roads, tunnels, bridges, public transportation systems, water supply and sewage systems, flood control systems, harbors, and air pollution control systems, among other projects. Civil engineers work with structures and are called upon to design solutions to problems such as polluted streams, rivers, and lakes and foul air in a workable and cost-effective manner. In the environmental sciences, civil engineers play an extremely important role in developing technology and structures that control or minimize pollution and are energy efficient.

Civil engineers often use computers to solve mathematical equations to determine how a structure or system operates. They also use computer-aided design (CAD) systems to produce and analyze designs. They spend a great deal of time writing reports and consulting with other engineers. Complex projects often require many engineers, each person working on a small part of the job.

In addition to working in design and development, many civil engineers work in testing, production, and maintenance. They supervise production in factories, test manufactured goods to determine quality, and estimate the time and cost to complete projects.

A particularly important subfield of civil engineering is environmental engineering. Environmental engineers, also called sanitary engineers, design, construct, and supervise programs to improve the environment and public health. They design and build wastewater treatment facilities, monitor treatment processing, devise strategies to deliver water during droughts, and build sanitation facilities in impoverished countries and refugee camps. They also design and build treatment processes to control air pollution, help industries comply with air pollution laws, and use computer simulations to help solve metropolitan air pollution problems. These engineers also work with government agencies responsible for maintaining clean air and water standards. Environmental engineering is one of the fastest-growing subfields in the engineering sciences, and a large number of these engineers are being called upon to help solve some of the nation's most pressing environmental problems.

Several other subfields of civil engineering are involved with air and water issues. Water resource engineers design dams and plan the diversion of rivers, streams, and floodwaters. Structural engineers design large projects, such as dams, bridges, smokestacks, and buildings. Geotechnical engineers develop excavation techniques and construction methods for tunnels, aqueducts, and other works. Public works engineers plan and design environmentally friendly cities with large-scale public transportation systems, clustered and central retail centers, and efficient highway systems.

RELATED PROFESSIONS

Mechanical Engineer	Industrial Engineer
Architect	Earth Scientist
Computer Scientist	Environmental Planner
Hydrologist	Chemist
Geophysicist	Oceanographer

EDUCATIONAL REQUIREMENTS

The minimal educational requirement for a career in engineering is a bachelor of science degree in engineering. There are presently about 320 colleges and universities offering bachelor's degree programs that are accredited by the Accreditation Board for Engineering and Technology (ABET), and about 250 colleges offer bachelor's degrees in engineering technology. A large number of these institutions offer a specialty degree in civil engineering; however, an engineer trained in one branch can easily work in another area. Some college graduates in the physical sciences or mathematics may be qualified to work as engineers, especially in the emerging high-technology fields. Schools with civil engineering programs may stress different specialties within the field. For example, a program may stress environmental engineering or geotechnical classes. Some programs emphasize industrial practices, preparing students for jobs in industry, while others are more theoretical and are better for students preparing for graduate work. Carefully investigate curricula before selecting a college.

Graduate training is essential for engineering faculty positions but is not required for the majority of entry-level engineering positions. Many engineers obtain a master's degree to learn new technology, to broaden their education, or to enhance promotion opportunities. Many engineers are obtaining M.B.A. degrees to advance to management and sales positions.

Bachelor's degree programs in engineering are usually designed to take four years; many students find they need five years to complete their studies.

In a typical four-year curriculum, students spend the first two years studying the basics, such as mathematics, physics, chemistry, introduction to engineering, English, the social sciences, and humanities. During the last two years, students take courses in the civil engineering concentration. Courses are specific to the subfield in civil engineering that the student chooses. Some schools offer a general engineering curriculum in which students are not able to choose a concentration until reaching graduate school. In addition, some institutions offer five-year master's degree programs.

PROFESSIONAL CERTIFICATION

All fifty states and the District of Columbia require registration for engineers whose work affects life, health, or property or who offer their services to the public. The Accreditation Board for Engineering and Technology (ABET) offers the Professional Engineer (PE) license. Attainment of the license is based upon the acquisition of an engineering degree from an ABET-approved institution, successful completion of the Engineering-in-Training examination, four years of relevant work experience, and the successful completion of a state examination. Licenses are generally transferable among states. Contact ABET, listed at the end of this chapter, for further information.

The American Academy of Environmental Engineers (AAEE) has established the designation Diplomat Environmental Engineer (DEE) for those who have excelled in the area of environmental engineering. A number of criteria must be met before taking a qualifying examination: All candidates must possess an AAEE-recognized bachelor's degree in engineering or a closely related field; candidates must already hold a valid PE license; they must have eight years of experience prior to taking the acceptance exam; and they must be of high moral character. Applicants then take an examination in one of the following eight areas: air pollution, water supply and wastewater, general environmental engineering, solid waste management, hazardous waste management, industrial hygiene, radiation protection, or sanitary engineering. Contact AAEE, listed at the end of this chapter, for further information.

SETTINGS

While members of many branches of engineering spend all or most of their time indoors working in laboratories, industrial plants, or offices, civil engineers often spend a good amount of time outdoors at construction or work sites. However, a good number of civil engineers work almost exclusively in offices. Many engineers work a standard forty-hour week, but, at times, deadlines or design standards may bring extra pressure to the job. When this happens, engineers may be required to work long hours and sometimes experience considerable job stress.

EMPLOYMENT STATISTICS AND MAJOR EMPLOYERS

Civil engineers held about 196,000 jobs in 1996. That same year more than 1.3 million engineers were employed in the United States. According to the U.S. Department of Labor, employment opportunities in all branches of engineering are expected to be good through the year 2006, because employment is expected to increase faster than the average for all occupations, while the number of degrees granted in engineering may not increase as fast as employment. Certain industries such as the bloated defense contracting sector have experienced declines, but these adjustments are expected to affect civil engineers very little.

About 39 percent of civil engineers work for federal, state, and local government agencies. In the federal government, civil engineers work for the departments of Transportation, Defense, the Interior, and Energy and in the National Aeronautics and Space Administration. In state and local government agencies, civil engineers are employed mainly in departments of water resources and transportation.

Almost 47 percent of civil engineers work for research and development firms, construction companies, and consulting firms. Many federal agencies contract out much of their actual work to engineering consulting firms in and around Washington, D.C., and around the country. In addition, civil engineers work in every large- and medium-sized urban area and in many rural communities. Many engineers teach and conduct research at colleges and universities. Also, about thirteen thousand civil engineers were self-employed in 1996, many as consultants.

SALARY STATISTICS

In 1996, the average starting salary for a civil engineer with a bachelor's degree was $33,119, while the starting salary for civil engineers with a master's degree was $45,400, and for Ph.D. holders it was $59,200. A typical civil engineer with a bachelor's degree can expect to earn $46,000 annually after five years in the field and more than $56,000 after ten years. Engineers with advanced degrees can expect to earn 10 percent to 15 percent more than entry-level bachelor's degree holders.

The average salary for civil engineers working for the federal government in nonsupervisory, supervisory, and managerial positions was $61,950 in 1997. In academia, assistant engineering professors earn an average salary of around $46,000. Associate professors have an average income of $52,896, while full professors earn around $77,721 per year. Part-time engineering instructors earn an average of $27,000 per year.

SOURCES OF FURTHER INFORMATION

Accreditation Board for Engineering and Technology
111 Market Place
Suite 1050
Baltimore, MD 21202-4012
Internet address: www.abet.ba.md.us

American Academy of Environmental Engineers
130 Holiday Court
Suite 100
Annapolis, MD 21401

American Society of Civil Engineers
1801 Alexander Bell Drive
Reston, VA 20191-4400
Internet address: www.asce.org

Junior Engineering Technical Society
JETS—Guidance Project
1420 King St.
Suite 405
Alexandria, VA 22314-2794
Internet address: www. asce.org/jets
The society describes careers for many different engineering
concentrations. For further information on a certain area of
engineering or a listing of accredited programs, send a self-
addressed envelope to JETS.

National Society of Professional Engineers
Education Foundation
1420 King St.
Alexandria, VA 22314-2794
Internet address: www.nspe.org

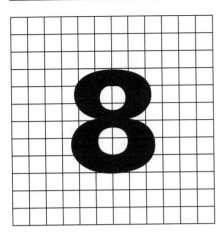

GROUNDWATER PROFESSIONAL

including
Geologist
Geophysicist
Hydrologist

Groundwater professionals apply scientific knowledge and mathematical principles to solve water-related problems around the globe: problems of quantity, quality, and availability. They may be concerned with finding water supplies for cities or to irrigate farms or controlling river flooding or soil erosion. In addition, they may work in environmental protection, protecting or cleaning up pollution or locating sites for safe disposal of hazardous waste. Today, we are experiencing record water consumption, uncertain supplies, and growing demands for protection from pollution and flooding. Many of the water resource regions in the United States are threatened by pollution and sedimentation, and there are concerns that in the twenty-first century there will not be an adequate supply of groundwater or surface water to quench the thirst of our growing population. In many nations around the world water shortages have led to mass famine, starvation, and death, and water contamination has resulted in outbreaks of dysentery and cholera.

Water is a vital resource that Americans use abundantly in industry and agriculture. About 1,500 gallons of water are used to produce the hamburger, fries, and soft drink typical of a fast-food lunch. To produce the amount of finished steel in just one automobile requires 32,000 gallons of water. In addition to supplying the population with a basic sustenance, water resources are part of the very fabric of our economic and social systems.

A variety of physical scientists make up the group known as groundwater professionals. Geologists and geophysicists, also known as geological scientists or geoscientists, study the physical aspects and history of the earth. They identify and examine surface rocks and buried rocks recovered by drilling, study information collected by satellites, conduct geologic surveys, and construct maps. Some geoscientists use two- or three-dimensional computer modeling to demonstrate how water moves through layers of rock and other sedimentary materials. They also analyze information collected through seismic prospecting, a process by which sound waves are bounced off deep buried rocks to determine the density of solids and to detect the presence of water, oil, or natural gas. Geophysicists are also playing an increasingly important role in cleaning up the environment. Many of these scientists design and monitor waste disposal sites, preserve water supplies, and reclaim contaminated land and water to comply with strict federal and state environmental regulations. Other earth and life scientists who work with geoscientists are chemists and civil engineers, who are discussed elsewhere in this book.

Hydrology is a field that is related to geology and geophysics. Hydrologists study the fundamental transport processes of water—evaporation, precipitation, stream flow, infiltration, and groundwater flow—to be able to describe the location, quantity, and quality of water. They look for new sources of water for cities and agricultural and industrial areas. They work with engineers and other scientists to provide creative ways of extending water supplies. Their work may include investigating the feasibility of increasing water supplies by methods such as desalting ocean water, cloud seeding to increase rainfall, or capturing storm runoff for replenishing groundwater. Working with other environmental specialists, hydrologists help write environmental impact reports (EIRs) and advise policy-makers on the best way to clean up polluted sites, safely dispose of any waste, and keep drinking water sources free of contaminants. Some hydrologists specialize in the study of water in just one part of the hydrological cycle; limnologists (lakes); oceanographers (oceans); hydrometeorologists (atmosphere); glaciologists (glaciers); geomorphologists (landforms); geochemists (groundwater quality); and hydrogeologists (groundwater).

RELATED PROFESSIONS

Geographer	Seismologist
Chemist	Soil Scientist
Environmental Engineer	Mineralogist
Waste Management Engineer	Environmental Analyst

EDUCATIONAL REQUIREMENTS

The minimal educational requirement for a groundwater professional is a bachelor of science degree in hydrology, geology, chemistry, civil engineering, or geophysics. Most large colleges and universities and many smaller colleges have one of more of these programs. Hundreds of schools offer degree programs in geology; a smaller number offer programs in geophysics and other geosciences. While a bachelor's degree is adequate to enter the field, most groundwater professionals have some type of advanced degree, and many colleges offer graduate degrees in the groundwater sciences. Because this field is developing rapidly in terms of knowledge and technology, most professionals continue their educations throughout their careers.

While students can choose among several avenues of study in the groundwater sciences, all students should approach their studies with strong math and science backgrounds. Some good preparatory undergraduate courses are groundwater geology, inorganic chemistry, hydrology, calculus, physics, computer science, fluid mechanics, hydrology, and water chemistry. In addition to having backgrounds in the basic sciences, many groundwater professionals are skilled in mapping and computer modeling. Students who also have experience in data analysis and integration, digital mapping, remote sensing, and geographic information systems (GIS) will be best prepared for the job market. Laboratory and field experience are essential because many groundwater professionals conduct research, experiments, and fieldwork such as drilling and mapping.

PROFESSIONAL CERTIFICATION

There are several certificate programs and some licensing requirements for groundwater professionals. About half of the states require geologists to be registered in order to practice geology in those states. The designation Professional Geologist (PG) is granted only after applicants pass a written examination and provide evidence of work experience and references to the state licensing board.

Registration as a Professional Geologist, Professional Hydrogeologist, or Professional Hydrologist is conducted by the American Institute of Hydrology. The certification process requires applicants to hold a college degree in hydrology or a related field, demonstrate substantive work experience including original investigations, furnish five letters of reference, and pass a written examination.

A groundwater professional can also register as a Certified Groundwater Professional through the Association of Ground Water Scientists and Engineers. Applicants must possess a baccalaureate degree and have at least seven years of work experience. Explicit descriptions of qualifying work experience must be provided to demonstrate initiative, decision making, and sound scientific and engineering judgment. Two review committees judge the applicants' qualifications. While there is no examination, the selection process is very stringent and many applicants are rejected. For further information on all of the certificate programs, contact the appropriate society, listed at the end of this section. For information on state licensing requirements, contact the state departments of geology.

SETTINGS

Groundwater professionals work in a variety of settings, sometimes behind a desk or in a lab and sometimes flying a helicopter or driving a four-wheel drive vehicle to a remote setting. Sometimes they even need to cover large distances on foot. Many divide their time among fieldwork, office work, and laboratory work. They may spend time in the field drilling, mapping, and sampling in all types of climates and weather conditions. Generally, less-experienced groundwater professionals do the majority of fieldwork, while those with more experience remain indoors. Some groundwater professionals work overseas or in remote areas involving frequent job relocation.

Working hours are also highly variable. Groundwater professionals working in offices or laboratories work regular forty-hour weeks. Deadlines or the need to monitor projects in the field may require overtime. Those conducting fieldwork are usually on no fixed time schedule. While a forty-hour week is not unusual for them, many field professionals work overtime and irregular hours.

EMPLOYMENT STATISTICS AND MAJOR EMPLOYERS

Employment opportunities for groundwater professionals are expected to grow faster than the average for all occupations through the year 2006. The search for new sources of water for expanding populations and the adoption of strict environmental protection and regulatory practices, such as the national Safe Drinking Water Act, the designation of Superfund sites, and state initiatives, have made the groundwater profession a high-growth field. Activities associated with ensuring clean drinking water supplies will provide many new jobs for the next several years. These professionals will also be needed to work in areas of environmental protection and reclamation. By most estimates, the high demand for geoscientists and particularly hydrologists will continue to increase well into the foreseeable future. There is presently a shortage of qualified groundwater professionals, and the number of new graduates will be far less than the number of new and replacement job openings.

More than half of all groundwater professionals work for private consulting firms. These firms, commonly known as *environmental service firms*, conduct tests and perform remediation services for government agencies, private and public water utilities, mining and lumber companies, gasoline retailers, and other manufacturing and retailing companies. Many of these environmental service firms prepare environmental impact reports (EIRs), which are required by state and federal agencies for many public and private projects. For a detailed discussion of EIRs, see Part VII of this book. Most preliminary studies and actual cleanup work directed by the federal and state governments are done by these service firms.

The next largest employers are the federal, state, and local governments. In the federal government, groundwater professionals work primarily for the Environmental Protection Agency, Department of Energy, Department of Defense, U.S. Geological Survey, Soil Conservation Service, Bureau of Reclamation, Bureau of Land Management, and Peace Corps. In these jobs, groundwater professionals enforce federal regulations, monitor site remediation work, help establish present and future public policy, and assist developing nations with their water needs.

State agencies provide groundwater professionals employment opportunities in departments of public health, water and sewage management, and environmental protection and in irrigation districts. In addition, nearly half of all water utilities are owned by local government agencies that employ a good number of groundwater professionals.

Other groundwater professionals work for large companies in private industry, research companies, or private foundations or are self-employed. Colleges and universities hire a good number of groundwater professionals to teach and conduct research. Normally, a Ph.D. is required for these positions.

SALARY STATISTICS

According to the National Association of Colleges and Employers, starting salaries for entry-level geoscience majors was $30,900 in 1997. However, salaries can vary greatly, depending on the industry. For example, in 1996 the average salary for geoscientists with less than two years' experience in the oil and gas industry was

$48,000. The average entry-level salary for master's degree holders was $36,333 and for doctorate holders, $47,827. A recent report issued by the Michigan State University listed the average salary for hydrologists and related geoscientists as $41,580.

In the federal government, the average salary for geophysicists was $67,100 in 1997; for hydrologists the average was $54,800.

According to the American Association of University Professors, the average starting salary for a geoscience professor is $37,012. The average salary for a tenured professor is $62,764, while part-time instructors earn about $27,000.

SOURCES OF FURTHER INFORMATION

American Geological Institute
4220 King St.
Alexandria, VA 22302-1502
Internet Address: www.agiweb.org

American Geophysical Union
2000 Florida Ave. NW
Washington, DC 20009
Internet address: www.agu.org

American Water Works Association (AWWA)
6666 West Quincy Ave.
Denver, CO 80235
Internet address: www.awwa.org

Association for Women Geoscientists
4779 126th St. N
White Bear Lake, MN 55110-5910

Geological Society of America
P.O. Box 9140
Boulder, CO 80301-9140
Internet address: www.geosociety.org
The Society distributes free *Careers in Geosciences.*

The National Ground Water Association
601 Dempsey Road
Westerville, OH 43081
Internet address: www.nga.org

Water Environment Federation
601 Wythe St.
Alexandria, VA 22314-1994
Internet address: www.wef.org

WATER POLLUTION CONTROL TECHNICIAN

including
Wastewater Treatment Technician
Water Treatment Technician

Water pollution standards have become more and more stringent in the last thirty years. The Clean Water Act of 1972 established a national system for regulating the amount of pollutants that can be discharged. The Safe Drinking Water Act of 1974 established standards for drinking water. Since then, amendments have been added that set standards for monitoring such contaminants as cryptosporidium and giardia, two biological organisms that can cause serious health problems.

Clean water is important in many aspects of life, such as health, recreation, fish and wildlife, and commerce. It is the job of water pollution control technicians to ensure a clean water supply. These technicians help identify sources of water pollution and methods of reducing it. They collect samples from natural water bodies like lakes, rivers, streams, and reservoirs; from industrial sites; and from sewage treatment facilities. They then perform chemical and physical tests to identify the purity of the water. In public health alone, an army of water pollution control technicians monitor drinking water supplies, purification plants, and waste disposal plants to keep these facilities operating within the strict guidelines set by federal laws governing drinking water.

Most water pollution control technicians work as water treatment plant operators who treat water so it is safe to drink and wastewater treatment plant operators who remove harmful pollution from domestic and industrial wastewater. In both of these occupations, operators control processes and equipment to remove solid materials, chemical compounds, and microorganisms from water to render it harmless or safe to drink. Operators control pumps, valves, and other processing equipment and use gauges, wrenches, pliers, and other tools to maintain and operate water control systems. They read and interpret meters and gauges to make sure plant equipment and processes are working properly. They operate chemical feeding devices, take samples of water or wastewater, perform chemical and biological laboratory analyses, and test and adjust the level of chemicals added to the water.

Water and wastewater treatment plant operators increasingly rely upon computers to help monitor equipment and processes and analyze test results. They must be familiar with the operation of computers and the monitoring devices that are connected to these systems. They often use specialized software to record and check sampling results. If problems occur, they can quickly retrieve data in order to determine the cause of malfunctions.

RELATED OCCUPATIONS

Boiler Operator   Stationary Engineer
Gas-Compressor Operator   Chemical Plant Operator
Power Plant Operator   Petroleum Plant Operator
Chemical Technician   Biological Technician

EDUCATIONAL REQUIREMENTS

The minimal educational requirement for a career as a water treatment operator or a wastewater treatment operator is a high school diploma. Because of the hands-on nature of the work, most operators are trained on the job. There are, however, some skills and knowledge that employers look for in prospective employees. Because of the increasing use of computers, operators should have taken high school computer courses or have an understanding of the operation of these machines. In addition, employers prefer those who have had high school courses in chemistry, biology, and advanced mathematics.

There are one-year certificate programs and at least sixty two-year associate's degree programs in water pollution control offered at technical schools and community colleges. Courses leading to a certificate or degree teach the technical aspects of running a water or wastewater treatment plant. Employers prefer to hire college-trained technicians because they are trained specifically in the water treatment field. As the operation of these plants becomes more complex, employers are increasingly requiring educational training beyond high school.

Most state water pollution control agencies require their employees to attend continuing education courses and in many cases offer these classes at the plant or pay at least partial tuition at local colleges. These courses cover the principles of treatment processes and process control, laboratory procedures, odors and their control, safety, chlorination, sedimentation, biological oxidation, sludge treatment and disposal, and flow measurements. The completion of these courses can lead to an associate's degree in science or engineering, which in turn can lead to greater employment opportunities.

SPECIAL CERTIFICATION

In forty-nine states, operators must pass a certifying examination to demonstrate their ability to oversee wastewater treatment plant operations. A voluntary certification program is in effect in the remaining state. Typically, different classes of certification apply to different-sized treatment plants. Operators of a simple plant serving a small town, for example, may need a high school diploma and one year of on-the-job experience and be required to take a written examination, while the operator of a large and complex municipal treatment facility may need four years of experience and a number of specific technical classes and be required to take a more difficult examination. For further information on certification procedures, check with the state board of licensing or the Association of Boards of Certification (ABC), listed at the end of this chapter. The ABC seeks to establish uniform certification requirements and reciprocity of certification for water utilities and pollution control operations across the nation.

SETTINGS

Water treatment facilities are located in every part of the country in both urban and rural areas. Water and wastewater treatment plant operators work both indoors and outdoors in all types of weather. They may be exposed to noisy machinery and some unpleasant odors, although chlorine and other chemicals are used to minimize these odors. Operators sometimes use dangerous chemicals, so safety procedures must be followed carefully. This type of work requires operators to be in good physical condition because they are required to lift heavy objects, stoop, and climb slippery ladders to do their work.

Most operators work forty-hour weeks. Because plants operate continuously for twenty-four hours every day, operators work one of the three eight-hour shifts and often weekends and holidays on a rotational basis.

EMPLOYMENT STATISTICS AND MAJOR EMPLOYERS

Water and wastewater plant operators held around ninety-eight thousand jobs in 1996. They are employed around the country, primarily by local governments in larger towns and cities. Employment of water and wastewater plant operators is expected to grow faster than the average for all occupations through the year 2006. The growing population and rapid expansion of urban and suburban areas are expected to increase demand for water and wastewater treatment services. As new plants are constructed to meet these demands, employment of these operators will increase. Also, many older plants are being reconditioned and expanded; this will create new job openings. In addition, many job openings occur as experienced operators transfer to other occupations or retire.

Although local government has traditionally been the largest employer of water and wastewater treatment plant operators, increased reliance on private firms specializing in the operation and management of water and wastewater treatment facilities should shift some employment demand toward these companies. Increased water-monitoring activities by manufacturing firms should also create new job opportunities. Employment in this field is little affected by economic and employment swings because water services are essential.

SALARY STATISTICS

Annual salaries of water and wastewater plant operators averaged about $30,800 in 1996, or about $551 a week. The lowest 10 percent earned about $313 a week, the middle 50 percent between $392 and $703 a week, and the top 10 percent about $808 a week. Superintendents of large water treatment facilities earn more than $50,000 per year. Fringe benefits for plant operators are usually generous because many are city or municipal employees. They usually receive generous health plans, sick and vacation time, and extra pay for working second or third shifts.

SOURCES OF FURTHER INFORMATION

Association of Boards of Certification
208 Fifth St.
Ames, IA 50010-6259
Internet address: www.abccext.org
The Association distributes an information brochure free of charge.

American Water Resources Association
950 Herndon Parkway
Suite 300
Herndon, VA 20170-5531
Internet address: www.awra.org

American Water Works Association
6666 West Quincy Ave.
Denver, CO 80235
Internet address: www.awwa.org

National Ground Water Association
601 Dempsey Road
Westerville, OH 43081
Internet: www.ngwa.org

Association of State and Interstate Water Pollution Control
    Administrators
444 North Capitol St. NW
Suite 330
Washington, DC 20002

Association of State Drinking Water Administrators
1120 Connecticut Ave. NW
Suite 1000
Washington, DC 20036
Internet address: www.asdwa.org

Water Environment Federation
601 Wythe St.
Alexandria, VA 22314-1994
Internet address: www.wef.org

Water Quality Association
4151 Naperville Road
Lisle, IL 60532
Internet address: www.wqa.org

Part Two
Energy and Resource Engineering

OVERVIEW

**Total Employment
1.5 million**

Employment Breakdown by Job Sector

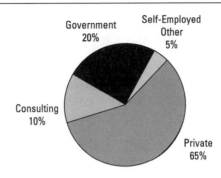

Government
20%

Self-Employed
Other
5%

Consulting
10%

Private
65%

Projected Growth

Employment in energy and resource engineering is expected to grow slower than the average for all occupations through the year 2006. The employment outlook varies greatly by industry. Employment in the coal industry is expected to decline, while opportunities in nuclear engineering will increase slightly. Oil, natural gas, and alternative energy industries should experience mild growth. Petroleum engineers should experience a declining job market. Mechanical, electrical, and electronics engineers, on the other hand, should find ample job opportunities.

Salary Range

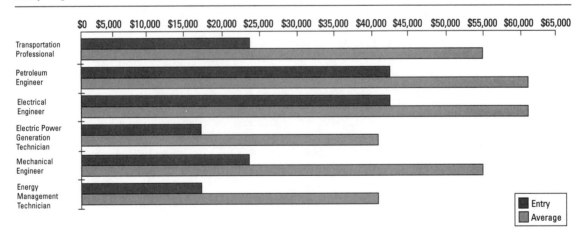

A CLOSER LOOK AT ENERGY AND RESOURCE ENGINEERING

As we enter the twenty-first century, the United States is, by far, the leading user of the world's energy resources. With only 4.8 percent of the world's population, the United States uses 25 percent of all the energy generated on the planet. The burning of nonrenewable and highly polluting fossil fuels, such as oil, coal, and natural gas, accounts for 89 percent of our raw energy consumption. While the rest of the world derives about 20 percent of its energy needs from renewable energy sources, such as hydroelectric, geothermal, biomass, solar, and wind power, only 4 percent of U.S. energy needs are provided by these sources. Being a world economic power and a nation that enjoys a very high standard of living requires the use of massive amounts of energy, but just how long can this country depend upon sources that pollute the earth and atmosphere and that will be used up in as little as seventy-five years? Perhaps our failure to exploit energy sources that exist plentifully within our own borders and are well within our technical reach is reckless and shortsighted. At present, we cannot free ourselves from our energy dependency on other countries because, aside from coal, the energy resources that we most use lie outside our national borders.

In the 1950s, the government and scientific community assured the nation that the ambitious pursuit of nuclear power technology would make energy so plentiful and cheap that we could literally disconnect our home power meters. Atomic-powered automobiles, planes, and durable goods were all advertised as being the wave of the near future. Today, nuclear power supplies the United States with only 7 percent of its energy needs, and none of the promised nuclear-powered consumer goods have been developed. Power from nuclear reactors has turned out to be much more expensive than that from conventional sources, and both the disposal of radioactive waste, some of which has a half-life of ten thousand years, and the dismantling and disposal of older plants are logistical and financial nightmares. Public opinion about nuclear power has never been particularly favorable, and the construction of these plants has become prohibitively expensive. No new plants are slated to be built, and more than half of the facilities operating today will be shut down within the next twenty years. At present and well into the foreseeable future nuclear power is not an alternative energy option.

National energy policy was jump-started in the early 1970s because of the oil embargo by the OPEC oil cartel. The government created many plans and laws designed to make the United States less energy dependent on foreign countries. Measures aimed at energy conservation, the development of alternative energy sources, and technological advances for designing energy-efficient machines all proved successful. During the next several years, overall use of oil dropped several percentage points, automobile gasoline efficiency standards were created, and solar, wind, and geothermal power were vigorously researched.

In the 1980s presidents Ronald Reagan and George Bush downplayed the need for a national energy policy based on anything but economic expansion and the continued use of nonrenewable fossil fuels. The Gulf War in 1991 was not about the restoration of "democracy" in Kuwait, for there was never any, but was a well-coordinated international effort to keep the political balance of oil-producing nations aligned with the largest industrial nations. Will international aggression become even greater when fossil fuel supplies become scarce?

Under the Clinton Administration, the United States refocused on creating a more sensible national energy policy agenda that will meet and exceed many of the objectives set in the early 1970s. National transportation policy now calls for a reasonable mix of public transportation and national highway projects. Fuel economy standards are again on the rise, and manufacturers are moving ahead on production of automobiles that run on propane and other gases as well as electric and solar-powered vehicles. Federal funding of research into alternative energy has also been expanded. What this country needs is a clear vision of its present and future energy needs, and it appears that we are moving in the right direction again.

PROFESSIONS RELATED TO ENERGY AND RESOURCE ENGINEERING

Civil Engineer	Geophysicist
Marine Engineer	Paleontologist
Mining Engineer	Engineering Technician
Chemical Engineer	Laboratory Technician
Chemist	Computer Programmer
Geologist	Solar Engineer
Environmental Engineer	Architect
Design Engineer	Architectural Technician

MAJOR EMPLOYERS

Most energy and resource engineering workers are employed in the private sector. Equipment manufacturers employ engineers, physical scientists, and laboratory and installation technicians to research, design, build, and install many machines and devices. A large segment of the energy manufacturing industry are builders of heating and cooling systems. The petroleum industry also employs a large number of workers in the United States. While there has been a slowdown in oil and natural gas production, the refining and distribution sectors of the industry offer many job opportunities. Energy consulting firms also comprise a big share of the energy employment market. Companies specializing in petroleum, chemical, and mining engineering as well as firms involved in developing alternative energy technology, are leaders in the field of energy employment. Many small, start-up solar and wind power companies operate around the nation. While the market for their services is small, continuing technological breakthroughs and competitive pricing are starting to make these companies real players in the energy marketplace. Contracting companies responsible for installing and maintaining energy equipment also hire a large number of technicians.

Both public and private power utility companies make up the next largest pool of energy employers. Electrical, electronics, and mechanical engineers, power plant operators and distributors, and many support technicians work in this industry. Federal, state, and local governments also hire a good number of workers in a variety of agencies. Local and regional public service agencies and public utility districts provide jobs for thousands of professionals and technicians, while the U.S. Department of Energy is the largest federal employer.

The transportation industry also employs energy and resource engineering personnel. Engineers and technicians work on energy efficiency and pollution improvements in the automobile industry, while transportation planners and designers are busy working on the nation's various transportation needs.

PROJECTED TRENDS AND EMPLOYMENT GROWTH

The employment outlook for the energy and resource engineering field is mixed. Opportunities in the petroleum industry are not strong. There has been a downturn in oil exploration and production in the United States because the world price of oil has been low for several years. New methods of exploration and extraction are vital to companies trying to continue domestic oil and gas production, so petroleum engineers are expected to have a bright job future. If oil prices rise, renewed domestic interest in exploration and production should occur and the general job market should expand.

Employment opportunities in energy production are expected to remain steady for the next several years. Changes in U.S. energy law several years ago have partially deregulated the power utility industry. An increase in the number of private utility companies and greater competition in the field is expected. The effects of these actions on employment are not known.

Companies and consulting firms involved in the development, application, and installation of improved energy technology should face the brightest future. This type of work will have the greatest impact in several areas:

- **Utilities.** New electric generation technologies are being developed that will increase the conversion efficiency of raw material to usable energy from 33 percent to 45 percent. Utilities will be installing this new technology to offset the need to build new power generation plants.

- **Transportation.** In accordance with regulations in the Clean Air Act, the Corporate Automotive Fuel Economy (CAFE) standard of 1975, and the Gas Guzzler Act of 1979, automobile fuel efficiency standards are supposed to rise each year. From 1974 to 1986, fuel economy almost doubled, but since that time a slight decrease in fuel economy has occurred. The 1990 Clean Air Act requires cars to have under-the-hood systems to determine if pollution control devices are working accurately and requires automobile makers to begin the process of creating cars that use clean fuel. Because automobiles emit the greatest percentage of carbon monoxide—a greenhouse gas—development of autos that are much more fuel efficient and spew less pollutants is necessary. This development will also have an impact on the petroleum refining industry, which produces methanol as a gasoline additive.

- **Residential and commercial buildings.** Improved building technology will save about 50 percent of energy used in older buildings and nearly 80 percent of energy used in newer buildings. Among the technological improvements are passive solar heating in windows, computer-controlled heating and cooling controls, more efficient lighting, better insulation, and condensing furnaces. The market for appraising and producing energy needs and producing and installing this technology has grown tremendously during the past few years.

- **Renewable energy.** Energy sources such as solar, geothermal, wind power, and hydroelectric are becoming more cost competitive with conventional energy sources. Improvement in energy conversion rates and lower start-up costs have spurred the growth of these energy supplies.

SOURCES OF FURTHER INFORMATION

American Council for an Energy-Efficient Economy
1001 Connecticut Ave. NW
Suite 801
Washington, DC 20036

American Nuclear Society
555 North Kensington Ave.
LaGrange Park, IL 60525
Internet address: www.ans.org

Also consider the following publications:

Opportunities in Energy Careers (1992), by John H. Woodburn, published by VGM Career Horizons, NTC/Contemporary Publishing Group. Describes energy careers and energy issues in detail in the oil, coal, natural gas, solar, nuclear, and electric energy generation fields.

The Occupational Outlook Handbook (annual), compiled by the United States Department of Labor, published by VGM Career Horizons, NTC/Contemporary Publishing Group. Lists and describes many energy-related careers, including engineering careers, using Department of Labor data and statistics.

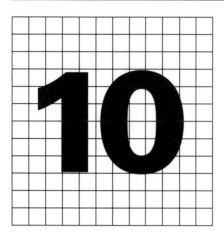

TRANSPORTATION PROFESSIONAL

including
Transportation Designer
Transportation Planner
Transportation Operator

Transportation professionals plan, design, construct, and operate the streets and highways, public transit systems, airports, railroads, ports, and harbors of the United States. It takes a great deal of strategic planning and coordinated execution to see that people and goods move on the roads, sea, and air safely and economically. Another aspect of the job is determining the most environmentally sound methods of transportation.

Because a great deal of energy is used in transporting people and goods from one place to another, it is the job of transportation professionals to make this process as efficient as possible. In the United States, billions of dollars and millions of barrels of oil are wasted each year due solely to the time people spend stuck in roadway traffic jams. Traffic professionals are concerned with ways to relieve traffic congestion by designing roads with carpool lanes and encouraging the use of public transportation. Regional mass transit systems are being developed around the nation, even in Los Angeles, former bastion of the automobile. Transportation professionals also investigate, upgrade, and correct work to minimize the negative effects of new developments and proposed highway projects on air and noise pollution, wetlands, and other aspects of the environment. They design and control computerized traffic control systems to allow more efficient traffic flow and invent ways through the use of high-technology equipment to increase the capacity and safety of roadways. Researchers also are working with new technologies such as superconductivity, which can propel highly energy-efficient trains at speeds reaching 300 miles per hour.

Because of the breadth of work in the transportation field, which encompasses not only engineering but also planning, landscaping, computers, and environmental concerns, transportation professionals come from a variety of backgrounds. Transportation designers are concerned with the structural and aesthetic aspects of transportation projects. Their work backgrounds and educational experience include civil and mechanical engineering, architecture, drafting, landscape architecture, and construction management. These people provide mechanical and construction expertise when planning and building roadways, bridges, rails, and other transportation infrastructure. Transportation designers may be asked to build an automobile ramp for a busy intersection, design a tunnel under a river or bay, or engineer a roadway through a mountain pass. They must consider the unique environmental aspects of the natural landscape. Such work is carried out by landscape designers who handle aesthetic considerations. Roadway overpasses, for example, must blend in with or complement the surroundings, and tunnel and bridge approaches are landscaped to blend the beauty of the indigenous flora with the human-made concrete and steel structures. Construction engineers make sure that the project is built and designed with the correct materials and that the best in new technology is applied.

Transportation planners work with other transportation professionals as well as with people in technical vocations, neighborhood groups, and public officials. Most projects require the preparation of environmental documents or environmental impact statements, and a project's success may depend on its ability to minimize negative effects on air, water, and wildlife. Noise barriers, landscaping, or special design considerations may be required. Planners must meet each challenge and present solutions that both do the job from the design standpoint and address the concerns of the public. Transportation planners may be called upon to justify projects to neighborhood groups, lawyers, business leaders, news media, and elected officials.

Transportation operation is another important field of the transportation profession. Traffic engineers are responsible for design, implementation, and maintenance of traffic controls, signs, and pavement markings. Traffic control is essential for safe travel on ordinary roads, in construction work zones, on detours, and for special events. Traffic engineers use computers to monitor the flow of traffic onto freeways, control parking decks, analyze accident locations, determine roadway capacities, improve traffic flow at intersections, and coordinate the operation of traffic signals throughout a city. This work also includes public transportation engineering to determine the routes and service frequency of buses and trains in the most cost-effective manner. Overall, traffic engineers must work with developers, planners, and designers to meet the challenge of providing a safe, affordable, and efficient transportation system.

RELATED PROFESSIONS

Architect	Environmental Landscaper
Surveyor	Hydrologist
Urban Planner	Geographer
Recreation Planner	Geologist

EDUCATIONAL REQUIREMENTS

Most transportation professionals hold at least a bachelor of science degree from a four-year college. Many transportation professionals have degrees in engineering, particularly civil, electrical, mechanical, or chemical engineering. However, due to the diverse nature of the transportation profession, many professionals have educational backgrounds in urban and regional planning, environmental planning, computer science, landscape architecture, construction management, and a number of other related fields.

While few schools have specific transportation science programs, most offer degrees in one or more of the related majors. There are, for example, nearly 320 ABET-certified engineering programs in American colleges and universities, 130 undergraduate and graduate-level planning programs, 90 architecture programs, and 25 surveying programs. However, not all transportation careers require a four-year degree. Draftspersons, computer programmers, traffic signal technicians, and construction inspectors are needed. Many technical schools and community colleges offer two-year associate degrees in these areas.

Transportation professionals should have strong educational backgrounds in mathematics and the sciences. High school students are encouraged to take advanced mathematics courses such as calculus and statistics and science courses in the earth sciences, geology, physics, and chemistry. In college, transportation courses may include transportation planning, traffic engineering, railroad engineering, highway design, airport design, and related courses, such as computer science, statistics, urban planning, geography, economics, business management, and public administration. Additional transportation training can be obtained through training conferences and short courses on various transportation issues offered by employers, universities, and professional societies.

PROFESSIONAL CERTIFICATION

All fifty states and the District of Columbia require registration for engineers whose work affects life, health, or property or who offer their services to the public. The Accreditation Board for Engineering and Technology (ABET) offers the Professional Engineer (PE) license. An applicant must have an engineering degree from an ABET-approved institution, pass the Engineering-in-Training examination, have four years of relevant work experience, and pass a state examination. Licenses are generally transferable among states. Contact ABET, listed at the end of this chapter, for further information.

The American Planning Association (APA) offers members the opportunity to join the American Institute of Certified Planners (AICP). To qualify, members must have a combination of education and professional experience and pass a written examination. The level of experience required for consideration ranges from eight years for those without college degrees to two years for those with graduate degrees in planning from APA-accredited universities. Contact the APA, listed at the end of this chapter, for further information.

Most states also require surveyors and construction managers to be licensed. Contact the state licensing agency for more information on licensing requirements.

SETTINGS

While members of many branches of the transportation profession spend all or most of their time working outdoors on job sites, measuring traffic flows, and installing equipment, other professionals, including design engineers and draftspersons, spend a good amount of time working in offices. Working conditions for field workers vary greatly. Engineers and construction managers may be required to work many hours in the hot sun in the summer or in cold and windy conditions in the winter. Those monitoring traffic flow may be exposed to dangerous conditions when working on narrow roadways, in tunnels, or high up on bridges.

Most transportation professionals work standard forty-hour weeks, but at times deadlines or design standards may bring extra pressure to the job. When this happens, transportation professionals may be required to work long hours and sometimes experience considerable job stress. Those working on job sites may be required to work night shifts when traffic flow is lightest, particularly in the summer, when weather conditions are most favorable for construction. Working hours can be long, particularly when incentives and bonuses are offered by state and federal transportation agencies for work that is completed ahead of schedule.

EMPLOYMENT STATISTICS AND MAJOR EMPLOYERS

Employment opportunities for transportation professionals are expected to grow faster than average for all professionals up to the year 2006. The availability of new jobs comes primarily from three sources: new transportation technologies, the emphasis on public transportation projects by the federal government and many large municipal governments, and the expected retirement of up to one-third of the current workforce of transportation engineers. In addition, the pool of civil and mechanical engineering graduates, which makes up more than one-half of all transportation professionals, has been steadily dropping during the last nine years. Employment opportunities are therefore quite good for new graduates.

The majority of all transportation engineers work for federal, state, and local governments. At the federal level, most transportation professionals work for the Department of Transportation. In state governments, transportation professionals are employed at highway and transportation departments. Most professionals employed in local government work for city and regional transportation agencies that operate mass transit systems across the nation. Some of these systems, like the New York Metropolitan Transit Authority, the San Francisco Bay Area Rapid Transit (BART), and the Washington, D.C., Metro system move several hundred thousand people per day.

In private industry, transportation professionals work primarily for transportation consulting firms. These firms serve clients in the public and private sectors, including business leaders, neighborhood groups, and government officials. Typical projects cover anything from assessing transportation needs for a major land development firm to controlling traffic at a busy intersection. Many transportation professionals must prepare environmental impact statements because the success of most projects lies with proving that they will have minimal negative effects on air, water, and wildlife. In addition, some transportation professionals conduct research at consulting firms and private transportation foundations.

A good number of transportation professionals are engaged in research and in teaching at colleges and universities. Most are employed in departments of engineering. A Ph.D. is usually required for these positions.

SALARY STATISTICS

According to the Bureau of Labor Statistics, the average entry-level salary for junior transportation engineers, planners, or analysts and traffic engineers was around $40,000 in 1997. Professionals working independently with a minimum of two years of experience earned $51,000, on average, while supervisors such as project engineers and senior transportation planners earned an average salary of $54,500. Directors of transportation departments, senior partners, and presidents of private firms earned $83,000 or more.

Entry-level transportation engineers working for the federal government with a bachelor's degree can expect to earn about $25,000, depending upon experience. The holder of a master's degree will earn around $56,700, while those with a Ph.D. can expect a salary of $64,000 or more. The mean salary for all transportation professionals in the federal government was $61,950 in 1997.

In academia, assistant transportation engineering professors earn an average salary of $45,753. Associate professors have an average income of $51,000, while full professors earn about $76,655 per year. Part-time engineering instructors earn an average of $27,000 per year.

SOURCES OF FURTHER INFORMATION

American Planning Association
1776 Massachusetts Ave. NW
Washington, DC 20036
Internet address: www.planning.org
The APA provides a wealth of information regarding current planning issues, how to become an American Institute of Certified Planner (AICP), fellowships and scholarships, and careers.

Accreditation Board for Engineering and Technology, Inc.
111 Market Place
Suite 1050
Baltimore, MD 21202
Internet address: www.abet.org

American Association of State Highway and Transportation
    Officials
444 N. Capitol St. NW
Washington, DC 20001

American Public Transit Association
1201 New York Ave. NW
Suite 400
Washington, DC 20005
Internet address: www.apta.com

American Public Works Association
2345 Grand Blvd.
Suite 500
Kansas City, MO 64108-2641
Internet address: www.apwa.net

American Road & Transportation Builders Association
501 School St. SW
Eighth floor
Washington, DC 20024-2713
Internet address: www.artba.org

Institute of Transportation Engineers
525 School St. SW
Suite 410
Washington, DC 20024-2729
Internet address: www.ite.org

Transportation Research Board
National Research Council
2101 Constitution Ave. NW
Washington, DC 20418

Department of Transportation
Nassif Building
400 Seventh St. SW
Washington, DC 20590
Internet address: www.dot.gov

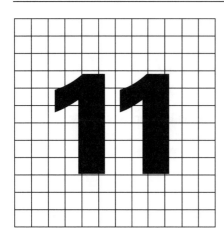

PETROLEUM ENGINEER

Petroleum engineers conduct searches to find underground reservoirs of natural gas and oil. After locating one, they work with geologists and other specialists to determine what drilling methods to use to extract the oil or gas, and they monitor the drilling and production operations.

While these are nonrenewable resources and their supplies will be depleted one day, much of the world still depends on these resources for its energy needs. In the United States, nearly 66 percent of our energy needs are satisfied by oil and natural gas. At best, there is a 75-year supply of large oil and about a 250-year supply of natural gas reserves that can be reached easily and processed relatively inexpensively. While this nation must soon cut back on its massive energy appetite and rely much more heavily upon renewable energy sources such as solar and wind power, petroleum and natural gas are central to the nation's social and economic health.

Petroleum engineers use their technical skills to extract and process crude oil and natural gas. These engineers, along with petroleum geologists, drill deep into the earth and use satellite imagery and sophisticated computer models to explore for and find new energy reserves. When a workable reservoir containing oil or natural gas is discovered, petroleum engineers work to find the maximum profitable recovery from the reservoir. At present, only about 32 percent of oil is recovered from reservoirs, so petroleum engineers use their skills to find ways to recover the remaining 68 percent. They use various enhanced recovery methods, such as injecting water, chemicals, or steam into an oil reservoir to force more of the oil out and horizontal drilling or fracturing to connect more of the gas reservoir to a well. They also estimate the number of wells that can be drilled economically and simulate future performance using sophisticated computer models.

RELATED PROFESSIONS

Geologist   Chemical Engineer
Geophysicist   Mining Engineer

Environmental Engineer   Geographer
Oceanographer   Computer Programmer

EDUCATIONAL REQUIREMENTS

The minimal educational requirement for a career as a petroleum engineer is a bachelor of science degree in engineering. About 320 schools offer bachelor's degree programs in engineering that are accredited by the Accreditation Board of Engineering and Technology. Because there is a relatively small number of petroleum engineers compared with the engineers from other major disciplines, fewer schools have such programs. An engineer trained in one branch of the field can, however, easily work in another area, and many mechanical engineers work in the petroleum field. Also, students majoring in geology, geology engineering, and other earth science programs may be qualified to work as petroleum engineers.

In a typical four-year engineering program, classes during the first two years include mathematics, physics, chemistry, introduction to computing, principles of engineering, and social science and humanities courses. During the final two years, students take more specialized engineering courses, such as well drilling, petroleum production, reservoir analysis, properties of reservoir fluids, advanced geology, and computer programming. Some schools offer a general engineering curriculum in which students are not able to choose a concentration until graduate school. In addition, some institutions offer five-year master's degree programs.

Graduate training is becoming more of the norm for professionals working in the energy resources field. Many petroleum engineers obtain either advanced degrees in petroleum engineering or M.B.A. degrees in order to work in management and sales positions.

PROFESSIONAL CERTIFICATION

All fifty states and the District of Columbia require registration for engineers whose work affects life, health, or property or who offer their services to the public. The Accreditation Board for Engineering and Technology (ABET) offers the Professional Engineer (PE) license. Attainment of the license is based upon the acquisition of an engineering degree from an ABET-approved institution, successful completion of the Engineering-in-Training examination, four years of relevant work experience, and the successful completion of a state examination. Licenses are generally transferable between states. Contact ABET, listed at the end of this chapter, for further information.

The Association of Engineering Geologists also provides the designation Certified Engineering Geologist. An applicant must demonstrate considerable experience before being able to take the registration examination and in some states must be a registered geologist before taking the examination. For further information on all of the certification programs, contact the organizations listed at the end of this chapter.

SETTINGS

Most petroleum engineers work where oil and gas are found. They work at drilling sites to oversee the application of new drilling technologies. At these sites, petroleum engineers have access to offices and computer equipment. Large numbers of these engineers are employed in the United States in Texas, Oklahoma, Louisiana, Colorado, and California as well as in the Middle East, Russia, Venezuela, Ecuador, the North Sea, and many other ocean-based locations.

Because drilling is done in shifts around the clock, petroleum engineers can be working during any shift. They usually work forty-hour weeks. During times of peak oil and gas output or critical drilling phases, they may be required to work more hours. Explosions and fires are hazards that petroleum engineers may confront. Those working on ocean oil platforms are exposed to the greatest risks because they are isolated, and rough seas sometimes wreak havoc on these structures.

EMPLOYMENT STATISTICS AND MAJOR EMPLOYERS

In 1996, petroleum engineers comprised more than 13,000 of the more than 1.3 million engineers employed in the United States. Employment of petroleum engineers is expected to decline through the year 2006, unless oil and gas prices unexpectedly rise enough to encourage new oil exploration. While expansion in the petroleum industry is unlikely, there will be ample employment opportunities for petroleum engineers because fewer engineers graduate each year than retire or switch to other industries. Those with advanced degrees, particularly Ph.D.'s, should find the best employment opportunities.

Petroleum engineers work primarily in the petroleum industry and closely allied fields. Employers include major oil companies and hundreds of smaller, independent oil exploration, production, and service companies. They also work for engineering consulting firms, oil field services, and equipment suppliers; still others are independent consultants. Because petroleum engineers specialize in the discovery and production of oil and gas, relatively few are employed in the refining, transportation, and retail sectors of the oil and gas industry.

Relatively few petroleum engineers work in government. In the federal government they work primarily at the Department of Energy, while some work for state agencies in oil-producing states like Texas, Oklahoma, California, and Ohio. Petroleum engineers also teach and do research in colleges and universities.

SALARY STATISTICS

According to the National Association of Colleges and Employers, petroleum engineering graduates with bachelor's degrees had an average starting salary of $43,674 in 1997. A survey of workplaces in 160 metropolitan areas reported that in 1995 experienced mid-level engineers with no supervisory responsibilities had median annual earnings of about $59,100, with the middle half earning between $54,000 and $65,000 per year. Median annual earnings for engineers at senior managerial levels were about $99,200. Because petroleum engineers are in the highest-paid engineering professions, expect average salaries for them to be somewhat higher.

The average salary for engineers in the federal government in nonsupervisory, supervisory, and managerial positions was $61,950 in 1997; petroleum engineers more often fall on the higher end of the wage scale.

In academia, assistant engineering professors earn an average salary of $45,753. Associate professors have an average income of $52,896, while full professors earn $77,721 per year. Part-time engineering instructors earn an average of $27,000 per year.

SOURCES OF FURTHER INFORMATION

Accreditation Board for Engineering and Technology
111 Market Place
Suite 1050
Baltimore, MD 21202
Internet address: www.abet.org
The board publishes a listing of accredited schools of engineering throughout the country.

American Association of Petroleum Geologists
Box 979
Tulsa, OK 74101
Internet address: www.aapg.org

American Institute of Mining, Metallurgical, and Petroleum
    Engineers
345 East 47th St.
New York, NY 10017

American Society for Engineering Education
Eleven Dupont Circle
Suite 200
Washington, DC 20036
Internet address: www.asee.org
The society publishes two directories annually, one for undergraduate study and the other for graduate study and research in all areas of engineering.

Association of Engineering Geologists
Dept. of Geology and Geophysics
Texas A&M University
MS-3115
College Station, TX 77843-3115

Association of Energy Engineers
4025 Pleasantdale Road
Suite 420
Atlanta, GA 30340
Internet address: www.aeecenter.org

National Society of Professional Engineers
1420 King St.
Alexandria, VA 22314-2794
Internet address: www.nspe.org

Society of Petroleum Engineers
P.O. Box 833836
Richardson, TX 75083-3836
Internet address: www.spe.org

ELECTRICAL AND ELECTRONICS ENGINEER

Electrical and electronics engineers design, develop, test, and supervise the manufacturing and installation of electrical and electronic equipment, components, or systems for commercial, industrial, military, or scientific use. They employ science, technology, and problem-solving skills to design, construct, and maintain products, services, and information systems. These engineers play an important role in the environmental sciences because they develop technology that is applied to energy-related problems. Among some of the applications that these engineers have developed are high-powered computers that can be used to design and monitor more efficient energy generation and delivery systems, automobile electronic fuel-injected systems that boost gas mileage, geoscience and remote-sensing technology, and technology for satellites and space exploration.

Generally, electrical and electronics engineers specialize in two distinct areas of their profession. Electrical engineers specialize in the creation and transmission of large amounts of electricity at power generation stations. Electronics engineers usually work with much smaller amounts of power and concentrate their attention on developing electronic equipment, such as computers, microprocessors, and communication and other high-tech equipment.

Two very important areas of energy conservation and development that electrical and electronic engineers have been involved in are the development of more-efficient power lines and transmission systems and the use of wind power. As electricity moves through power lines from the generation plant to the home or factory, a good amount of that energy is absorbed, in a process called *resistance*, by the lines themselves. When power is sent a long distance, a substantial percent of the electricity is lost. Electrical and electronics engineers are researching the use of less-resistant metals and alternative power transmission methods to overcome this problem. In addition, more and more power lines are being placed underground, which complicates matters even further because these lines must be insulated against moisture.

The use of windmills or wind turbines to generate power is another interest of electrical and electronics engineers. Presently, more than 95 percent of all research on wind-generated power takes place in the United States; most of this activity takes place in California. Two of the largest stations, one at Altamont Pass near San Francisco and the other in the Tehachapi Mountains near Los Angeles, are run by power utility companies. The use of wind to generate power is promising because this energy source is clean and renewable. Electronics engineers have contributed to the knowledge of wind turbine technology, and as research and development of wind energy continues, both electrical and electronic engineers will be instrumental in making it a technically viable and financially feasible endeavor for power utility companies.

RELATED PROFESSIONS

Quality Control Engineer	Mathematician
Software Engineer	Chemical Engineer
Computer Scientist	Environmental Engineer
Mechanical Engineer	Architectural Engineer

EDUCATIONAL REQUIREMENTS

The minimal educational requirement for a career as an electrical or electronics engineer is a bachelor of science degree in engineering. About 390 U.S. schools offer bachelor's degree programs in engineering that are accredited by the Accreditation Board for Engineering and Technology (ABET). Because electrical and electronics engineering is the largest subfield in engineering, a large number of these institutions offer a specialty degree in electrical and electronics engineering. An engineer trained in one branch of the field can, however, easily work in another area. In addition, some college graduates in the physical sciences or mathematics may be qualified to work in an emerging high-technology field such as this one.

In a typical four-year engineering program, classes during the first two years include mathematics, physics, chemistry, introduction to computing, principles of engineering, and social science and humanities courses. During the final two years, students take more specialized engineering courses, such as mechanics and thermodynamics, electromagnetic fields, circuits and electronics, linear systems, and energy conservation. Schools sometimes stress specific specialties within the field, and students with specific interests should investigate curricula carefully before selecting a college. Some schools offer a general engineering curriculum in which students are not able to choose a concentration until reaching graduate school. In addition, some institutions offer five-year master's degree programs.

Graduate training is essential for engineering faculty positions but is not required for the majority of entry-level engineering positions. Many engineers get master's degrees to learn new technology, to broaden their education, or to enhance promotion opportunities. Many engineers are obtaining M.B.A. degrees to advance to management and sales positions.

PROFESSIONAL CERTIFICATION

All fifty states and the District of Columbia require registration for engineers whose work affects life, health, or property or who offer their services to the public. The Accreditation Board for Engineering and Technology (ABET) offers the Professional Engineer (PE) license. Attainment of the license is based upon the acquisition of an engineering degree from an ABET-approved institution, successful completion of the Engineering-in-Training examination, four years of relevant work experience, and successful completion of a state examination. Licenses are generally transferable among states. Contact ABET, listed at the end of this chapter, for further information.

SETTINGS

Electrical and electronics engineers work in laboratories and other research facilities, classrooms, offices, and manufacturing facilities where they inspect, supervise, and solve on-site problems. They may spend a substantial amount of time conducting research using computers to design and test projects and writing reports. These engineers also work extensively with other engineers; complex projects often require the services of many engineers, each working on a small part of the job.

Many engineers work standard forty-hour weeks. At times, deadlines or design standards may bring extra work pressure to the job. When this happens, engineers may work long hours and experience considerable stress.

EMPLOYMENT STATISTICS AND MAJOR EMPLOYERS

In 1996, electrical and electronics engineers comprised about 367,000 of the more than 1.3 million engineers employed in the United States. Electrical and electronics engineering is the largest subfield within the discipline. According to the Engineering Manpower Commission, the number of engineers graduated from colleges and universities during the past nine years has dropped steadily. According to the U.S. Department of Labor, employment opportunities in all branches of engineering are expected to be good through the year 2006 because employment is expected to increase faster than the average for all occupations, while the number of degrees granted in engineering is not expected to increase much above present levels. In addition, opportunities for electrical and electronics engineers have been strong for several years as the computer field and other high-technology areas have continued to expand. Recently, the demand for electrical and electronics engineers in the military-industrial complex has declined; this sector has been bloated for years because of disproportionately high spending by government. Government reinvestment in other high-tech areas, such as space exploration, environmental studies, and the information superhighway, should balance the loss of electrical and electronics engineers from the military sector.

The majority of electrical and electronics engineers work for firms that manufacture electrical and electronic equipment, business machines, professional and scientific equipment, and aircraft and aircraft parts. A substantial number conduct research and development for these companies or work for engineering consulting firms. Some electrical and electronics engineers are self-employed. Additionally, many electrical engineers work for private and public power utility companies around the nation. Employment with power utilities is expected to increase slowly but steadily as power use rises in the United States.

The remainder of electrical and electronics engineers work in government. At the federal level, these engineers are employed by the departments of Transportation, Energy, and Defense and by the National Aeronautic and Space Administration. A good number of electrical and electronics engineers work for state energy agencies.

SALARY STATISTICS

According to the National Association of Colleges and Employers, electrical and electronics engineering graduates with bachelor's degrees have an average starting salary of $39,513, while those with master's degrees earn, on average, $45,400 per year. Holders of Ph.D. degrees earned an entry-level salary of $59,200 per year in 1997. A survey of workplaces in 160 metropolitan areas reported that experienced mid-level engineers with no supervisory responsibilities had median annual earnings of about $59,100, with the middle half earning between $54,000 and $65,000 per year. Median annual earnings for engineers at senior managerial levels were about $99,200.

Entry-level engineers with bachelor's degrees who work for the federal government can expect to earn about $25,000. The holder of a master's degree will earn around $56,700, while those with Ph.D.'s can expect a salary of $64,000 or more. The average salary for engineers in the federal government in nonsupervisory, supervisory, and managerial positions was $61,950 in 1997.

In academia, assistant engineering professors earn an average salary of $45,753. Associate professors have an average income of $52,896, while full professors earn about $77,721 per year. Part-time engineering instructors earn an average of $27,000 per year.

SOURCES OF FURTHER INFORMATION

Accreditation Board for Engineering and Technology
111 Market Place
Suite 1050
Baltimore, MD 21202-4012
Internet address: www.abet.org
The board publishes a listing of accredited schools of engineering throughout the country.

American Society for Engineering Education
Eleven Dupont Circle
Suite 200
Washington, DC 20036
Internet address: www.asee.org

The society publishes two directories annually, one for undergraduate study and the other for graduate study and research in all areas of engineering.

Institute of Electrical and Electronics Engineers
1828 L St. NW
Suite 1202
Washington, DC 20036-5104
Internet address: www.ieee.org
The institute publishes the *Employment Guide for Engineers and Scientists,* which includes a directory of companies that employ electrical, electronics, and computer engineers.

National Society of Professional Engineers
1420 King St.
Alexandria, VA 22314-2794
Internet address: www.nspe.org

ELECTRIC POWER GENERATION TECHNICIAN

including
Power Plant Operator
Power Distributor

Electric power generation technicians are entrusted with the enormous task of keeping power steadily flowing from power generation plants and substations to the public. The power generation and distribution infrastructure of the United States is truly massive, with virtually every urban home and more than 98 percent of rural homes being supplied with electric power. Without electricity, most Americans could not heat or air condition their homes, cook food, work or play at their computers, or watch television.

The two types of electric power generation technicians can most readily be differentiated by their places in the power generation and distribution process. Power plant operators control the machinery that generates electricity. They control equipment that distributes power among generators, combine the current for several generators, and regulate the flow of electricity into power lines. When power requirements change, they start or stop generators and connect them to or disconnect them from circuits. Their most important task is to make sure that electricity is flowing from the plant properly and at the correct voltage.

Power distributors and dispatchers control the flow of electricity through transmission lines to users. They operate current converters, voltage transformers, and circuit breakers. Their job requires them to anticipate power needs, such as those caused by changes in weather, and call control room operators to start or stop boilers and generators in order to maintain the supply of electrical power. Power dispatchers are also responsible for handling emergencies, such as those caused by substation damage, transformer failures, or power line problems, which are most often caused by downed trees. They also operate substations where they can step up or step down voltage and operate equipment to control the flow of electricity in and out of substations.

RELATED OCCUPATIONS

Water and Wastewater
Treatment Plant Operator

Petroleum Refinery Operator
Chemical Plant Operator

Waterworks Pump Station Operator   Science Technician
Sanitary Landfill Operator   Solar Collector Technician
Air Pollution Control Technician

EDUCATIONAL REQUIREMENTS

The minimal educational requirement for a job as an electric power generation technician is a high school diploma. Many entry-level technicians are trained on the job, but a strong background in high school mathematics and science is preferred by employers. Most trainees are first assigned as assistants, power plant laborers, or power line construction workers and are later evaluated for operator and distributor positions. Future assignments generally depend on the results of aptitude tests, work performance, and the availability of openings. Workers selected for technician positions receive extensive in-house and classroom training provided by the employer. Several years of training and experience are required to become a fully qualified control room operator or power distributor. Some two-year colleges and technical institutes offer certificates and training in electric plant operation. Graduates generally bypass the plant apprenticeship period and are hired directly as plant operator or power distributor trainees. In addition to undergoing initial training, all operators and power distributors are given periodic refresher courses and information on new operation technologies and techniques.

SPECIAL CERTIFICATION

Outside of in-house training programs, there are no special certification or licensing requirements for this occupation.

SETTINGS

Electric power generation technicians work at plants around the country in both rural and urban areas. Urban areas offer more employment opportunities because power demand is highest in these locations. Operators and distributors who work in control rooms generally sit or stand at control stations. While this work is not physically demanding, it requires a great amount of focus. At older generation stations, controls are not centralized, so operators move throughout the plant, operating and monitoring valves, switches, and gauges. Operators working outside the control room may be exposed to electric shock, falls, or burns.

Technicians work forty-hour weeks, but because plants operate twenty-four hours a day, seven days a week, they are required to work nights and weekends, usually on a rotating schedule. Workers periodically rotate to different daily shifts so that less desirable shifts are shared by all operators. These schedule shifts can be fatiguing because of the changes they require in sleeping and living patterns.

EMPLOYMENT STATISTICS AND MAJOR EMPLOYERS

In 1996, about forty thousand electric power generation technicians were employed in the United States. Overall, employment opportunities for electric power generation technicians are expected to grow slightly more slowly than the average for all occupations up to the year 2006. Because of vigorous electric plant construction projects during the past several years, the construction of new plants and upgrading of older facilities is expected to slow during the next several years. In addition, newer plants are constructed with a far greater number of automated systems that require the services of fewer technicians. As educational requirements are moderate and wages and job benefits are high, competition for jobs is keen. Most job openings will occur as workers leave the workforce or transfer to other occupations.

More than 90 percent of electric power generation technicians work for public and private electric utility companies and government agencies that produce electricity. In the federal government, technicians work at Department of Energy facilities, located primarily in the southeastern United States. The Bureau of Reclamation in the U.S. Department of Agriculture, which runs many hydroelectric plants at dam sites primarily in the Southwest and far West, hire these technicians. In addition, some technicians are employed by private companies that run their own power generation plants.

SALARY STATISTICS

Compared to the salaries of technicians in related industries, the weekly earnings of electric power generation technicians are relatively high. In 1995, annual earnings for the most junior workers were about $20,200, with the middle half earning between $17,700 and $22,800 a year. Those with more experience earned about $32,700 a year, and those in supervisory or senior positions, $54,800.

In the federal government, salaries are based on the General Schedule (GS); however, salaries depend heavily upon education, experience, and type of work performed. For entry-level technicians with two-year degrees, salaries range from $43,510 for industrial engineering technicians to $46,040 for electronics technicians.

SOURCES OF FURTHER INFORMATION

International Brotherhood of Electrical Workers (IBEW)
1125 15th St. NW
Washington, DC 20005
Internet address: www.ibew.org

Institute of Electrical and Electronics Engineering, Inc.
1828 L St. NW
Suite 1202
Washington, DC 20036-5104
Internet address: www.ieee.org
The society distributes a free pamphlet describing engineering and engineering technology careers.

Utility Workers Union of America
815 16th St. NW
Washington, DC 20006
Internet address: www.uwua.org

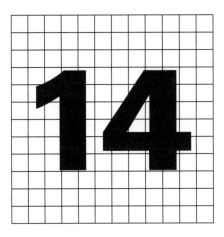

MECHANICAL ENGINEER

including
Solar Power Engineer

Mechanical engineering is a very broad discipline. It is concerned with mechanical design, heat transfer, energy conversion, fuel combustion technology, noise control and acoustics, robotic controls, solar energy, and other technical impacts on society. Mechanical engineers focus on the forces that convert natural energy into practical uses by studying the motion of gases, liquids, and solids and the heating and cooling of objects. They use the basic building blocks of science—combustion of matter, interaction of materials, and transfer of energy—to design everything from robots, computers, automobiles, and airplanes to power plants, furnaces, and solar energy cells.

Because mechanical engineering is such a broad engineering discipline, extending across many interdependent specialties, the work of individual engineers is highly specialized. Specialties include applied engineering, design engineering, heat transfer, power plant engineering, underwater technology, aerospace engineering, bionics, and plastics engineering. These engineers tackle a multitude of environmental science problems including ways to dispose of nuclear waste, how to design earthquake-proof structures, how to design space stations and underwater structures, and how to harness alternative forms of energy.

The development of solar energy is one particularly important area of energy development that mechanical engineers have been investigating. In this developing subfield, which has received progressively more funding from the federal government during the past few years and generated renewed interest in private industry, engineers are called solar power engineers. Each year, the sun sends toward earth thirty thousand times as much energy as is used by the entire world's industries. Harnessing this energy has proved to be a challenge because the solar cells used to collect the sun's rays have been very inefficient, and the cost of using solar technology is higher than the cost of conventional energy sources. Because it is not cost competitive, solar technology has not been adopted on a large scale. During the past several years, however, mechanical engineers have made strides in building a more efficient and cheaper solar cell. A silicon-based cell that is twice as efficient as its predecessors and can be mass produced at a low cost was recently developed. There are several large-scale solar power generation stations in the United States at which solar power engineers are experimenting with ways to collect and distribute this free, unlimited, and nonpolluting energy source. As oil and coal reserves diminish and the nuclear power industry proves to be too costly and unreliable, the need to more fully develop solar power is becoming apparent.

RELATED PROFESSIONS

Aerospace Engineer	Electrical and Electronics Engineer
Civil Engineer	Environmental Engineer
Mining Engineer	Forest Engineer
Physicist	Geophysicist

EDUCATIONAL REQUIREMENTS

The minimal educational requirement for a career as a mechanical engineer is a bachelor of science degree in engineering. More than 320 schools offer degrees in engineering in programs certified by the Accreditation Board of Engineering and Technology (ABET), and a large number of these institutions offer a specialty degree in mechanical engineering. An engineer trained in one branch of the field can, however, easily work in another area. In addition, some college graduates in physics or mathematics may be qualified to work as mechanical engineers because many of the principles of engineering are rooted in these disciplines.

In a typical four-year engineering program, classes during the first two years include mathematics, physics, chemistry, introduction to computing, principles of mechanical engineering, and social science and humanities courses. During the final two years, students take more specialized engineering courses, such as mechanics and thermodynamics, electromagnetic fields, heat transfer, fluid dynamics, and energy conservation. Laboratory experience is very important because it provides students with the practical application of their scientific concepts. In addition, computers are used extensively throughout the engineering curriculum.

Schools sometimes stress specific specialties within the field; students with specific interests should investigate curricula carefully before selecting a college. Some schools offer a general engineering curriculum in which students are not able to choose a concentration until reaching graduate school. In addition, some institutions offer five-year master's degree programs.

Graduate training is essential for engineering faculty positions but is not required for the majority of entry-level engineering positions. However, many engineers do obtain master's degrees to learn new technology, to broaden their educations, or to enhance promotion opportunities. Many engineers are obtaining M.B.A. degrees to advance to management and sales positions.

PROFESSIONAL CERTIFICATION

All fifty states and the District of Columbia require registration for engineers whose work affects life, health, or property or who offer their services to the public. The Accreditation Board for Engineering and Technology (ABET) offers the Professional Engineer (PE) license. Attainment of the license is based upon the acquisition of an engineering degree from an ABET-approved institution, successful completion of the Engineering-in-Training examination, four years of relevant work experience, and successful completion of a state examination. Licenses are generally transferable among states. Contact ABET, listed at the end of this chapter, for further information.

SETTINGS

Mechanical engineers work in laboratories and other research facilities, classrooms, offices, and manufacturing facilities where they inspect, supervise, and solve on-site problems. They may spend a substantial amount of time conducting research, using computers to design and test projects, and writing reports. These engineers also work extensively with other engineers, because complex projects often require the services of many engineers, each working on a small part of the job.

Many engineers work standard forty-hour weeks. At times, deadlines or design standards may bring extra work pressure to the job. When this happens, engineers may work long hours and experience considerable stress.

EMPLOYMENT STATISTICS AND MAJOR EMPLOYERS

In 1996, mechanical engineers held about 228,000 of the more than 1.3 million engineer jobs in the United States. According to the Engineering Manpower Commission, the number of engineers graduated from colleges and universities during the past nine years has dropped steadily. According to the U.S. Department of Labor, employment opportunities in all branches of engineering are expected to be good through the year 2005 because employment for engineers is expected to increase faster than the average for all occupations, while the number of degrees granted in engineering is not expected to increase much above present levels.

The majority of mechanical engineers work in the private sector, and more than three of five jobs are in manufacturing. Because mechanical engineering is the broadest engineering discipline, there are employment opportunities in many different job sectors and industries. Industries employing a large number of mechanical engineers include those that produce machinery, transportation equipment, electrical equipment, instruments, and metal products. Mechanical engineers are well represented throughout the organizational structure of most companies. They work as production supervisors, quality control agents, research and development specialists, and sales and marketing personnel, and they work in upper management. Most mechanical engineers start out as junior production engineers, and many advance to management positions. Research and development and consulting firms also hire a number of mechanical engineers.

Some mechanical engineers work in government. At the federal level, these engineers are employed by the Department of Agriculture in the Bureau of Reclamation, by the U.S. Army Corps of Engineers, by the National Aeronautic and

Space Administration, and by the Department of Transportation, Energy, and Defense.

SALARY STATISTICS

According to the National Association of Colleges and Employers, mechanical engineering graduates with bachelor's degrees had an average starting salary of $38,113, while those with master's degrees earned, on average, $45,400 per year. Holders of Ph.D. degrees earned an entry-level salary of $59,200 per year in 1997. A survey of workplaces in 160 metropolitan areas reported that experienced mid-level engineers with no supervisory responsibilities had median annual earnings of about $59,100, with the middle half earning between $54,000 and $65,000 per year. Median annual earnings for engineers at senior managerial levels were about $99,200.

Entry-level engineers working for the federal government with bachelor's degrees can expect to earn about $25,000. The holder of a master's degree will earn about $56,700, while those with Ph.D.'s can expect a salary of about $64,700. The average salary for engineers in the federal government in nonsupervisory, supervisory, and managerial positions was $61,950 in 1997.

In academia, assistant engineering professors earn an average salary of $45,753. Associate professors have an average income of $52,896, while full professors earn about $77,721 per year. Part-time engineering instructors earn an average of $27,000 per year.

SOURCES OF FURTHER INFORMATION

Accreditation Board for Engineering and Technology
111 Market Place
Suite 1050
Baltimore, MD 21202-4012
Internet address: www.abet.org
The board publishes a listing of accredited schools of engineering throughout the country.

American Society for Engineering Education
1818 N St. NW
Suite 600
Washington, DC 20036-2479
Internet address: www.asee.org
The society publishes two directories annually; one for undergraduate study and the other for graduate study and research in all areas of engineering.

American Society of Mechanical Engineers
345 East 47th St.
New York, NY 10017
Internet address: www.asme.org

American Society of Heating, Refrigerating, and Air-
  Conditioning Engineers, Inc.
1791 Tullie Circle, NE
Atlanta, GA 30329
Internet address: www.ashrae.org

National Society of Professional Engineers
2029 K St. NW
Washington, DC 20006
Internet address: www.nspe.org

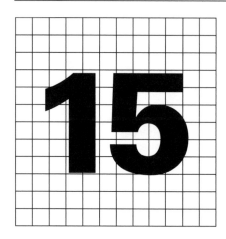

ENERGY MANAGEMENT TECHNICIAN

including
Energy Research Technician
Energy Production Technician
Energy Conservation Technician

Energy management technicians play an increasingly important role as energy costs continue to rise steeply and as people search for ways to make their homes, offices, and factories more energy efficient and less costly. These technicians perform several functions, which can be divided into three work areas: energy-related research and development, energy production, and energy conservation.

Energy research technicians work at public and private energy research facilities. They assist in the design and operation of laboratory experiments involving mechanical, electrical, hydraulic, or chemical properties in order to better understand and improve the energy budget of machinery. Energy research technicians work closely with engineers, chemists, physicists, and other research scientists. These technicians perform tests and measurements using complex measuring instruments and computers. Their work often leads to modifications that improve system functions and reduce energy inputs.

Energy production technicians work with engineers and other technicians to install, operate, modify, and repair systems and devices that convert raw energy inputs into usable energy supplies. Examples of these devices are home and industrial temperature control systems, including steam, electric, and hot water furnaces, air-conditioning systems, and solar heating systems. Technicians typically supervise other technicians in the installation and repair of these systems. Increasingly, these types of systems are controlled by complex computer control panels that require a knowledge of both mechanics and electronics.

Energy conservation technicians are involved with appraising the energy use of existing structures and suggesting ways to increase energy conservation. These technicians work with energy engineers and other technicians to determine building measurements and energy system specifications and to suggest methods to increase mechanical efficiency and structural modifications to save energy. Many public and private utility companies dispatch these technicians to private homes to assess energy problems, such as leaks in doors and windows and clogged furnaces and filters, and to suggest measures to correct these problems. In some cases, energy conservation technicians also fix diagnosed problems.

RELATED OCCUPATIONS

Power Plant Operator	Air-Conditioning, Heating, and
Power Distributor	Refrigeration Technician
Solar Collection Technician	Electromechanical Technician
Chemical Technician	Petroleum Technician
	Mechanical Engineering Technician

EDUCATIONAL REQUIREMENTS

While there are no formal requirements for an energy management technician position, most employers prefer applicants who have associate degrees from two-year community colleges or technical institutes or who have apprenticed with energy management specialists for at least six months. Many community college and technical institute programs in energy management are available. Most technical institutes offer programs that are quite specific and deal explicitly with the installation, maintenance, and repair of certain types of heating or air-conditioning systems. Conversely, community colleges tend to offer more broad-based programs, familiarizing students with the principles and applications of physics, electronics, energy conservation, computers, instrumentation, and energy economics. These majors are often called *energy conservation* or *energy management technology*. At these colleges, typical first programs include classes in mathematics, chemistry, physics, the fundamentals of energy technology and engineering, introduction to electricity and electrical devices, and energy production systems. Second-year classes may include electrical power and illumination systems, mechanical and fluid systems, energy conservation codes and regulations, blueprint reading, and heating, ventilating, and air-conditioning maintenance. Students must like working with their hands and have mechanical aptitude. Students spend a considerable amount of time in the laboratory assembling, disassembling, adjusting, and operating a variety of energy systems. Most graduates of energy management programs secure jobs before leaving college because school job placement offices do a good job of placing them.

SPECIAL CERTIFICATION

There are presently no state licensing requirements for this occupation.

SETTINGS

Energy management technicians work in laboratories, manufacturing facilities, and power plants and at homes and small businesses. Research technicians work primarily in laboratories or engineering departments. They usually work normal schedules and standard forty-hour weeks. Research technicians work with machinery and instruments that can cause harm by electric shock, and they must exercise good judgment and caution. In most cases facilities are clean, safe, and comfortable with advanced machinery and instruments.

Production technicians work primarily in manufacturing facilities and power plants and at work sites installing and maintaining equipment. Depending on their duties, these technicians can spend part or all of their time making service and installation calls. Their places of work can be dirty, noisy, and sometimes hot or cold. For the most part, they travel only locally and are usually assigned company vehicles. These technicians also work regular forty-hour weeks, but occasionally they must work more when equipment installation or repair deadlines are tight.

Conservation technicians work primarily in the field at homes and businesses. They typically make appointments with clients and meet them at the sites they are inspecting. They frequently talk with clients and make return calls to check up on improvements or make additional inspections; therefore, they must possess good communication skills. These technicians may need to climb and squeeze into tight locations and are occasionally required to work in dirty, noisy, and hot or cold places. Most are assigned company vehicles and must possess valid driver's licenses. In some cases these technicians must drive far from their home base, but overnight stays away from home are rare. Conservation technicians work typical forty-hour weeks, and overtime is generally not required.

EMPLOYMENT STATISTICS AND MAJOR EMPLOYERS

Several thousand energy management technicians are employed in the United States. The employment outlook for these technicians is better than the average for all occupations through the year 2006. As nonrenewable energy sources are depleted and energy prices rise, the demand for skilled energy technicians will increase. Citizens wishing to keep energy bills down, businesses wishing to install more efficient energy systems, and firms wishing to develop the best in energy technology contribute to healthy job growth in this field.

Most energy management technicians work for public and private utility companies, contract service companies, or energy research and development firms, or they are self-employed. Local community public service agencies, such as public utility districts, also hire a number of these technicians.

SALARY STATISTICS

The pay for energy management technicians is above the average for technicians in similar fields. Most entry-level technicians with only high school diplomas and no experience can expect to earn between $17,500 and $20,000, while those with two-year college degrees can earn between $19,500 and $25,000 per year. Technicians with three to six years' experience can earn as much as $35,000 per year. Local government agencies have similar starting pay scales and usually offer more generous benefit packages, such as family health insurance and sick and vacation pay.

SOURCES OF FURTHER INFORMATION

American Council for an Energy-Efficient Economy
1001 Connecticut Ave. NW
Suite 801
Washington, DC 20036

U.S. Public Interest Research Group
218 D St. SE
Washington, DC 20003
Internet address: www.pirg.org

Part Three
Planning and Design

OVERVIEW

**Total Employment
290,000**

Employment Breakdown by Job Sector

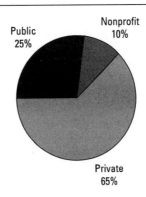

Public
25%

Nonprofit
10%

Private
65%

Projected Growth

According to the U.S. Department of Labor, employment opportunities in planning are expected to increase by about 19 percent by the year 2006. This rate of increase is about as fast as the average for all occupations. Employment opportunities in design should increase about 24 percent by the year 2006, which is slightly higher than the average for all occupations. The growing commitment to environmental planning will make landscape architecture the most lucrative career area in this field.

Salary Range

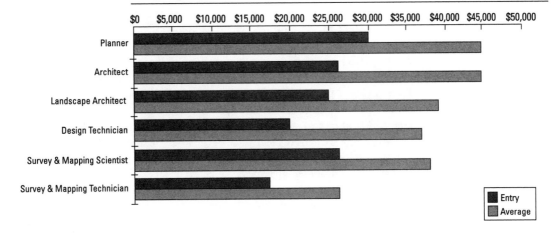

$0 $5,000 $10,000 $15,000 $20,000 $25,000 $30,000 $35,000 $40,000 $45,000 $50,000

Planner

Architect

Landscape Architect

Design Technician

Survey & Mapping Scientist

Survey & Mapping Technician

■ Entry
▨ Average

A CLOSER LOOK AT PLANNING AND DESIGN

When people think of the environment, the first images that come to mind are scenes of tall trees, babbling brooks, snowcapped mountains, beautiful flowers, and abundant wildlife. What are missing from our romanticized visions are the throngs of people and artifacts of civilization that occupy the real environment of our everyday lives. Because more than 75 percent of Americans now live in urban areas, they are more likely to relate to the features and environs of small towns like Manchester, Vermont, cozy cities like Paris, Florida, and Santa Fe, New Mexico; or metropolitan centers like San Francisco and Baltimore than to small rural communities or pristine wilderness areas. For urban dwellers, the most pressing environmental issues are smog, crime, traffic, and the lack of open and green space.

During the past 200 years there has been a dramatic shift in where people live and work. In 1800 only 6 percent of the U.S. population lived in urban areas. In addition to the general urbanization there has been a move from large cities to the suburbs. Both the initial migration from rural communities to cities and the subsequent move from larger cities to the suburbs have had profound effects on the environment.

Urban sprawl creates numerous environmental and infrastructure problems. What do we do with the old cities as the population literally empties from them? How do we accommodate suburban growth and preserve the landscape? How can we mitigate increased traffic congestion and the corresponding air pollution? What can be done to preserve open space as urban developments pave over the landscape? These are the difficult questions that planners and designers are being asked to solve.

Several forces will change the urban landscape in the future. The urban sprawl is likely to continue into "exurbia" (the undeveloped or relatively underdeveloped areas adjacent to the suburbs). The developments in exurbia will likely include very low-density and large-lot single-family homes; retirement communities; and resorts and second-home communities. Examples of this type of development can be seen in the western suburbs of Washington, D.C., and Miami and around Kansas City, Missouri, and Tucson, Arizona. Features like public transportation centers, centralized retail areas, concentric residential communities, and centralized park and recreation areas are essential to master plans. All of these features make communities more easily accessible to the residents and promote lifestyles that have a lower impact on the environment.

Finally, environmental issues, including the preservation of wetlands, open space, natural habitats, and endangered species and the need to enhance the quality of life for people living in all areas, need to be addressed. Increased development of rural communities and nondeveloped areas places additional burdens on the land, water, and other natural resources.

The increased urban population combined with the need to preserve natural habitats have created a strong demand for planners and design professionals. Planning and design professionals can shape the future of our cities while preserving vital natural resources as well as historical landmarks, thus making a positive contribution to the quality of life for everyone.

PROJECTED GROWTH AND EMPLOYMENT TRENDS

Overall employment for planners is expected to grow about as fast as the average for all occupations through the year 2006. Most job openings will arise from the need to replace experienced planners that are leaving the profession. The need for planners will vary by region, with the best opportunities arising in states that have mandated planning programs.

The design profession is expected to grow as fast as the general economy. This field is closely tied to the construction industry, and employment growth is therefore cyclical. Employment growth will vary depending on the location, with most growth anticipated in more rural and underdeveloped communities.

THE PLANNING PROFESSION

When we think about the quality of our lives we often focus on our homes, neighborhoods, jobs, and recreational environments. For a person who wants to make a significant contribution in all these areas, a career in planning offers this unique opportunity. Essentially, planners work on establishing land-use plans and implementing programs that ensure that the objectives of the plans are fulfilled. The land-use plans may involve preserving natural habitats, such as the San Francisco Bay, or controlling the development of urban areas. This exciting and rewarding career allows professionals to protect the environment, enhance the quality of life for others, and help shape the future development of cities.

In general, planners can be divided into two broad categories: those who work within a *geographic boundary* and those who work within a *policy area* or on a specific issue. Often these two overlap. Planners who work within a geographical boundary include city, regional, and state planners. These planners may focus on a specific urban center or a wider area, such as entire metropolitan zones or unique geographic areas such as mountain and island communities. Planners who focus on a geographic area are generally responsible for developing a plan that addresses public-use issues. These issues may include the preservation of a natural area, protection of historical landmarks, or protection of a certain type of land use (such as making sure residents are not displaced by industrial uses). After a plan for an area has been established, the planner is responsible for implementing a program to ensure that the planning objectives are met.

Planners also protect and preserve natural resources. These planners are generally responsible for a specific natural resource or geographic area. A planner who works in a particular area may, for instance, work to preserve wetlands or the historical character of an area. Examples of this type of work include preservation work on the California coast and the massive restoration project on the Kissimmee River in the wetlands of southern Florida. These types of environmental planning activities are fueled by public concern and federal mandates. Other planners work on specific issues. These planners include transportation planners, solid waste management planners, and wetland planners.

Planners working with policy issues include federal and some state planners. Instead of working with specific and limited planning projects, these planners develop general policy areas, funding priorities, and guidelines that regional and local planners follow.

Regardless of the type of planning, the planning process involves developing plans and implementing programs to address public policy issues. Generally these plans focus on land-use issues. Planners usually develop plans that specify the best use of a community's land, based on the existing pattern of development. These plans typically consider residential, commercial, industrial, recreational, and environmental issues. In addition, planners consider social service, transportation, public health, and public infrastructure issues. Implementing the plan often requires a coordinated effort among government agencies, such as the transportation department, the zoning department, school districts, and other agencies. In addition, implementing the plan requires a coordinated effort between the public and private sectors and includes working with the residents of communities as well as developers and quasipublic agencies such as hospitals.

Planners are also responsible for capital improvements, such as the building of new schools, public housing, and sewage systems and the extension of services to other areas. Often planning involves the preservation of existing uses or natural resources. The planning agency may try to preserve existing land use such as low-income housing, residential hotels for the poor, or small businesses located in a depressed area. Planners also address a wide range of environmental issues, including ensuring air and water quality, pollution control, locating hazardous waste sites, and implementing recycling programs. Often planners work to reach a balance between economic development and preserving the environment.

PLANNING-RELATED PROFESSIONS

Growth Management Planner
City Manager
Building and Zoning
  Administrator
Architect
Draftsperson
Survey and Mapping Technician
Landscape Architect

Planning Consultant
Planning Director
Development or Redevelopment
  Administrator
Designer
Surveyor
Architect and Construction
  Technician

THE DESIGN PROFESSIONAL

Several political decisions, acts of nature, and technological advances have drastically influenced the nature of work and employment opportunities in the design profession. First, in July 1992 the Americans with Disabilities Act (ADA) was signed by President George Bush. This sweeping legislation was designed to extend civil rights protection to persons with disabilities by making public and private structures more accessible to them. Second, a series of California earthquakes focused national attention on the risks associated with living near active and inactive faults and created a demand for design professionals who can design and retrofit structures that will withstand a major earthquake. Finally, new technologies including Graphic Information Systems (GIS) and Global Positioning

Systems (GPS) have changed the way we measure, map, and analyze geographic information and have opened up new and exciting career avenues for design professionals.

Design professionals include architects, landscape architects, designers, drafters, design technicians, engineers, surveyors, and other professionals who plan and design structures as well as public and private parks, roads, and open space. Architects are responsible for the planning and design of buildings. Landscape architects plan and design parks, plazas, residential yards, office parks, and special-use properties such as golf courses. Surveyors measure and establish elevation points, contours, and boundaries. The information compiled by surveyors is used for construction projects and mapmaking. Design professionals are supported by survey, architecture, and construction technicians who carry out much of the actual work.

Americans with Disabilities Act (ADA)

The Americans with Disabilities Act covers four broad areas: employment, public services and transportation, public accommodations, and telecommunications. Design professionals are primarily concerned with Title III, the public accommodations provision. This provision includes the definition of *disability* (which includes mental impairments) and calls for the removal of barriers in public accommodations. The ADA requires that barriers be removed in existing "public accommodations" if such removal is "readily achievable." In addition, alterations made to a public building must be made accessible in line with specific technical requirements. The law further states that public accommodations must take whatever steps are necessary to ensure that no one with a disability is excluded, denied services, segregated, or otherwise treated differently from anyone else because of the absence of ancillary aids and services—unless it can be demonstrated that taking those steps would fundamentally alter the nature of the goods, services, or accommodations being offered or would result in an "undue burden."

This law was written broadly and has resulted in a bonanza of employment opportunities for architects, surveyors, civil engineers, construction technicians, and real estate consultants who estimate costs, make design modifications, and work on remodeling properties in order to provide access to the disabled. Specifically, architects and construction experts provide ADA compliance surveys, which provide detailed inventories of potential barriers, recommend ways of removing barriers, estimate the cost of removing the barriers, and supervise remodeling projects.

Seismic Designs and Retrofitting

In October 1989 the Loma-Prieta earthquake caused an estimated $980 million in damage to the Bay Area, and in January 1994 the Northridge earthquake caused an estimated $3 billion in damage to the Los Angeles area. These two earthquakes have increased the need to retrofit buildings to be seismically safe and develop new design features that will protect against future earthquakes. In contrast to widely held beliefs in southern California, only a handful (four hundred) of Los Angeles's thousands of multistory buildings are seismically reinforced. In addition, many of the safety designs developed and installed in the 1970s failed during the latest spate of moderately strong earthquakes, which points to the need to apply new and better seismic technology. Thus, architects and engineers will continue to develop ways to design structures that can withstand major earthquakes. In addition, older properties, particularly brick structures, require seismic retrofitting. The challenge to architects and engineers is to retrofit older properties without destroying the architectural integrity of the structures. This type of work is not limited to California; other seismically active areas of the country are the Seattle metropolitan region, the Alaska coastal region, the Midwest, and much of the Northeast, including New York City, which has major faults running under the island of Manhattan. Better seismic technology will benefit all these locations.

GIS and GPS

The work of mapping scientists is changing rapidly due to new technologies; the most important of these is the Geographic Information Systems (GIS). GIS science is a new and exciting field that will drastically change our understanding of the planet as well as the amount of information that can be analyzed within a geographic area. GIS scientists combine computer technology with geographic information and databases in order to simultaneously study geomorphic, landscape, and human settlement patterns on the earth's surface.

These systems are extremely powerful tools that can be used to study both urban land-use patterns and environmental conditions. Urban planners can combine census data on employment, and income and other economic and demographic data with maps in order to understand current land-use patterns as well as changes in land-use patterns. Planners can also use GIS to analyze the physical features of an undeveloped area in order to plan the development of a site based on the physical features of the property, soil characteristics, and presence of wetlands, endangered species, and other wildlife. The GIS can then be used to develop the property in a way that will minimize environmental damage. Within the environmental field, the GIS can be combined with satellite imagery to map the destruction of natural resources, measure drought conditions, and note changes in the botanical features of an area. This science has created a demand for computer programmers to link large databases with mapping software. Mapping software facilitates the collection of a wide variety of information based on geographic perimeters. It can be used to establish the most-efficient delivery systems as well as assist planners annualizing traffic patterns in order to design new roads and public transportation routes. This field is promising for those interested in mapping, surveying, engineering, demography, planning, forestry, and the life sciences.

Global Positioning Systems (GPS) use a satellite that precisely locates points on the earth using radio signals. The system was designed by the military for the navigation of planes, tanks, ships, and other equipment. The GPS program has been adopted by surveyors and other scientists who use signals transmitted by small receivers placed at specific geographic locations to analyze all types of information. Some applications are the study of ozone depletion, global warming, environmental destruction caused by overgrazing, and changes in water flow. GPS has been used with heat sensors that can detect the amount of heat on the planet's surface. When insects consume large quantities of plants, the amount of heat generated declines, indicating that a pesticide program may be required. Thus, the use of pesticides can be targeted, which cuts down on blanket spraying.

DESIGN-RELATED PROFESSIONS

Civil Engineer	Planner
Interior Designer	Engineer Technician
Drafter	Traffic and Highway Engineer
General Contractor	Graphic Designer

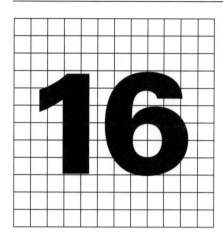

PLANNER

including
City Planner
Urban Planner
Regional Planner
State Planner
Federal Planner

CITY PLANNER

Much of the damage that we do to the environment takes place in the urban setting. Some environmental problems, such as smog, are primarily due to industrialization, increased automobile traffic, and other urban conditions. Efficient planning can reduce traffic congestion, contain urban sprawl (which decreases commuter time), and increase the availability and convenience of public transportation. Thus, city planners and urban planners can help ease human and environmental stresses by modifying the infrastructure of urban areas. In addition to enhancing the quality of life within an urban area, urban planners have the opportunity to solve complex social problems, such as crime, poverty, affordable housing, and urban blight. They can also enhance the aesthetic and environmental quality of communities by preserving parks, natural areas, and open space.

The vast majority of urban planners work for government agencies. The most jobs by far are found in city and municipal planning departments. Fewer jobs are found at regional, state, and federal agencies. Planners help develop master plans, program objectives, and timetables to complete civic projects. Almost all metropolitan areas have general plans designed to protect, preserve, and enhance the quality of the urban area. Furthermore, the general plan serves as a basis for coordinating public and private services and growth and development within the urban area and adjacent parcels.

In larger cities, planners divide the general plan into specific planning jurisdictions and oversee the implementation of the plan's various elements. These elements may include transportation, recreation, preservation, open space, and community facilities. Planners also develop expertise in economic and conservation issues and work in specialized areas, such as wetland preservation, business district development, greenbelt preservation, and the development of specific neighborhood plans. Planners must also consider specific objectives such as maintaining the historical character of a neighborhood and encouraging or discouraging specific uses.

REGIONAL PLANNER

Because people have begun to recognize the complexity of urban areas and natural resources, the need for regional planners has increased dramatically. Regional planners address issues that influence more than one jurisdiction or a highly sensitive area. Areas of concern to a regional planner tend to be somewhat broader than those of an urban planner and may focus on economic development, the preservation of natural resources, or reducing conflicts among municipalities. They focus on issues like traffic congestion and infrastructure that transcend community boundaries. Regional planners can assist in solving problems common to several urban areas; for example, they may control pollution, find more efficient ways to handle household waste, implement recycling programs, or find a location for an undesirable land use such as landfill. Regional planning organizations can attempt to protect vital natural resources that cross the boundaries of several cities, counties, or even states. These agencies may protect a specific natural resource like a bay or harbor or, in the case of California, the entire coastline. Often these agencies seek to find a balance between preservationists and economic developers. As you may imagine, regional planners can find themselves caught between two or more groups that have drastically different opinions regarding the best use of a particular natural resource.

Regional planning agencies that address more than one jurisdiction include the Metropolitan Council of the Twin Cities of Minnesota, the Association of Bay Area Governments in California, the Cape Cod Commission, and the San Diego Regional Planning and Growth Control Board. Other regional planning agencies focus on geographic areas that are considered sensitive to uncontrolled development. Examples of these agencies include the Tahoe Regional Planning Agency, the California Coastal Commission, and Bay Vision 2020. These agencies were created to address regional issues involving important natural resources, but there is an inherent conflict between local and regional government. Local governments are likely to resist giving up control of the management of land within their jurisdiction to a regional planner. The local government may be perceived as incompetent to manage natural resources or development. Regional agencies must also work with other local, state, and federal agencies. The Tahoe Regional Planning Agency was formed in 1970 and was then immediately subjected to the conflicting interests of two states, five local governments, and twenty-two federal agencies with jurisdiction over the Tahoe Basin, not to mention the thousands of property owners whose ability to develop their properties would potentially be restricted by the agency.

As is the case for urban planners, regional planners are responsible for establishing land-use plans and implementing programs that ensure that the objectives of the larger program are fulfilled. Regional planning offers a unique opportunity to balance the use and protection of our natural resources.

STATE PLANNER

State planning began in response to the Great Depression of the 1930s and was influenced by New Deal programs. State planning agencies faded away as the nation entered World War II and during the postwar economic boom. Beginning in the mid-1950s, the federal government again began supporting state, regional, and local planning efforts. Only recently have agencies begun to take on more proactive roles in managing growth, due primarily to the major environmental and infrastructure problems caused by rapid metropolitan growth. Among the objectives of state planning are the management of environmental concerns. For example, in Florida's State Comprehensive Plan, seven of the twenty-five goals pertain to the environment. Likewise when Vermont enacted Act 200 (growth control legislation), half of the state policies established involved the preservation of natural resources. In the 1970s several states enacted state planning programs. Generally, there are two types of state planning agencies. The first are those agencies founded to protect unique environmental resources and accorded powers to override local government regulations that might compromise their mission. The second type are mandated by the state to create regional entities to develop regional plans and to coordinate local plans according to stated land-use objectives. The specific concerns most often cited are environmental protection, cost-efficient infrastructure, and affordable housing and economic development. The planning process for state planners is much the same as that for regional planners, although the objectives are much broader. Nearly all state planning jobs are with state agencies.

FEDERAL PLANNER

Federal agencies do not become involved in the local planning process. They focus on larger issues, such as transportation, housing, and environmental protection. While the federal government does not work directly with communities on specific planning issues, it does provide major funding for development, redevelopment, transportation, subsidized housing, and many other programs.

Community development programs have never recovered from the stigma attached to the Urban Renewal Programs established under the Housing Act of 1949 and eventually dropped in 1973. Under the Urban Renewal Program, "undesirable uses" such as low-income housing and small businesses were razed for new developments. As a result of urban renewal, 600,000 dwelling units were demolished, displacing approximately two million people, most of whom were poor. A total of 250,000 new dwelling units were built, and most were occupied by middle-income and high-income households. Because of the problems with the original urban renewal plan, future federal programs are likely to be more focused on what is referred to as *categorical grants*: money designated for housing, economic development, transportation, and so on.

Employment opportunities exist in many federal agencies and planning consulting firms hired by the federal government. The Department of Housing and Urban Development (HUD) hires a number of planners. Those interested in air quality and transportation issues can find employment with the Department of Transportation. The government is presently changing its focus on transportation needs from automobile to long- and short-distance rail systems. This project, which requires input from transportation planners, will benefit the environment because it will result in less carbon monoxide being released into the environment. With the planned closing of military bases throughout the nation, the Department of Defense will need planners who can implement programs to convert the former military bases to civilian uses.

EDUCATIONAL REQUIREMENTS

The basic requirement for a career in planning is an undergraduate bachelor of science (B.S.) degree in planning. In addition to a planning degree, study in real estate, architecture, landscape architecture, engineering, public policy, or political science can be beneficial. While a master's degree in planning is not required, it is becoming essential. According to the American Planning Association (APA), fifty-five undergraduate and eighty-seven graduate programs offered an APA-certified degree in planning in 1993.

Students are encouraged while still in college to work with planning professionals to gain practical work experience. Check with city, regional, and state planning agencies. Because these agencies have only a limited capacity to accommodate students, experience can also be gained in college departments involved in the school planning process or in real estate consulting firms, the offices of large developers, and nonprofit organizations working with government planning agencies.

PROFESSIONAL CERTIFICATION

The American Planning Association offers members the opportunity to become members of the American Institute of Certified Planners (AICP). To qualify, a person must have a combination of education and professional experience, and pass a written examination. The level of experience required for consideration ranges from eight years for those without college degrees to two years for those with graduate degrees in planning from APA-accredited universities. Contact the APA, listed at the end of this chapter, for further information.

SETTINGS

Most planners work for government agencies. Federal planners work primarily in Washington, D.C., but some work in locations outside of the capital. State planning professionals work at the state capitals or in field offices located throughout a state, while regional and city planners work locally. Government offices are usually comfortable, well-lit facilities located in the downtown area.

Planners work forty hours per week with regular work schedules. Some government agencies may offer more flexible work schedules, such as four ten-hour days rather than the traditional five-day workweek. Occasionally planners are required to work nights and weekends, particularly when they are required to meet with concerned citizens or elected officials. Because most planning jobs are with city and county agencies, planning departments are usually small.

Planners work in a politically charged environment. They are often asked to solve planning issues that involve competing political parties, various government agencies, and concerned business and citizen organizations in a range of social, economic, environmental, or preservation issues. In general, planners seek to find one solution to multiple problems and competing interests. Given these circumstances, political conflicts are bound to arise. Planners need to arbitrate between opposing groups and are often required to find solutions that are both practical and politically feasible. Those who enjoy the challenge of working with a variety of interest groups in a political atmosphere should pursue a planning career.

EMPLOYMENT STATISTICS AND MAJOR EMPLOYERS

In 1996, there were about 29,400 planners employed in the United States. Approximately two-thirds of the planners worked for local government agencies; most others were employed in state and federal agencies. The remaining positions were found in the nonprofit sector, development firms, or related private businesses, such as architectural firms or consulting firms.

The Bureau of Labor Statistics estimates that employment of urban and regional planners will increase by about 5 percent before the year 2006. Overall, however, the employment outlook for planners is mixed. Certain government agencies are likely to have a strong need for planners. One is the Department of Defense, which is closing bases and reshuffling existing personnel. The Department of Transportation is likely to require planners to solve increasing transportation problems into the foreseeable future. At the same time, the huge federal deficit combined with the swelling demands created by entitlement programs, such as Social Security, medical insurance, and Medicare, are likely to result in a significant decrease in the funds available for categorical grants or comprehensive planning policies.

On the state level, the demand for planners is likely to increase as the trend toward suburbanization continues to engulf surrounding areas.

The demand in local government planning agencies, which employ the majority of planners, is expected to rise as small communities grow. Planning needs will increasingly be met by regional agencies. Employment in private industry will also increase because planning departments at all levels of government hire consulting firms to research planning needs.

Overall, the Department of Labor estimates that employment in the planning field is expected to grow about as fast as the average for all occupations through the year 2006. Most job openings will arise from the need to replace experienced planners leaving the profession. The need for planners will vary by region. The best opportunities are in those states that have mandated planning objectives.

SALARY STATISTICS

The earning potential for planners generally increases with the size of the planning agency and the experience and education level of the planner. According to the Department of Labor, in 1997 the median annual salary for urban and regional planners was $41,400. Entry-level planners earned an average of $30,000, compared to $40,000 for those with five to ten years' experience. Those with bachelor's degrees earned, on average, $40,000, compared to $44,000 for those with master's degrees and $53,000 for those with Ph.D.'s. In general, the average salaries in local governments are lower than those for state and federal workers. Likewise, salary levels are generally higher in larger communities where the cost of living is also higher. Private consulting firms pay an average salary of $50,000. Development firms offer the highest salaries, while nonprofit organizations pay the lowest.

SOURCES OF FURTHER INFORMATION

American Planning Association
1776 Massachusetts Ave. NW
Washington, DC 20036
Internet address: www.planning.org
The APA provides a wealth of information regarding current planning issues, membership in the American Institute of Certified Planners (AICP), fellowships and scholarships, and careers. The APA publishes numerous books and articles covering a wide range of planning issues including the following:

Guide to Undergraduate Education in Urban and Regional Planning and Related Fields, 3d edition

Guide to Graduate Education in Urban and Regional Planning Accredited University Planning Programs

This is a list of undergraduate and graduate programs that are accredited by the Planning Accreditation Board:
Government Job Finder
Non Profits' Job Finder
Where to Find Employment Advertisements for Planners

The Urban Land Institute
625 Indiana Ave. NW
Washington, DC 20004-2930
Internet address: www.uli.org
The ULI, a membership organization for students, professors, and librarians, publishes Metro Packets, which include information on selected topics related to urban development. The ULI also publishes "project reference files," which provide detailed information on specific development or redevelopment projects.

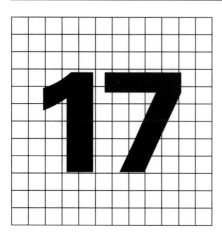

ARCHITECT

Architects are responsible for influencing how we feel about the structures, from single family homes to skyscrapers that are virtual cities and from schools to stadiums, which we work in and inhabit. They design new buildings and prepare plans for remodeling existing properties. The process of designing a building starts with interviewing the client in order to understand what the client—an individual, organization, or government body—wants. After the architect understands the needs of the client, he or she designs the building. In order to design a property the architect considers local and state building regulations, city zoning requirements, and the client's specific needs. The local climate, site features, and neighborhood characteristics are considered. The architect must design a structure that can be constructed within a predefined budget.

Architects work closely with other professionals to determine the type of materials to be used, interior design features, and engineering considerations. The final design will show the location and type of structure, building features, and location of utilities, windows, doors, and plumbing. It will detail interior finishes, cabinetry, and other building features. After the building plans are complete, the architect may assist the client in hiring contractors. The architect is also responsible for assisting the client with the construction of the building and may be required to change the design as the construction progresses.

Architects design a wide variety of buildings: industrial buildings, shopping centers, homes, apartments, hospitals, offices, churches, and other structures. Architects also design public buildings: airports, schools, libraries, government buildings, and housing for the poor. Architects may specialize in a specific type of property or in one phase of work. Some of the larger firms have departments of architects who specialize in urban design, master plan designs for residential communities, or collaboration with government planning departments.

RELATED PROFESSIONS

Civil Engineer
Interior Designer
Drafter
General Contractor
Technician

Surveyor
Architectural Technician
Traffic and Highway Engineer
Graphic Designer

EDUCATIONAL REQUIREMENTS

In order to be a practicing architect, a person must have a college degree. Most architecture schools offer four- or five-year programs leading to a bachelor of architecture degree (B.S.) or a six-year master's degree. Architecture schools are accredited by the National Architectural Accrediting Board (NAAB). While there are more than ninety accredited schools of architecture, the competition to enter these programs can be fierce.

Many people think that the ability to draw and other artistic abilities are required of an architect. While these skills may be helpful, they are not required. The most important ability is the ability to conceptualize spatial relationships and understand engineering principles. Most college programs include courses in architectural history, building design, math and engineering, graphic design, computer programming, physical sciences, and liberal arts.

PROFESSIONAL CERTIFICATION

All states require architects to be licensed or registered before practicing architecture. Architects who are not licensed must work for licensed architects who are responsible for the unlicensed architects' work. Most states grant a license only if a candidate graduates from an accredited school of architecture, has completed three years of practical experience, and has successfully completed a four-day examination. Contact the American Institute of Architects, listed at the end of this chapter, or the state architectural licensing board for further information.

SETTINGS

While architects spend most of their time indoors, their office settings are frequently more casual than traditional offices, and often suits and ties are not required. An architect in Boulder, Colorado, said he wears a tie to the office but takes it off as soon as he walks in the door. While the office setting may be casual, the work hours can be long. Architects may work nights, weekends, and holidays to meet important deadlines.

While most of architects' time is spent in an office, they also spend a considerable amount of time elsewhere meeting with clients and at construction sites. The daily routine varies. Architects must meet with clients, salespeople, contractors, and other professionals. While the job offers variety, architects spend a good deal of time working on the routine elements of a design. The routine tasks have been reduced by computer-aided design systems (CAD), which have, at the same time, increased the level of detail required.

EMPLOYMENT STATISTICS AND MAJOR EMPLOYERS

In 1996, about 94,000 people were employed as architects in the United States. Most of the jobs were in architecture firms. Most architecture firms are small; the majority employ five or fewer workers. More than 25 percent of all architects are self-employed. Other architects work for builders, real estate developers, consultants, or government agencies. Some of the government agencies that may employ architects are planning agencies; the departments of Defense, the Interior, and Housing and Urban Development; and the General Services Administration. While most architects work for small firms, some firms have offices nationwide, and larger firms may have several offices in a single region.

Employment opportunities for architects are expected to be good in the foreseeable future. Employment is expected to increase as fast as the average for all occupations. At the same time, the number of degrees granted in architecture is not expected to increase significantly. The need for architects depends on the demand for new construction. Construction is highly sensitive to cyclical changes in the economy. While the demand for architects is expected to be relatively strong, the employment outlook is shaded by the fact that economic and construction cycles affect the career opportunities for architects. When the construction industry is expanding, the need for office space increases (for architects, engineers, bankers, and other professionals involved in the construction industry), and when employment opportunities increase, more people buy homes and have greater incomes (which facilitates the construction of new homes and shopping centers). When the construction industry is shrinking, the demand for new homes, office space, and shopping centers decreases. Thus, while architecture is an exciting and interesting career, its cycles and fluctuations must be considered.

SALARY STATISTICS

For recently licensed architects, the average salary is about $27,000. Licensed architects who have been working for three to five years earned an average of $33,000 in 1997. According to The American Institute of Architects, the median salary for intern-architects was $27,000 in 1996. For architects with eight to ten years' experience, the median salary was $45,000, and for partners and the self-employed, the median salary was $75,000 to $100,000.

SOURCES OF FURTHER INFORMATION

Careers in Architecture Program
The American Institute of Architects
1735 New York Ave. NW
Washington, DC 20006
Internet address: www.aiaonline.org

National Architectural Accreditation Board
1725 New York Ave. NW
Washington, DC 20006
Internet address: www.naab.org

Society of American Registered Architects
303 South Broadway
Tarrytown, NY 10591
Internet address: www.sara-national.org

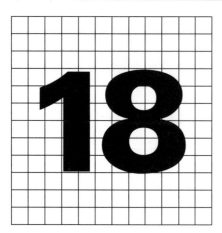

LANDSCAPE ARCHITECT

Landscape architects plan and design parks, plazas, residential yards, office parks, shopping centers, and special-use properties. They may also design large master plans for new communities, college campuses, golf courses, country clubs, or other special-use properties. Other design projects may involve working with government agencies, preparing environmental impact reports, restoring historic landscapes, managing waterfront improvement projects, or designing parks and recreational areas.

These architects design areas so that they are not only functional but also beautiful and compatible with the natural environment. In planning a site, landscape architects first consider the nature and purpose of the project and the funds available. They analyze the natural elements of the site, such as climate, soil, slope of the land, drainage, and vegetation. They observe where sunlight falls on the site at different times of the day and examine the site from various angles.

Landscape architects may plan the location of buildings, roads, walkways, and plazas. They select plants, grasses, trees, and shrubs and determine the location of each type of landscaping. Landscape architects are also responsible for the design of decks, patios, open space, and private outdoor areas as well as the irrigation systems, storm drains, signs, and other components of the site. Overall, landscape architecture is an exciting career that combines an understanding of landscape design, engineering, and construction with geology, hydrology, horticulture, botany, geology, and the humanities and arts.

RELATED PROFESSIONS

Drafter
Architect
Engineer
Botanist
Landscaper and Ground Manager

Rangeland Specialist
Arborist
Nursery Manager
Horticulturist

EDUCATIONAL REQUIREMENTS

Landscape architects must complete four- or five-year college programs in order to receive bachelor's degrees in landscape architecture. Recently, many landscape architecture students have been electing to receive additional training and earn master's degrees. Courses may include the history of landscape architecture, landscape design, engineering and math, graphic design, communication, and surveying. In addition, students study horticulture, botany, geology, hydrology, agronomy, meteorology, and other related subjects. The design studio is an important aspect of many landscape architecture curricula. Students are assigned real projects to work on, providing them with valuable hands-on experience. As is the case for architects, the ability to understand spatial relationships and conceptual designs is more important to the landscape architect than is artistic talent. According to the American Society of Landscape Architects, fifty-one accredited colleges and universities offer graduate and undergraduate degrees.

PROFESSIONAL CERTIFICATION

Most states require landscape architects to be licensed. In order to be eligible to receive a license, candidates must have a degree from an accredited university and two to four years of practical experience; they also must pass a comprehensive examination. A few states require additional examinations on laws and/or plant material indigenous to those states. For more information, contact the American Society of Landscape Architects, listed at the end of this chapter, or the individual state licensing agency.

SETTINGS

Landscape architects spend much of their time indoors, although they also work outdoors when inspecting sites or supervising construction. As is the case for architects, landscape architects need to spend time with clients, salespeople, and other professionals and may be involved in working with clients to hire and supervise contractors. While most landscape architects work standard forty-hour weeks, longer hours are required to meet client demands and construction deadlines. Given the nature of the work, the job can be somewhat seasonal with a reduced workload during the winter months.

The design process generally starts with understanding the needs of the client and inspecting the site. The landscape architect considers such site-specific features as topography, sunlight, existing structures and plants, soil conditions, and development restrictions. Then plans are developed that balance the building design with the physical features of the property.

EMPLOYMENT STATISTICS AND MAJOR EMPLOYERS

Approximately seventeen thousand landscape architects were employed in the United States in 1997. Forty percent of all landscape architects work for firms that offer landscape architecture services (which include both landscape architecture firms and traditional architectural firms). Most of the rest were employed by architecture firms. The federal government, particularly the U.S. departments of Agriculture, Defense, and the Interior, also employ landscape architects. Approximately three in ten landscape architects are self-employed.

Most employment for landscape architects is concentrated in urban and suburban areas in all parts of the country. Some landscape architects work in rural areas, particularly those in the federal government who plan and design parks and recreation areas.

The outlook for opportunities in landscape architecture is very promising, as jobs are expected to grow faster than the average for all occupations through the year 2006.

SALARY STATISTICS

Median annual earnings for all architects, including landscape architects, were about $39,500 in 1996. The middle 50 percent earned between $38,200 and $53,900; 10 percent earned less than $23,900, and 10 percent earned more than $65,800. Some partners and successful business owners earn more than $100,000 per year.

SOURCES OF FURTHER INFORMATION

American Society of Landscape Architects
636 Eye St. NW
Washington, DC 20001-3736
Internet address: www.asla.org
The society provides a free brochure, *A Guide to Educational Programs in Landscape Architecture,* which describes the landscape architecture profession, and a monthly magazine, *Landscape Architecture Magazine*, which gives information on career trends and employment opportunities.

Associated Landscape Contractors of America
150 Elden St.
Suite 270
Herndon, VA 20170
Internet address: www.alca.org

Council of Landscape Architectural Registration Boards
12700 Fair Lakes Circle
Suite 110
Fairfax, VA 22033
Internet address: www.clarb.org

DESIGN TECHNICIAN

including
Architecture Technician
Construction Technician

Design technicians can be intimately involved with designing, planning, and constructing environmentally sound buildings. Design technicians include architecture technicians and construction technicians. In architectural and engineering offices, technicians assist professionals in preparing drawings, completing cost estimates, calculating areas and materials, and preparing specifications. They may also assist architects in inspecting construction sites, estimating percentage of completion, and making sure construction is completed on schedule. These technicians may assist in making sure that the required corrections are made or help ensure that a project is completed in a cost-effective manner. Other jobs include architectural drafters who fill in the technical details on architectural plans, according to the specific codes and calculations of the engineers, surveyors, and architects. Structural drafters perform roughly the same duties as architectural drafters, but focus on concrete, steel, glass, and other structural components of a building.

Construction technicians' duties range from entry-level jobs such as materials checkers to advanced jobs such as construction supervisors. Construction technicians may also act as building inspectors to ensure that jobs are completed in a satisfactory manner. Construction technicians often work as construction salespeople, applying their knowledge of products, building codes, installation procedures, and the uses for the products they are selling. Other jobs include estimators, who help estimate the quantity and price of materials, and plant and building supervisors.

RELATED PROFESSIONS

Architectural Drafter
Structural Drafter and Detail Checker
Assistant Plant Engineer and
   Building Supervisor

Architect
Landscape Architect
Construction Inspector
Engineering Technician

Architectural Sales Representative   CAD Technician
Estimator   Landscaper
Clerical Methods Analyst   Cartographic Drafter
Drafter   Contractor
Building Inspector   Surveyor
Plant Engineer

EDUCATIONAL REQUIREMENTS

Technicians require either vocational school or technical institute training. Generally, these two-year programs result in a certificate, diploma, or associate degree. Because construction technicians deal with building and operations, vocational schools and technical institutes offer the best programs for them. A few technical colleges offer four-year degrees in architectural engineering technology. Graduates of four-year programs are referred to as *technologists* in order to distinguish them from two-year graduates. Almost all schools that train architectural and building construction technicians require two years of high school algebra, a year of trigonometry or geometry, and one or two years of physical science. Programs in architectural technology include courses in mathematics (including calculus), architectural drawing, technical mathematics, applied physics, building materials, construction methods, communication skills, construction planning and control, and architectural history. During the second year of an architectural or construction technician program, the courses include architectural drawing and model building, elementary surveying, advanced architectural drawing, technical reporting, building service systems, contracts, codes, specifications and office practices, computer applications, general and industrial economics, and construction cost estimating contracts.

PROFESSIONAL CERTIFICATION

Architectural and building construction technicians are not required to be licensed. Some technicians do, however, work toward obtaining licenses or become certified engineering technicians. If an architectural or building construction technician has the practical experience, he or she can take the examination to be a licensed land surveyor.

Although drafters are not required to be certified, the American Design Drafting Association has established a certification program. Applicants are tested on their knowledge of drafting essentials such as geometric construction, working drawings, and architectural terms and standards. Certification shows that a drafter has met nationally recognized standards.

SETTINGS

Working conditions vary with the type of work. Some architectural technicians can expect work almost exclusively in architectural or engineering offices. Architectural offices are almost always clean, comfortable, and well lighted. An architectural technician will do much of the work seated at a desk or drawing table.

Technicians who work at construction sites spend most of their time outdoors. An architectural technician spends many hours or days preparing detailed estimates or drawings. Paying attention to detail is a critical skill for these technicians. At a construction site, the construction technicians must make sure that the work meets exact specifications, and when reviewing drawings, technicians must focus on ensuring that the work has been performed according to the detailed specifications. Building projects may include homes, factories, apartment buildings, shopping centers, and public buildings such as libraries, schools, and prisons. Architecture and construction involve a wide variety of materials, including conventional pine, hardwood lumber, ceramics, glass, and metals; therefore, technicians need to understand the components of each of these materials.

EMPLOYMENT STATISTICS AND MAJOR EMPLOYERS

Drafters held about 310,000 jobs in 1996. This number includes architectural drafters as well as aeronautical, electrical, electronic, civil, mechanical, and pipeline drafters. More than 32 percent of all drafters worked in engineering and architectural firms. Another 29 percent worked in manufacturing industries; the remaining were mostly employed in the construction, communications, utilities, and personnel supply services industries. The need for architectural and construction technicians is expected to remain strong in the foreseeable future as technologies continue to increase the complex nature of building systems and computers increase the level of skill required by technicians.

SALARY STATISTICS

Architectural and building construction technicians earn salaries similar to those of other engineering technicians. Their starting salaries average around $20,700 per year. More experienced technicians generally earn between $36,100 and $40,900; some senior technicians earn $50,000 or more per year.

SOURCES OF FURTHER INFORMATION

Associated General Contractors of America
333 John Carlyle St.
Alexandria, VA 22314
Internet address: www.agc.org

The American Institute of Architects
1735 New York Ave. NW
Washington, DC 20006
Internet address: www.aiaonline.org

Society of American Registered Architects
303 South Broadway
Tarrytown, NY 10591
Internet address: www.sara-national.org

Accrediting Commission of Career Schools and Colleges of
  Technology
2101 Wilson Blvd.
Suite 302
Arlington, VA 22201
Internet address: www.accsct.org

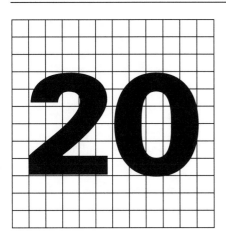

SURVEYOR AND MAPPING SCIENTIST

including
Land Surveyor
Mapping Scientist

In order to accurately designate property lines, park boundaries, and other geographical divisions on the earth's surface, it is necessary to survey and map the area in question. There are two groups of workers who are engaged in the process of measuring and mapping: land surveyors and mapping scientists. Land surveyors establish official land, air, space, and water boundaries; write descriptions of land for deeds, leases, and other legal documents; define airspace for airports; and measure construction and mineral sites. Land surveyors manage one or more survey parties who measure distances, directions, and angles between points and elevations of points, lines, and contours on the earth's surface. They plan the fieldwork, select known survey reference points, and determine the precise location of all important features of the survey area. They also research legal records and look for evidence of previous boundaries. Land surveyors also use the Global Positioning System (GPS) to make precise point surveys using satellites and ground-based receivers. The GPS is a satellite system that can pinpoint any location on earth using radio signals transmitted by satellite.

Mapping scientists, like land surveyors, measure, map, and chart the earth's surface but generally cover much larger areas. Mapping scientists include workers in several occupations. Cartographers prepare maps using information provided by geodetic surveys, aerial photographs, and satellite data. Photogrammetrists prepare maps and drawings by measuring and interpreting aerial photographs and using analytical processes and mathematical formulas; they make detailed maps of areas that are inaccessible or difficult to survey by other methods. Map editors develop and verify map contents from aerial photographs and other reference sources.

The work of mapping scientists is also changing due to new technologies, which include GPS and geographic information systems (GIS). The GIS is made up of computerized data banks of spatial data, new earth resources data satellites, and improved aerial photography. With these integrated tools, mapping scientists can generate much more accurate and detailed map information. The individual mapping science specialists, like cartographers and photogrammetrists, are presently merging into the single title geographic information specialists. This profession combines the jobs of mapping and surveying with collecting and analyzing geographic information.

RELATED PROFESSIONS

Geophysical prospecting surveyors locate points to take geophysical measurements in order to determine the geology of the earth. (Generally this work is petroleum related.)

Geodetic surveyors measure large areas of land, sea, or space and must account for the curvature of the planet.

Mining surveyors survey both surface and underground areas.

Seismologists study earthquake fault lines.

EDUCATIONAL REQUIREMENTS

The majority of practicing surveyors are prepared with a combination of postsecondary school courses and on-the-job training. However, new technological developments now often make it advisable to attain a bachelor's degree. Approximately twenty-five universities offer four-year programs that lead to a bachelor of science (B.S.) degree in surveying. Cartographers and photogrammetrists hold at least a bachelor's degree in geography and usually complete further graduate training. Because the GIS and GPS fields are relatively new, no formal degree programs have yet been established, but degree programs for geographic information specialists are being developed, primarily in college earth science departments, such as geography, meteorology, and geology. Geographic information specialists will need to command a solid understanding of surveying, mapmaking, and computer programming and have a knowledge of environmental conditions.

PROFESSIONAL CERTIFICATION

All fifty states license land surveyors. While the fastest way to become a licensed surveyor is to obtain a four-year degree, the degree is not a requirement in some states. Most states do require some formal education beyond high school and a combination of education and two to four years' experience along with successful completion of an examination. Given the increasing complexity of surveying, most states likely will eventually require four-year degrees. For further information on state licensing requirements, contact the American Congress on Surveying and Mapping, listed at the end of this chapter, or individual state licensing agencies.

SETTINGS

A career in surveying is for someone who enjoys spending a great deal of time outdoors. Generally surveyors work on a team that includes a party chief, several technicians, and assistants. Photogrammetrists prepare maps and drawings by reviewing aerial photographs and typically work in offices. GIS scientists are likely to spend most of their time indoors, although fieldwork is required in order to verify that the information presented on the GIS reflects actual conditions. The work of land surveyors can be quite strenuous; they must work outdoors in all kinds of weather, stand and walk for long periods, and carry heavy instruments and equipment. They may commute long distances to job sites. Although a normal workweek is forty hours, surveyors may work longer hours in the summer because this is the time when the construction industry is most active.

EMPLOYMENT STATISTICS AND MAJOR EMPLOYERS

Of the 101,000 surveyors and mapping scientists employed in 1996, approximately 60 percent work for engineering, architectural, and surveying firms. Federal, state, and local governments employ approximately 25 percent of all surveyors and mapping scientists. The major employers in the federal government include the U.S. Geological Survey, the Bureau of Land Management, the Army Corps of Engineers, the Forest Service, the National Oceanic and Atmospheric Administration, and the National Imagery and Mapping Agency (NIMA), formerly the Defense Mapping Agency. See Chapter 2 for a full description of most of these departments and agencies. State and local government agencies that hire surveyors include planning departments, highway departments, and environmental protection agencies. Some mapping scientists conduct research and teach at colleges and universities. The remaining surveyors and mapping scientists are employed by construction firms, mining and oil companies, consulting firms, utility companies, and developers, or they are self-employed.

Employment of surveyors and mapping scientists is expected to decline slightly through the year 2006, as the widespread uses of GPS, GIS, and remote sensing increase accuracy and productivity in the field. The demand for GIS and GPS scientists is expected to remain strong in the foreseeable future. According to the Department of Labor, little or no growth is expected in the federal government. Higher levels of technology and a trend of upgrading licensing requirements combined with the increased demand for geographical data will ensure that the best opportunities will be for the more educated surveyors and scientists. According to the Department of Labor, GPS and GIS may increase productivity for larger projects and enhance employment opportunities for mapping scientists, surveyors, and survey technicians who have the educational background to use the new technology and may decrease the demand for people with less training.

SALARY STATISTICS

In 1996, the median weekly earnings for surveyors and mapping scientists were about $694. The middle 50 percent earned between $547 and $849 a week; 10 percent earned less than $446 a week, and 10 percent earned more than $1,000 a week. In 1997, entry-level surveyors for the federal government earned between $19,520 and $29,580 per year, depending on their qualifications. A mapping scientist entering academia can expect an average starting salary of about $39,000 as an assistant professor and about $70,000 when fully tenured. While no firm salary data exist for surveyors and mapping scientists in the private sector, job seekers can expect starting salaries to be near or slightly above those in the federal government.

SOURCES OF FURTHER INFORMATION

American Congress on Surveying and Mapping
5410 Grosvenor Lane
Suite 100
Bethesda, MD 20814-2122

American Society for Photogrammetry and Remote Sensing
5410 Grosvenor Lane
Suite 210
Bethesda, MD 20814-2122
Internet address: www.asprs.org

American Geophysical Union
200 Florida Ave. NW
Washington, DC 20009
Internet address: www.agu.org

American Planning Association
1776 Massachusetts Ave. NW
Washington, DC 20036
Internet address:www.planning.org
The Planners Bookstore carries several books on GIS systems and the planning profession.

U.S. Geological Survey
U.S. National Center
Reston, VA 22092

SURVEYOR AND MAPPING TECHNICIAN

Surveying and mapping technicians help civil engineers, surveyors, and cartographers record geographic data. The surveying or mapping technician is a key worker who assists a chief instrument worker under the supervising surveyor. These technicians are responsible for operating surveying instruments such as the theodolite, transit, and level and electronic equipment to measure a distance or locate a point or for assisting in making elevation measurements.

New technologies such as the Global Positioning System (GPS), advances in measuring instruments, and computer data processing have made surveying and mapping technical careers more complex and dynamic in the last few years. These changes have increased the accuracy of surveying and mapping and extended their use beyond the surface of the land to the ocean floors and neighboring planets. These new technologies are increasingly demanded in the business world where planners and real estate professionals use Geographic Information Systems (GIS) to analyze land-use patterns, traffic patterns, and economic and demographic components of urban areas. Environmentalists are also using advanced mapping techniques to track endangered species, measure the destruction of environmentally sensitive areas, and study various ecosystems. The skilled technician can make a positive contribution to these new and exciting areas in the future.

RELATED PROFESSIONS

Architectural Drafter
Structural Drafter and Detail Checker
Engineering Technician
Landscaper
Cartographic Drafter
Survey Assistant
Photogrammetric Technician

Architect
Landscape Architect
CAD Technician
Drafter
Surveyor
Highway Technician
Rail and Waterway Technician

EDUCATIONAL REQUIREMENTS

Survey technicians and mapping technicians can attend junior and community colleges, technical institutes, and vocational schools, which offer one-, two-, and three-year programs in both surveying and mapping technology. For those who choose to enroll in two-year programs, the first-year classes generally include English, composition, drafting, applied mathematics, surveying and measurements, statistics, computers, and physics. The second-year courses include technical physics, advanced surveying, photogrammetry, mapping, soils and foundations, legal concerns, and technical reporting. High school students interested in surveying should take courses in algebra, geometry, trigonometry, drafting, mechanical drawing, and computer science.

SPECIAL CERTIFICATION

No professional certification is required for this occupation.

SETTINGS

Surveying technicians will spend most of their time outdoors; their working conditions are similar to those of surveyors. Conversely, mapping technicians spend most of their time working in office environments with mapping scientists. For both surveying and mapping technicians the ability to pay close attention to detail and work well with others is particularly important.

EMPLOYMENT STATISTICS AND MAJOR EMPLOYERS

Surveyor technicians are employed in the same areas as surveyors; architectural, engineering, and surveying firms; government agencies; mining, oil, gas, and utility companies; and construction firms. The demand for technicians is expected to decline in the foreseeable future. At the same time, new technologies combined with the demand for more sophisticated geographic data may enhance opportunities for those technicians with the required education and skills. This is a rapidly changing field that is best suited for those who enjoy learning and are willing to continually upgrade their skills in order to keep up with the latest changes in technology—particularly GIS and GPS processing.

SALARY STATISTICS

In 1996, the median weekly earnings for survey and mapping technicians were about $461. The middle 50 percent earned between $378 and $461 a week, 10 percent earned less than $294 a week, and 10 percent earned more than $942 per week.

SOURCES OF FURTHER INFORMATION

American Congress on Surveying and Mapping
5410 Grosvenor Lane
Suite 100
Bethesda, MD 20814-2122

American Society for Photogrammetry and Remote Sensing
5410 Grosvenor Lane
Suite 210
Bethesda, MD 20814-2122
Internet address: www.asprs.org

Part Four
Forestry and Outdoor Recreation

OVERVIEW

**Total Employment
70,000**

Employment Breakdown by Job Sector

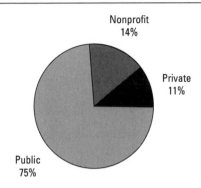

Nonprofit
14%

Private
11%

Public
75%

Projected Growth

According to the U.S. Department of Labor, employment opportunities in forestry and outdoor recreation are expected to increase by about 17 percent by the year 2006. This rate of increase is about as fast as the average for all occupations. Growth should be strongest in state and local governments where demand will be spurred by an ongoing emphasis on environmental protection and responsible land management. There will also be increased opportunities with private owners of timberland.

Salary Range

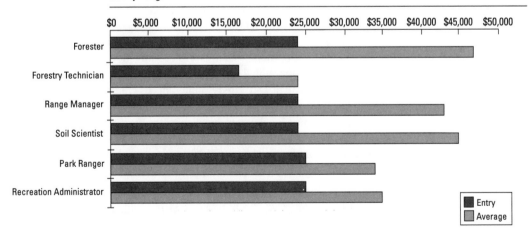

INTRODUCTION

The science of forestry was first established in the United States at the beginning of the twentieth century. At that time, vast sections of American forest had been cut down and no plans had been made for the future. In the past 100 years, foresters have worked hard to reestablish forests in the United States. The forests now grow nearly four times as much wood each year than they did in 1920. There are now about 730 million acres of forestland in the United States, about 67 percent as much as there was in 1600.

Forests are an essential part of the balance of nature. All life exists in a narrow zone between outer space and the solid mantle of the earth called the *biosphere*. Within this zone, life thrives in an interconnected balance, with each life form composing a piece of the complex web called the *global ecosystem*. The term *ecosystem* means the interacting of animals, plants, and bacteria in a natural hierarchy, from inorganic (nonliving) atoms and molecules to increasingly complex units of cells, tissues, and organs that make up biological communities, species, and populations. This is an incredibly complicated system that requires the simultaneous interaction of billions of organisms to produce and sustain even the simplest forms of life.

The part of the ecosystem that provides us with the resources for our food and shelter is a thin layer of rich earth called *topsoil*. This nutritious soil, averaging only 6 to 12 inches in depth around the globe, sustains all of land-dwelling life. The great forests of the world are its most monumental product. The forests are highly important; they are home to most species of plants and animals and provide humans with food, shelter, medicine, and recreation. They are also the global air purification system, for trees recycle carbon dioxide into oxygen. The root systems of trees and other vegetation also prevent erosion; they keep the fertile and life-sustaining soil from being washed away and lost forever.

Throughout the brief history of the human species, which spans only a few hundred thousand years, humans have been just one of the individually insignificant components of the great ecosystem. In the past few hundred years, however, humans have begun to strain the balance of nature. We have decimated the great forests; lost billions of tons of topsoil to the sea; polluted the land, water, and air; and strained the carrying capacity of the land through overpopulation.

The job of environmental scientists or conservation scientists, as they are often called, is to study the global and local ecosystems and determine how best to preserve the environment and satisfy human needs. In order to reverse our destructive practices, a new approach to the environment is needed. This approach should focus not only upon local issues, but also on the overall management of the ecosystem. Everything is interconnected. The forestry and outdoor recreation professions, with their emphasis on the management of large biological communities, will increasingly be called upon to carry out this work.

PROFESSIONS RELATED TO FORESTRY AND OUTDOOR RECREATION

Animal Scientist	Zoologist
Agricultural Scientist	Soil Scientist
Agricultural Engineer	Plant Pathologist
Agronomist	Horticulturist
Archaeologist	Landscape Architect
Biologist	Arborist

Earth Scientist   Toxicologist
Ecologist   Recreation Planner
GIS Specialist   Ornithologist
Environmental Planner

BACKGROUND AND RECENT HISTORY OF U.S. CONSERVATION WORK

The U.S. government has assumed primary responsibility for the management of our precious natural resources since the late part of the nineteenth century. In 1862, the U.S. Department of Agriculture was formed, and in 1872, Congress set aside Yellowstone as our first national park. In 1902 the Department of Agriculture formed the National Forest Service, and in 1916 the National Park Service was added to the Department of the Interior. In addition, most states in the early part of this century began to set aside land for public use. More recently, in 1970, the U.S. Environmental Protection Agency was created as an independent agency to monitor the overall environmental health of the nation.

Today, slightly less than one-third of the area of the United States is forested. Twenty-eight percent of this land is owned by the government, and the rest is owned by corporate or private interests. Forested land in the United States is comprised of a wide variety of ecosystems, from the hardwood forests of Appalachia and the great wetlands of Florida to the expansive prairie lands of the Midwest, the rugged alpine conifer forests of the Rockies, and the lush and misty stands of the giant redwood in northern California.

According to the Society of American Foresters, the natural resource management profession is divided into five broad areas: timber, wildlife, grazing, soil and water, and recreation. Forestry is an important part of the natural resource management field because forests provide us with two invaluable assets: a place to appreciate and reconnect with the earth and a source of wood products. Foresters are responsible for the maintenance and continued health of our vast timber stands. Rangelands are important for livestock grazing and recreation and essential for wildlife. Range managers ensure the balance between a healthy ecosystem and properly managed range use for commerce and recreation. Soil scientists are responsible for testing soils to ensure the growth of healthy vegetation and control erosion. Park rangers assist the public in understanding our natural surroundings, protect the public from any dangers the wilds may present, and protect the wilds from dangers the public may present. Finally, recreation administrators make sure that the public receives maximum enjoyment from its leisure time.

MAJOR EMPLOYERS

About 30 percent of workers in this field are employed by the federal government. The major federal employer is the U.S. Department of Agriculture (USDA), where conservationists are concentrated in the Natural Resource Conservation Service. Conservation professionals also work for the Department of the Interior, the Environmental Protection Agency, the Department of Energy, and the Department of Defense. In addition, the National Recreation and Park Association estimates that about 75,000 full-time workers are employed at approximately 100,000 state and local recreation sites throughout the United States. While this represents a large workforce, only a fraction of these workers are conservation scientists; the rest are administrators, maintenance workers, and support staff. See Chapter 2 for an in-depth discussion of government employment opportunities.

The majority of resource managers in the private sector work for timber and timber consulting companies that supply lumber and paper products to the public, fish hatcheries, mining operations, livestock and ranch operations, and nonprofit land conservation projects. Some of the largest forest product companies are Boise Cascade Corp., Georgia-Pacific Corp., International Paper Co., Mead Corp., and Weyerhauser Co. Major nonprofit organizations involved in the acquisition of land for preservation include the Trust for Public Land, Rails to Trails, The Nature Conservancy, and the World Wildlife Fund.

PROJECTED TRENDS AND EMPLOYMENT GROWTH

Job opportunities in the conservation sciences will grow about as fast as the average for all other occupations through the year 2006. Growth will be strongest in state and local governments, to meet the demand for environmental protection and responsible land management. For example, the nationwide Stewardship Incentive Programs, funded by the federal government, provide funding to the states and encourage landowners to practice multiple-use forest management. In addition, more professionals trained in the conservation sciences will be absorbed by consulting firms to conduct environmental impact analyses. Conservation scientists will be needed to assess the impact of various land-use projects and proposals on local ecosystems and suggest ways to minimize potential or existing damage caused by development. Also, the recreation industry is growing steadily due to the increase in leisure time for many Americans. Recreation professionals will find solid employment opportunities in the hospitality and travel industries.

In the public sector, overall job growth is expected to grow slowly through the year 2006. This slow growth is mainly due to present budget constraints at all levels of government. The public sector of the conservation field was saturated with conservation workers in the early 1970s; as they retire, however, another wave of workers will be required during the early part of the twenty-first century. In other federal agencies, however, there will be a greater need for conservation scientists.

SOURCES OF FURTHER INFORMATION

American Forest Foundation
1111 19th St. NW
Suite 780
Washington, DC 20036
The American Forest Foundation conducts education and research programs. AFF supports the American Tree Farm System, 71,000 private landowners managing 95 million acres of

forests, and Project Learning Tree, an environmental training program.

Also consult the following publications:

The Complete Guide to Environmental Careers in the 21st Century (1998), by the Environmental Careers Organization, published by Island Press. Contains information on recreation and forestry careers.

Conservation Directory (annual), by the National Wildlife Federation. Includes a detailed list and description of government and nongovernment organizations engaged in conservation work both nationally and internationally.

Directory of the Forest Products Industry, published by Miller Freeman Publications. A 748-page who's who of the forest products industry, including sawmills, wood treatment plants, and plywood mills. Includes individual company information such as addresses, product and volume, and names and telephone numbers of key contacts. Look in the reference section of your local college or university for a copy.

Timber Harvesting (monthly magazine), by Hatton-Brown Publishers. Each January issue contains a listing of personnel employed by the wood supply and forestry departments of all major pulp and paper companies and industrial timber firms in the United States.

FORESTER

Foresters are responsible for the protection, management, and development of forest lands and their resources. They receive training in the conservation sciences and intensively study forest ecosystems, concentrating largely on trees. Foresters often specialize in one interest area, such as wood technology, forest resources management, urban forestry, or forest economics. According to the Society of American Foresters, foresters typically spend a majority of their time outdoors during their first few years of employment and later take on more administrative and management duties. Outdoor duties include crew supervision, measuring and grading trees, conducting land surveys, evaluating insect outbreaks, fighting wildfires, managing controlled fires, laying out road systems, supervising timber harvests, planning tree planting and trail construction programs, and doing research and interpretive teaching. More experienced foresters concentrate on forest use planning, contracting, preparation of environmental impact reports, and budget management. Experienced foresters often become top executives in public conservation agencies, conservation organizations, and forest product corporations. Many are consultants who offer forestry advice to private landowners, corporations, and public agencies.

Foresters are intensely interested in the preservation of wildlife habitats and must seriously weigh the balance between economic interests and the health of the ecosystem when overseeing timber cutting or the extraction of other resources. The process of tree harvesting can damage wildlife habitats, creek beds, water quality, and soil stability. Foresters must continuously monitor tree-cutting areas to ensure that no irreversible damage is done. Instruments used in surveying the health of a forest include clinometers to measure height and increment bores and bark gauges to measure growth of trees. Increasingly, advanced survey methods like photogrammetry and remote sensing (taking photographs from airplanes and satellites) are used for mapping large forest areas and detecting the effects of forest and land use. Computer programs are often used to evaluate forest growth patterns and simulate the effects of forest fires, climate changes, recreational use, and timber cutting.

RELATED PROFESSIONS

Forest Ranger
Forestry Technician
Service Forester
Forest Fire Officer
Farm Manager
Forest Entomologist

Ranch Manager
Soil Scientist
Conservation Technician
Environmental Scientist
Forest Hydrologist

EDUCATIONAL REQUIREMENTS

The minimal educational requirement for a professional forester is a four-year bachelor's degree in forestry. Most land grant colleges and universities offer a bachelor's or more advanced degree in forestry, and the Society of American Foresters has accredited forty-eight of these programs. A typical college program stresses an understanding of mathematics, computers, and science. Students are required to take a core curriculum of science and math courses, which includes biology, chemistry, ecology, agronomy, physics, and calculus. The use of computers to monitor and simulate forestry and land-use practices, especially with the powerful geographic information systems (GIS) program, is common in many forestry programs. Students are usually required to do a field project on the specialty of their interest. Students are also encouraged to do a summer internship or paid training program in a forest or park, working with professionals in the field. In addition, most programs offer courses in forest economics and business administration, which help prepare students for administrative and managerial responsibilities.

PROFESSIONAL CERTIFICATION

Fifteen states have mandatory licensing or voluntary registration requirements that a forester must meet in order to earn the title *professional forester* and provide professional consulting services. Contact the Society of American Foresters, listed at the end of this chapter, for further information.

SETTINGS

Due to the nature of their work, foresters spend a fair amount of time outdoors. Most national forests are large, and foresters are required to travel deep into the woods, sometimes for several days. This can be very physically demanding work, involving long distance hiking and even forest fire fighting. Foresters should be comfortable living in remote and rural areas since most live in or near their place of work. Many foresters are provided housing in the national forest, and living conditions vary from basic with no electricity or running water to comfortable with modern accommodations. Others live in rural communities or towns that border national parks.

EMPLOYMENT STATISTICS AND MAJOR EMPLOYERS

Foresters work for federal, state, and local governments and in private industry and academia. In 1996, about 37,000 foresters were employed in the United States; it is predicted that there will be about 43,400 employed by the year 2006. While foresters are employed in every state, they are most heavily concentrated in the West and Southeast, which have the majority of private and public forests and where most of the lumber and pulpwood operations are located. About 50 percent of all foresters work for private industry, mainly as caretakers of forest stands for wood and paper product companies. A small percentage of foresters work in urban settings as tree care specialists.

Approximately 40 percent of foresters work for the federal, state, and local governments. In the federal government, foresters are employed mostly at the U.S. Department of Agriculture and the Department of the Interior. State and local government forestry departments employ most of the rest of these professionals. The remaining 10 percent work as consultants or in academic settings.

SALARY STATISTICS

According to the Department of Labor, the average annual salary range for foresters was about $40,900 in 1997; the majority of foresters were earning salaries between $32,800 and $49,300.

In 1997, foresters entering federal government jobs with bachelor's degrees earned between $19,500 and $24,200 a year. Those with master's degrees earned starting salaries between $24,200 and $29,600. Foresters with doctoral degrees earned starting salaries of $35,800 to $42,900 in research positions. In 1997, the average salary for foresters working for the federal government was $47,600.

SOURCES OF FURTHER INFORMATION

American Forest Foundation
1111 19th St. NW
Suite 780
Washington, DC 20036

American Forests
P.O. Box 2000
Washington, DC 20013
Internet address: www.amfor.org

National Association of State Foresters
444 N. Capital St. NW
Suite 540
Washington, DC 20001

Society of American Foresters
5400 Grosvenor Lane
Bethesda, MD 20814
Internet address: www.safnet.org

Also consult *Opportunities in Forestry* (1992), by Christopher M. Willie, published by VGM Career Horizons, NTC/Contemporary Publishing Group.

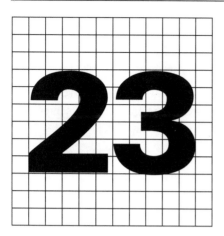

FORESTRY TECHNICIAN

Forestry technicians are indispensable members of the forestry team. Without their assistance, professional foresters would be unable to conduct their work. Forestry technicians help plan, conduct, and supervise all forest operations. Their work spans the breadth of the forestry field and includes timber production, water regulation, wildlife management, recreation planning, and research. Forestry technicians estimate the amount of timber to be cut in a harvest, survey and build roads through forestlands, supervise reforestation projects, survey forest genetics, supervise fire control crews, and collect data for disease and insect control, among other duties.

Whereas professional foresters often specialize in a particular area of work, forestry technicians must have a broad base of technical skills and knowledge of forestry issues. Forestry technicians must also possess sharp interpersonal and communication skills because they often write and present oral reports and supervise skilled work crews. They can advance to a number of conservation positions, including refuge manager, fish and game preserve manager, and forestry consultant. Some foresters, range managers, and other conservation professionals begin their careers as forestry technicians, receiving excellent field training before moving on to professional positions.

RELATED PROFESSIONS

Forester	Range Manager
Wildlife Technician	Biological Technician
Tree Nursery Management Assistant	Survey Assistant
Technical Research Assistant	Chemistry Technician
Forestry Consultant	Surveyor

EDUCATIONAL REQUIREMENTS

Most companies and government agencies hiring forestry technicians require at least a two-year associate's degree. More than eighty programs offer associate's degrees at junior or community colleges and technical institutes, and thirty-six of these have been sanctioned by the Society of American Foresters. Typical technician programs include courses in mathematics, botany, forestry, and engineering. A typical first-year's study program includes classes in forest surveying, technical reporting, forest measurement, technical drawing, botany of forests, and dendrology (tree identification). Second-year courses often include timber harvesting, wildlife ecology, forest fire control, aerial photographic interpretation, forest business management, advanced forest surveying, and map drafting and computer courses. Like foresters, technicians should be familiar with the geographic information systems (GIS) program.

Most technician programs include summer fieldwork as part of their curriculum. Check with a school to see if it arranges summer jobs for students.

SPECIAL CERTIFICATION

Some states require forestry technicians to be registered in order to provide consulting services, survey properties for legal purposes, or handle certain pesticides and chemicals. Contact the Society of American Foresters, listed at the end of this chapter, for further information.

SETTINGS

As is the case with forestry, the job of forestry technician can be strenuous and conducted in primitive places with little if any modern amenities. Most technicians work alone or supervising small crews under the overall supervision of professional foresters. Those entering this field must be comfortable living and working outdoors in rural and primitive areas. While working hours are generally regular, around forty hours per week, technicians can expect to work long hours during tree harvesting seasons and when fighting forest fires.

EMPLOYMENT STATISTICS AND MAJOR EMPLOYERS

Most forestry technicians are employed in private industry, mainly as surveyors for seasonal timber harvests and as caretakers for previously cut and replanted lands. Like foresters, forestry technicians are concentrated in the West and Southeast, where most of the lumber and pulpwood operations are located. Most other forestry technicians work in all tiers of government assisting professional foresters with their duties. According to the U.S. Department of Labor, more than forty thousand forestry technicians were employed in the mid-1990s. Employment opportunities in this field are expected to grow about as fast as the average until the year 2006.

SALARY STATISTICS

According to the Bureau of Labor Statistics, the average annual salary range for forestry technicians was $23,000 in 1997. Starting forestry technicians earned closer to $16,700, while those with more experience and responsibilities earned $31,400 or more.

SOURCES OF FURTHER INFORMATION

American Forest Foundation
1111 19th St. NW
Suite 780
Washington, DC 20036

American Forests
P.O. Box 2000
Washington, DC 20013
Internet address: www.amfor.org

Forest Management Trust
6124 SW 30th Ave.
Gainesville, FL 32608
Internet address: www.foresttrust.org

Forest Service Employees for Environmental Ethics
P.O. Box 11615
Eugene, OR 97440

National Recreation and Park Association
22377 Belmont Ridge Road
Ashburn, VA 20148
Internet address: www.nrpa.org

Society of American Foresters
5400 Grosvenor Lane
Bethesda, MD 20814
Internet address: www.safnet.org

Chief U.S. Forest Service
U.S. Department of Agriculture
P.O. Box 96090, SW
Washington, DC 20090
The U.S. Forest Service provides information on careers
in state and federal forestry organizations.

Also consult *Opportunities in Forestry* (1992), by Christopher M. Willie, published by VGM Career Horizons, NTC/Contemporary Publishing Group.

RANGE MANAGER/ RANGELAND SPECIALIST

Range managers or rangeland specialists are trusted to protect and preserve public rangeland ecosystems while maintaining the land for public recreational use and private economic activity. They maintain recreation areas and range improvements like reservoirs, fences, and corrals; manage range ecosystems; develop and carry out water facility, soil treatment, and erosion control plans; balance the environmental impact of private cattle grazing on sensitive range flora; conduct fire control and prevention measures; and control destructive pests. The most challenging task that range managers face is satisfying their missions of maintaining a healthy range ecosystem and allowing maximum public and private use of the land. Private interests, mainly oil and mining companies, have a financial stake in the energy and mineral resources found on the vast tracts of public land, and range managers monitor their activities to curtail any environmentally harmful resource extraction practices. Thus, range managers or range scientists, range ecologists, rangeland specialists, or range conservationists, as they are often called, use their knowledge of the conservation sciences to guide private and public land-use practices.

RELATED PROFESSIONS

Forest Ecologist
Fire Warden
Fire Ranger
Forest Worker
Wildlife Specialist

Wood Technologist
Soil Conservationist
Park Naturalist
Park Ranger

EDUCATIONAL REQUIREMENTS

The minimal educational requirement for a career as a range manager is a four-year bachelor's degree in range management or range science. Eighteen colleges and universities offer degrees in range management. A typical college curriculum includes courses in biology, chemistry, mathematics and physics, forestry, agronomy, wildlife management, and economics. Most programs offer specialized courses in soil, plant, and animal sciences, and most stress computer training. Communication and writing classes are encouraged because of the high level of professional and public interaction that occurs among range managers. Field experience is a clear career advantage for entry-level range managers, and summer employment and internship programs for college students are available primarily in the Forest Service, Bureau of Land Management, and Soil Conservation Service.

PROFESSIONAL CERTIFICATION

There are no special certifications for this occupation.

SETTINGS

The more than one billion acres of public rangeland in the United States are concentrated mainly in the western states and Alaska. This land is generally vast open space in or near mountainous regions; it supports mainly grass, shrub, and sporadic tree growth. Much of this land is found in semiarid zones where rainfall occurs in seasonal or semiannual cycles, and the landscape is dry and golden brown for several months and green and lush for a shorter time. Most public rangeland is found in sparsely populated areas in large states where large cities or towns are often hundreds of miles away. Those interested in a range management career can expect to spend a majority of their time outdoors and should be comfortable living in a rural setting. Range managers are often required to spend a considerable amount of time away from home participating in field projects that are physically demanding and often conducted in remote areas.

EMPLOYMENT STATISTICS AND MAJOR EMPLOYERS

In 1996, about ten thousand range managers were working in the United States. Most of these professionals were employed by the federal government, primarily in the Department of Agriculture in the Forest Service and the Soil Conservation Service and in the Department of the Interior in the Bureau of Land Management and the Bureau of Indian Affairs. Other range managers were employed by state government agencies in natural resource departments, fish and game departments, state land agencies, and extension services. Some professionals worked overseas with U.S. and United Nations agricultural and land development agencies. Also, a small number of professionals with advanced degrees taught at colleges and universities.

Employment growth in government is expected to be slower than average, and the overall number of range managers is expected to remain stable. This is due primarily to budget constraints in natural resource departments at all levels of government. The need for range managers may increase in the near future due to recent concerns about cattle overgrazing and the development of more wildlife habitats, particularly wetlands.

In the private sector, range managers are employed by mineral and coal mining companies, oil corporations, banks, trust companies, and a growing number of corporate ranches. In the mining and oil exploration industries, range managers work to reclaim land damaged by mining operations. They concentrate on ensuring healthy grazing environments for livestock on large ranches. Employment opportunities in the private sector are growing due to the push to clean up the waste from dormant mining operations and the proliferation of large corporate ranches.

SALARY STATISTICS

Range managers entering the federal government with bachelor's degrees and minimal work experience can expect to earn between $19,000 and $24,200 per year, and those who have earned master's degrees can expect an average starting salary between $24,200 and $29,600. The average salary for all range managers working for the federal government is $43,000 per year. Those with Ph.D.'s can expect a starting salary of between $35,800 and $42,900. Salaries in state government are slightly lower, while those in the private sector tend to mirror federal salaries, except for executive positions in which private range managers typically have higher salaries.

SOURCES OF FURTHER INFORMATION

Society for Range Management
1839 York St.
Denver, CO 80206
Internet address: www.srm.org

Also consult the following publications:

Careers for Nature Lovers and Other Outdoor Types (1993), by Louise Miller, published by VGM Career Horizons, NTC/Contemporary Publishing Group. Included is a chapter on forestry careers and a description of range managers.

Opportunities in State and Local Government Careers (1993), by Neale A. Baxter, published by VGM Career Horizons, NTC/Contemporary Publishing Group.

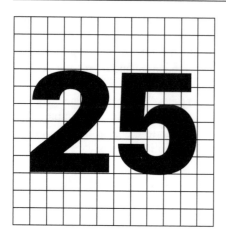

SOIL SCIENTIST

Soil scientists or soil conservationists focus on land-use practices and conservation measures that minimize soil erosion. They work on public lands, advise farmers and ranchers, and consult with landowners to control the loss of fertile soil. Soil scientists conduct chemical analyses of soils to determine the most suitable irrigation schemes and vegetation planting techniques to control wind-borne erosion. They also design and construct pond and terrace systems to save water and keep streams and rivers free from land-borne sediments. Some soil scientists concentrate on classifying soils according to their properties, such as composition, ability to hold water, level of nutrients, and resistance to erosion, while others study and map the land to determine erosion paths and areas of maximum fertility.

Soil conservationists working on public and private forest lands work closely with foresters and range managers. In timber-cutting areas, soil scientists help lay out cutting zones and help revegetate clear-cut lands. They help foresters and rangers design recreation areas and restore overused areas to their natural state. Working closely with range managers, soil scientists advise ranchers on grazing practices on public land and monitor and test soils in areas in which vegetation may be irreversibly damaged by overgrazing. Soil scientists are also consulted on building foundation, road building, and waterway, waste disposal, and reclamation projects.

RELATED PROFESSIONS

Agronomist
Crop Scientist
Botanist
Range Manager

Forester
Horticulturalist
Microbiologist
Plant Pathologist

EDUCATIONAL REQUIREMENTS

Few colleges offer majors in soil science, so most soil science professionals earn degrees in agronomy, forestry, range management, wildlife biology, regional planning, or agricultural engineering. Each state supports a land grant university with a focus on agricultural and forestry studies, such as the University of Wisconsin—Madison, which has an excellent degree program (bachelor's, master's, and Ph.D.) in soil science. Some of the areas that soil science students specialize in are soil biochemistry and microbiology, soil fertility and plant nutrition, forest soil science, soil classification and land use, soil and environmental physics, and soil and water management. Students take a wide range of science courses, including chemistry, forestry, plant pathology, botany, geology, meteorology, and physics. Numerous summer work and internship opportunities are provided by the U.S. Forest Service, Soil Conservation Service, and Bureau of Land Management.

PROFESSIONAL CERTIFICATION

The American Society of Agronomy offers its members a certification called the American Registry of Certified Professionals in Agronomy, Crops, and Soils. Contact the society for information on testing procedures and personal requirements.

SETTINGS

Soil scientists work in every region of the country and, like foresters and range managers, tend to be concentrated in the southern and western states. Most of their work is conducted outdoors and often in extreme weather conditions, such as rain or snowstorms, and in drought areas where they appraise the climate effects on soils. This fieldwork is often strenuous; soil scientists must be in good physical condition. At other times they are found in the laboratory analyzing soils and writing reports. Like professionals in other forestry and outdoor recreation careers, soil scientists should be comfortable living in rural settings and be prepared to spend stretches of time in the hinterlands under primitive living conditions. Good communication skills are also essential because soil scientists often must persuade landowners, ranchers, and other conservation scientists to follow soil-sensitive land-use practices.

EMPLOYMENT STATISTICS AND MAJOR EMPLOYERS

In 1997, more than seven thousand soil scientists were employed in the United States. The majority of soil scientists work for the federal, state, and local governments. The largest concentration of soil scientists is in the federal government, working in the Soil Conservation Service, Fish and Wildlife Service, Forest Service, Bureau of Land Management, Bureau of Reclamation, Bureau of Indian

Affairs, and Army Corps of Engineers. The Soil Conservation Service, in cooperation with state and local authorities, runs three thousand soil conservation districts around the nation. A small number of professionals work in the Environmental Protection Agency. State environmental and planning agencies also hire a number of soil scientists. States with erosion problems, fragile ecosystems, or large concentrations of grazing lands, located mainly in the West, have the greatest need for these professionals. Soil scientists also work for state and county Cooperative Extension services, which offer advice to farmers and ranchers. In private industry, soil scientists work for timber companies, mining operations, electric power companies, private sanitation firms, and agricultural equipment manufacturers. A growing number are employed by environmental consulting firms that inspect and clean up polluted land sites.

Job growth for soil scientists in government is expected to be level until the year 2006, due primarily to ongoing budget constraints. Normal worker turnover will create a fair number of job openings each year. In the private sector, job growth is expected to accelerate, particularly for workers involved in environmental cleanup operations, specifically the reclaiming of strip mine lands and wetlands and hazardous materials work.

SALARY STATISTICS

Entry-level soil scientists with bachelor's degrees and little work experience can expect a starting salary in the range of $20,000 to $26,000 per year. In the federal government, entry-level soil scientists with bachelor's degrees earn between $19,500 and $24,200. Most master's degree holders earn a starting salary of $24,200 to $29,000, while Ph.D. recipients earn between $35,800 and $42,900. These starting salaries are generally higher than those offered in state and local governments and comparable to salaries in the private sector.

SOURCES OF FURTHER INFORMATION

National Association of Conservation Districts
   Headquarters
509 Capitol NE
Washington, DC 20002
Internet address: www.nacdnet.org
The Association offers a free information pamphlet called the
Guide to Services.

Natural Resources Council of America
1025 Thomas Jefferson St. NW
Suite 109
Washington, DC 20007-5291

Soil Science Society of America
677 South Segoe Road
Madison, WI 53711-1086

Soil and Water Conservation Society
7515 Northeast Ankeny Road
Ankeny, IA 50021-9764
Internet address: www.swcs.org
The society offers a limited number of college scholarships in
conservation and has an excellent selection of books (discounted
for members) on a wide range of soil and water conservation
issues.

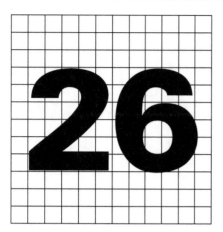

PARK RANGER

Of all the jobs in conservation science, park rangers have the most varied roles. They carry out multiple duties in managing parks, historical sites, and recreational areas. They supervise, manage, and perform work in the conservation and use of resources in national parks and other federally managed areas, including forest fire control, education of the public, law enforcement, and search and rescue.

The first responsibility of rangers is to ensure the safety and well-being of all park visitors, the wildlife, and land under their supervision. In order to protect visitors, rangers must enforce all laws and regulations that pertain to their parks. All rangers are trained in first aid and rescue procedures. Rangers in parks with treacherous terrain, changeable weather conditions, or potentially dangerous wildlife must make sure that hikers, campers, and backpackers follow all outdoor safety regulations. They are expected to maintain the parks and help visitors fully appreciate the natural and cultural history of their surroundings by leading interpretive talks and hikes. Rangers plan and supervise hiking trail and road building projects and assist in the planning of long-term land-use and recreation objectives. Conversely, rangers need to protect parks and their natural inhabitants from any human disturbance.

Rangers are also responsible for taking conservation measures separate from visitor use. They use their conservation knowledge to study wildlife behavior, plant species, and the health of the forest; they monitor water quality, pollution, and erosion problems, and they survey the overall health of a park's ecosystem. Many rangers are specialists in the unique environs of their parks. Some who work in mountainous zones are experts in mountain climbing, mountain search and rescue, and avalanche control; those in coastal areas are knowledgeable about the local marine biology; and those in desert climates may have a special knowledge of arid-dwelling flora and fauna.

Park rangers are responsible for supervising all park workers and their activities. In addition, they spend a good deal of time managing and performing administrative duties. As rangers gain seniority, they may be promoted to the position of head park ranger or district supervisor. Any promotion means less outdoor work and contact with the public and more administrative responsibilities.

RELATED PROFESSIONS

Campground Director
Environmental Interpreter
Interpretive Specialist
Museum Director
Natural Resource Manager
Outdoor Recreation Manager

Park Maintenance Director
Park Manager
Park Police
Park Technician
Ranger Aid

EDUCATIONAL REQUIREMENTS

Employment as a federal, state, county, or municipal employee in park management and natural resources usually requires a four-year bachelor's degree in parks and recreation management. More than three hundred degree programs in parks and recreation are offered by colleges and universities in the United States. The National Recreation and Park Association has accredited more than ninety of these programs. Additionally, there are more than one hundred graduate degree programs in this field.

Students are required to take courses in forestry, geography, geology, botany, biology, mathematics, and history and classes in the behavioral sciences, such as communications, psychology, sociology, and public speaking as well as a core curriculum of recreation management classes. Students in other academic disciplines like forestry or wildlife ecology who wish to pursue jobs as park rangers are required to take at least twenty-four semester hours of credit in park recreation and management.

Students are encouraged to work in park systems before college graduation. Numerous part-time and full-time summer job opportunities in parks are available at all levels of government. While most jobs require students to do menial tasks like maintenance or fee collection, exposure to and observance of rangers will certainly focus their career aspirations. In addition, many conservation organizations organize park volunteer work programs that expose students to ranger duties.

Park rangers in nonsupervisory positions need at least two years of college with at least twelve credits in science and criminal justice. Many rangers start as part-time, seasonal workers with the U.S. Forest Service before moving into full-time positions.

PROFESSIONAL CERTIFICATION

The National Recreation and Park Association offers a document of certification for those who meet the requirements of professionalism and technical knowledge. Contact the NRPA, listed at the end of this chapter, for information on testing procedures and personal requirements.

SETTINGS

The places in which park rangers work are as diverse as their job duties. Parks are spread throughout the country in urban, suburban, rural, and even desolate areas. At the federal level, the Forest Service runs 360 national parks, monuments, and historical areas. There is a great variety of parks. Parks such as Yosemite, Great Smoky Mountain, Everglades, and Grand Canyon are immensely popular and crowded; they grow to populations of small cities during the peak summer months. Parks like Badlands, Glacier, Redwood, and Zion are more isolated. There are parks in urban settings in and around Washington, D.C., and historical areas such as Gettysburg, Harpers Ferry, and the Statue of Liberty. There are also many archaeological sites where the history of native North Americans is preserved, like Aztec and Bandelire in New Mexico and Ocmulgee in Georgia.

There are more than 100,000 state, county, and municipal parks in this country. Many rangers work in inner-city or suburban parks where they expose citizens, especially children, to conservation issues. These parks and others in more rural areas serve the majority of Americans who seek outdoor recreation. Rangers must often be innovative because budgets for park facilities and maintenance are often thin.

In most federal and many state parks, rangers are supplied housing on park premises. These accommodations range from quite elaborate to military-style barracks. In addition, senior park rangers are usually given vehicles. Working hours can be quite long, especially during the summer months when the parks are busiest.

EMPLOYMENT STATISTICS AND MAJOR EMPLOYERS

The National Recreation and Park Association estimates that about seventy-five thousand full-time conservation workers were employed in all federal, state, county, and municipal parks in the late 1990s. Only a small number of these workers were park rangers. According to the U.S. Department of Labor, the employment outlook for rangers is average with slight growth in the field expected. By the year 2006, the number of ranger openings will increase because the last wave of entry-level rangers hired in the 1970s will be reaching retirement age. In the National Park Service, competition for park ranger openings is fierce. There are one hundred qualified applicants for every one park ranger hired. The National Park Service advises students interested in ranger positions to acquire the widest variety of applicable skills possible, including a knowledge of natural and human history, forestry, wildlife management, and law enforcement. Students are advised to concentrate their job searches in state, county, and local park departments where the majority of Park Ranger positions exist and where the turnover rate is much higher.

SALARY STATISTICS

Overall, salaries for park rangers tend to cluster in the middle pay range for government workers. Starting pay for National Park Service rangers is between

$24,200 and $29,600, depending on grades and previous experience. The average pay for all rangers is around $40,000. Federal rangers receive salary adjustments (locality pay) if they work in regions with a high cost of living, such as Washington, D.C., or northern California. Starting salaries in state and local parks are a bit higher. Entry-level rangers can expect to earn from $23,000 to $28,000 and experienced rangers may earn more than $50,000 per year. Some senior administrators earn as much as $75,000 to $100,000.

SOURCES OF FURTHER INFORMATION

American Recreation Coalition
1225 New York Ave.
Suite 450
Washington, DC 20005

National Parks and Conservation Association
1776 Massachusetts Ave. NW
Washington, DC 20036
Internet address: www.npca.org
A nonprofit organization devoted to conservation efforts in national parks, NPCA sponsors local groups that organize volunteer activities in parks and offer students summer field experience.

National Recreation and Park Association
22377 Belmont Ridge Road
Ashburn, VA 20148
Internet address: www.nrpa.org
This active association provides its members with professional developmental services, job fairs, and employment bulletins.

Also consult *The Complete Guide to Environmental Careers in the 21st Century* (1998), by the Environmental Careers Organization, published by Island Press. Included is an entire chapter on park and outdoor recreation careers.

RECREATION ADMINISTRATOR

The focus of recreation administration careers is on providing the public with exercise, entertainment, and outdoor activities. With the increase in leisure time for many Americans, the need for well-planned and well-executed recreation programs is becoming very important. Recreation administrators plan, organize, and direct activities that help people enjoy and benefit from leisure hours. They mobilize financial and human resources in both the private and public sector and are responsible for budgeting, marketing, trend forecasting, and other promotional activities that attract the public to their organizations. Some of the job titles for recreation administrators are director of parks and recreation, recreation supervisor, recreation center director, recreation leader, and park planner.

RELATED PROFESSIONS

Resort Manager
Cruise Ship Activity Director
Youth Agency Director
Corrections Recreation Specialist
Senior Citizens Center Director
Eco-Tour Guide

Recreation Leader
Fitness Club Manager
Recreation Worker
Park Planner
Conventions Coordinator
Adventure Travel Coordinator

EDUCATIONAL REQUIREMENTS

Most recreation administrators have completed at least a bachelor's degree, but more and more professionals are going on to complete master's degrees. The most popular degree programs are in parks and recreation, leisure studies, fitness management, physical education, and related fields. According to the National Recreation and Park Association (NRPA), more than 300 baccalaureate programs and more than 280 associate's degree programs in parks and recreation are offered by colleges and universities in the United States. The NRPA, in association with the

American Association of Leisure and Recreation, has accredited more than ninety associate's and bachelor's degree programs. For students interested in completing master's degrees, there are one hundred such programs in the United States. Because business skills are essential for recreation managers, students should take courses in management, accounting, business administration, and finance.

PROFESSIONAL CERTIFICATION

The National Recreation and Park Association offers a document of certification for those who meet the requirements of professionalism and technical knowledge. Contact the NRPA, listed at the end of the chapter, for information on testing procedures and personal requirements.

SETTINGS

Recreation administrators work for the federal, state, and local governments in park and recreation departments and in agencies that have in-house recreation programs. They work in physical education departments and run sports facilities at colleges and universities. They are employed by quasipublic or nonprofit city or community organizations that run community activity programs, youth and senior centers, and nursing homes. A growing number of professionals work in the private sector for companies and corporations that run or sponsor employee leisure activities, such as physical fitness programs, travel programs, social functions, and softball and bowling leagues. They also work at vacation resorts and on leisure cruise ships throughout the world.

Administrators spend about 60 percent of their time indoors doing administrative and managerial duties and another 40 percent outdoors running programs, training workers, and interacting with the public. Professionals in the public sector oversee the facilities that range from old and in need of updated equipment to modern and well-funded. Those facilities in the private sector are generally better equipped and funded. Recreation administrators working in the resort and entertainment industry are often in charge of lavish and state-of-the-art facilities and equipment.

EMPLOYMENT STATISTICS AND MAJOR EMPLOYERS

In 1996, about 233,000 full-time recreation workers were employed in the United States, and many additional workers held summer jobs in recreation. In addition many more were working for U.S. and foreign vacation and entertainment companies around the world. Recreation administrators are needed in all of these settings. More than half work in government agencies, primarily in park and recreation departments at the municipal and county levels. Another 20 percent work in membership organizations with social, fraternal, or civic orientations, such as YMCAs, the Boy Scouts, or the Red Cross, and about 10 percent work for social service or nonprofit organizations like youth and senior programs.

Recreation administrators employed in the private sector work for a variety of organizations. Private fitness and recreation centers employ a large number. Companies and corporations like IBM, Transamerica Life, and Proctor and Gamble provide employment opportunities because they often offer their employees access to on-site fitness facilities and encourage employees to participate in company-sponsored social functions and team sports. In the hospitality industry, recreation administrators work in large hotels across the world. In addition, many hotels in gambling cities like Las Vegas and Atlantic City have opened family-oriented hotel/casinos with lavish recreation facilities.

Competition in recreation administration will be intense through the year 2006, as all college graduates are eligible for these jobs, regardless of major. However, there will be a rise in job openings, due to the increase in leisure time for many Americans, the rising number of retired Americans who need recreational opportunities, and the overall increased interest in fitness and health. Job opportunities in local government are expected to slow slightly due to budget constraints. Employment opportunities in the private sector are expected to grow slightly faster than average.

SALARY STATISTICS

According to the National Comprehensive Salary and Benefits Study conducted by the National Recreation and Park Association (1993), the average salary for all recreation professionals is about $30,000. Park superintendents in 1993 received the highest average salary of $43,269, and recreation directors and recreation supervisors were close behind with average salaries of $42,675 and $42,510, respectively. Recreation supervisors earned an average of $28,935, and recreation center directors made $27,939. Salaries in the private sector, particularly for recreation directors and supervisors, were expected to be much higher.

SOURCES OF FURTHER INFORMATION

American Alliance for Health, Physical Education, Recreation,
   and Dance
1900 Association Drive
Reston, VA 22091
Internet address: www.aahperd.org

American Association for Leisure and Recreation
1900 Association Drive
Reston, VA 20191
Internet address: www.aalr.org

National Employee Services and Recreation Association
2111 York Road
Suite 207
Oakbrook, IL 60521
Internet address: www.nesra.org

National Recreation and Park Association
Division of Professional Services
22377 Belmont Ridge Road
Ashburn, VA 20148
Internet address: www.nrpa.org
The NRPA publishes the *National Job Bulletin,* which lists career openings for its members.

Part Five
Biological and Life Sciences

OVERVIEW

**Total Employment
360,000**

Employment Breakdown by Job Sector

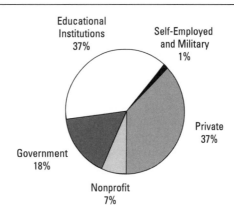

Educational Institutions 37%

Self-Employed and Military 1%

Private 37%

Nonprofit 7%

Government 18%

Projected Growth

According to the U.S. Department of Labor, employment opportunities in the biological sciences are expected to increase much faster than the average for all occupations through the year 2006. By the year 2006, there are expected to be 25 percent more biological scientists and 13 percent more science technicians than there are today. Although there is opportunity in this field, there is also very intense competition for coveted research positions, which are affected by budget cuts in federal funding.

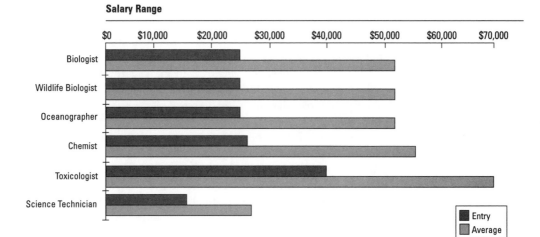

Salary Range

Biologist

Wildlife Biologist

Oceanographer

Chemist

Toxicologist

Science Technician

$0 $10,000 $20,000 $30,000 $40,000 $50,000 $60,000 $70,000

■ Entry
■ Average

HISTORY OF THE BIOLOGICAL AND LIFE SCIENCES

The mysteries of animal and plant life have long intrigued humans. The ancient Egyptians were the first to demonstrate a detailed knowledge of the human body and an understanding of other animal and plant life some four thousand years ago. When the Egyptians mummified bodies, they removed and preserved the major organs for study. There is written evidence that they found the heart to be of special importance and described it as central to the maintenance of life. This human curiosity led to the study of other aspects of anatomy and the biological life processes in general. While prehistoric humans can certainly be considered novice biologists—those who distinguished, sometimes fatally, between edible and inedible plants were certainly ancient taxonomists—there was only a most rudimentary study of living organisms until the time of the Egyptians.

Later the ancient Greeks became the first to systematically study, classify, and document the life processes. Around 500 B.C., Alcmaeon, a student of Pythagoras, the great philosopher and mathematician, conducted experiments that led him to distinguish between arteries and veins. Other Greeks studied sexual and asexual reproduction, categorized species, explored the anatomy of humans, and proposed the process of evolution. All of this accumulated knowledge was, however, lost to the West during the Christian Dark Ages when all scientific study was considered heretical and violently suppressed by the Church and its fanatical followers. The great library of Alexandria was burned, and many intellectuals were murdered. Arabs, who were beyond the territorial influence of the Christian zealots, continued the study of biology and the other sciences throughout this period. During this time, many important scientific advances were made, including enduring works on medicine, botany, and agronomy.

After several decades of intellectual suppression, reason finally reemerged in the West, and eventually many important scientific breakthroughs were made. In the thirteenth century, for example, Albertus Magnus wrote thirty-three books on botany with detailed descriptions of plant anatomy and propagation. In the sixteenth century, a complete anatomy of the human body was completed, and blood circulation was discovered. In the seventeenth century, the discoveries of cell and microscopic life were made. In the nineteenth century, Charles Darwin in his book *The Evolution of Species* detailed the process of evolution, and Louis Pasteur developed the field of immunology. In the late 1800s, Dmitri Mendeleev and Julius Meyer developed the periodic table of elements, which assigned an atomic weight and molecular count to all known elements.

In the last one hundred years, thousands of advances in the biological sciences have occurred. Just in the past twenty years, more discoveries have been made than in all of previous history combined! Among the most important are the isolation of the DNA (deoxyribonucleic acid) strand, which is the transmitter of genetic information for all living matter, and advances in biotechnology, the manipulation of genetic coding to alter certain traits or characteristics in living organisms. The biological sciences offer unlimited possibilities for study of global life processes. The scientists and technicians who work in this field are making important discoveries that will help solve pollution problems, decrease our dependence on nonrenewable energy sources, establish criteria for population control, and help feed the starving masses. The scientist or team behind each discovery needs only the proper tools and scientific imagination to help humanity achieve these important goals.

PROFESSIONS RELATED TO THE BIOLOGICAL SCIENCES

Forester	Agricultural Engineer
Range Manager	Veterinarian
Soil Conservationist	Animal Breeder
Horticulturist	Entomologist
Botanist	Medical Doctor
Agronomist	Medical Scientist
Animal Ecologist	Endangered Species Biologist
Aquatic Ecologist	Wetland Ecologist

MAJOR EMPLOYERS

Work in the biological sciences is heavily oriented toward research. Nearly half of all those employed in the biological sciences conduct basic research, either in the laboratory or in the field. More than one-third of biological scientists and technicians work at colleges, universities, and secondary schools, and a substantial amount of basic research is conducted on college campuses. In addition, biological scientists with advanced degrees often teach and conduct other routine academic duties.

About the same proportion of biological scientists and technicians work in private businesses and industry. The largest employers in industry are pharmaceutical, chemical, and food companies. In addition, a large number of research laboratories and consulting firms employ biological scientists.

Government agencies are also major employers of biological scientists and technicians. In the federal government, employment opportunities can be found in the Department of Agriculture at the Agricultural Research Service, Forest Service, Soil Conservation Service, and Extension Service. In the Department of the Interior, biological and life scientists work for the National Park Service, Fish and Wildlife Service, and Bureau of Land Management. State departments of agriculture and environmental protection are also large employers. Nonprofit organizations hire a number of biological science workers. Several organizations run nature and wildlife preserves, and some foundations conduct biological research. Finally, some biological scientists are self-employed, and some work for the military.

PROJECTED TRENDS AND EMPLOYMENT GROWTH

Employment forecasting in the biological sciences closely resembles weather forecasting: While there is the air of confidence in most predictions, the results are mixed at best. In the late 1980s and early 1990s, a severe shortage of science majors, particularly in the biological sciences, was predicted. College graduates a few years later found not the promised employment bonanza, but a highly competitive job market, largely the result of the unanticipated economic downturn during that period. The U.S. Department of Labor has predicted that, under an economy that experiences only "moderate growth," there will be a 24 percent increase in employment in the biological sciences to the year 2006. Most other employment studies also point to a probable shortage of qualified biological and life scientists in the first decade of the twenty-first century. With more than 100,000 people working in this field today, a substantial number of new jobs will be created in the coming decade even if these estimates are only partially correct.

Job growth is not expected to be uniform, especially in a field with so many areas of specialization. Growth is expected to be greatest in three areas.

Biotechnology is growing rapidly, particularly in the areas of plant genetic engineering and medical technology. There are more than seventy-five thousand edible wild plant species in the world that provide the genetic reservoir for biologists to use in recombining the genetic properties of crop strains to make them less susceptible to insects and disease and more productive. Also, about 25 percent of the prescription and nonprescription drugs produced in the United States are derived from wild plants. Worldwide, the sale of these drugs constitutes a more than $50 billion market. Wild plants are used to treat heart disease, cancer, and many other ailments. Intensive and promising research is involved in the search for a plant-based treatment for AIDS. Most estimates suggest more than one thousand new job openings each year for the next several years in these and related areas of research.

Ecosystem services encompass both the preservation of pristine plant and animal habitats and the cleanup of polluted areas. In the United States, more than ninety-five million people engage in outdoor recreation in wildlife areas, which generates more than $37 billion in revenue each year. Biological scientists are increasingly needed to ensure that a diverse population of plants and animal species maintain the healthy ecosystems in wilderness and other wildlife areas. In addition, Congress has reauthorized the Endangered Species Act, which calls for biological scientists to catalog sensitive and endangered species and make policy recommendations for the protection of their habitats. The Department of the Interior also plans a biological mapping of the entire nation; this will create a number of long-term jobs for biological and mapping scientists.

Environmental impact assessment will involve a large number of biological scientists in determining the effects of industry and government actions and in correcting environmental problems. Efforts to return previously developed or contaminated areas to their natural states will require the services of thousands of biological scientists and technicians. Military base closures will create a large market for biologists involved in evaluating potential hazardous and toxic waste problems and technologists involved in cleanup efforts. The same is true for industrial sites identified by the Environmental Protection Agency or state agencies as contaminated. See Part Seven for a complete description of these efforts.

SOURCES OF FURTHER INFORMATION

American Institute of Biological Sciences
1444 I St. NW
Washington, DC 20005
Internet address: www.aibs.org
The institute distributes, free of charge, a pamphlet entitled *Careers in Biology* and publishes the journal *BioScience*, which contains job listings.

Office of Opportunities in Science
American Association for the Advancement of Science
1200 New York Ave. NW
Washington, DC 20005
Internet address: www.aaas.org

Also consult the following publications:

Opportunities in Biology, by the Committee on Research Opportunities in Biology, published by National Academy Press.

Peterson's Job Opportunities for Engineering, Science, and Computer Graduates, published by Peterson's, P.O. Box 2123, Princeton, NJ 08543-2123. Lists hundreds of corporations and government agencies, many of which hire chemists.

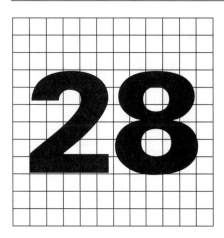

BIOLOGIST

including
Ecologist
Microbiologist
Zoologist

Biologists strive to understand how living systems work. Many scientists are involved in basic research—seeking knowledge for its own sake—while others are engaged in putting that knowledge to practical use. Biological scientists closely examine the relationship of living organisms to their environment. Organic life and the evolutionary developments in living organisms are so vast and complex that the biological sciences have been broken down into many areas of specialization. Almost any field that involves the study of living things requires the knowledge and services of biologists. Biologists are present in every aspect of the environmental sciences, from medical research and health and safety to wastewater and hazardous materials treatment. In Part Six, some agricultural biologists such as agronomists, botanists, and horticulturists are highlighted.

Biologists will play an increasingly important role in environmental sciences, particularly in the emerging science of biotechnology. Here, biologists use rapidly developing technology to recombine the genetic material of animals or plants, making organisms more productive or disease resistant. Most recently, this technology is being applied to produce bacteria that consume oil spills and dangerous radioactive isotopes. The present and potential uses of this technology are enormous. Several biological science fields will play a key role in the environmental sciences. Job growth in these areas is expected to be high. Ecologists or environmental biologists study the relationships among organisms, the relationships between organisms and their environments, and the effects on organisms of population size, pollutants, rainfall, temperature, and latitude. Some ecologists study the lives of specific kinds of organisms, such as microbes, plants, or animals. For example, an ecologist might study what makes a certain insect population rise and fall. Others study the whole spectrum of living beings within a particular habitat, such as prairies, ponds, or coral reefs. Some focus on the interactions among individuals of single species (population ecology) or among different species (community ecology) or between groups of species and the physical environment (ecosystem ecology). Regardless of their specific focuses, ecologists are united by an intense curiosity about how life works on planet earth. The work of ecologists has many practical applications related to environmental problems, such as understanding the effects of potential global warming or understanding how pollutants in rivers change species composition. Some ecologists may study the effects of farming practices on pest insects or methods of restoring damaged environments.

Microbiologists investigate the growth and characteristics of microscopic organisms, such as bacteria, algae, and fungi. They study the effects that these microscopic organisms have on humans and their environment. Microbiologists help answer such questions as, "How do cells use food and oxygen?" and "Which viruses pose the greatest threats to humans?" Their basic research can be applied to understanding the immunological and other biological functions of all plants and animals. Microbiologists may specialize in environmental, food, agricultural, or industrial microbiology, virology (the study of viruses), or immunology (the study of the mechanisms that fight infections). Many microbiologists are using biotechnology to advance knowledge of cell reproduction and human disease.

Zoologists are life scientists who study animals in both their natural environments and the laboratory. In particular, they study the origin and development of animal species, their habits and behavior, and the interaction between animals and their environments. Zoologists study mating practices, aggression, life histories, and the group behaviors of animals in their natural environments. Zoologists also conduct genetic research in order to discover how animal diseases develop and how traits are passed from generation to generation. Worldwide, thousands of species face extinction due to human settlements and activities in sensitive habitats and irresponsible hunting practices. Zoologists are scattered around the globe, from the Brazilian rain forests to the dense Siberian forests, conducting research and formulating policy positions on animal issues.

Other biologists working heavily in the environmental sciences are evolutionists, who study the development of plants and animals from the origin of the earth until the present; geneticists, who study the characteristics of heredity; morphologists, who study the form and structure of plants and animals; paleontologists, who study the fossilized remains of plants and animals that existed in former geologic periods; and taxonomists, who study the classification of animals and plants and create systems that categorize living organisms.

RELATED PROFESSIONS

Marine Biologist	Biochemist
Wildlife Biologist	Animal Breeder
Animal Scientist	Veterinarian

EDUCATIONAL REQUIREMENTS

The minimum requirement for a career in biology is a bachelor of science (B.S.) degree in biology or a closely related field. Almost every major university and college offers a degree in biology. Graduates with bachelor's degrees can enter the field as biological technicians or medical laboratory technologists or, with courses in education, high school biology teachers. Many with bachelor's degrees in biology enter medical, dental, veterinary, or other health profession schools. With master's degrees, students are qualified to teach, work as research assistants, or pursue careers in management, sales, and service. In order to take full advantage of this field, a doctoral degree is required. A graduate with a Ph.D. and a specific field of study can teach and conduct research in colleges and universities, become an academic administrator, or find a job as a senior staff specialist in government or private industry.

Students interested in biology should have a strong background in math and science. College courses offered during the first two years typically include calculus, statistics, general biology, chemistry, physics, computer science, humanities, liberal arts, and communication. Advanced courses depend heavily upon a student's interests but will require a good deal of laboratory work and usually a research paper. Curricula for advanced degrees often emphasize a subfield such as microbiology, ecology, or zoology, but not all schools offer all curricula. Advanced-degree programs include classroom and fieldwork, laboratory research, and a thesis or dissertation.

PROFESSIONAL CERTIFICATION

There are no special certifications or licenses for this profession.

SETTINGS

Biologists may work in classrooms, laboratories, offices, or the wilderness; their working conditions vary widely. Some biologists spend most of their time working in a laboratory or other research facility. These places tend to be clean and comfortable working environments. Many biologists will spend time in the office and classroom performing routine academic duties. Those who work outdoors, observing plants and animals in their own environs, are subject to a variety of working and living conditions. Depending upon the place and their field of study, biologists can find themselves observing Arctic animals in below-freezing conditions, identifying reptile species in the desert, recording gorilla mating rituals in the humid African jungle, or discovering new fungi in the Siberian forests. Biologists should be in good physical condition because they may be required to do strenuous physical work, walk long distances, and manage for extended periods with the absence of modern conveniences.

Working hours are also highly variable. Biologists working in the classroom or laboratory can expect regular forty-hour workweeks. Sometimes when conducting experiments, biologists need to work around the clock or into the evening hours to record and monitor the progress of their work. Those conducting field observations or experiments usually work at the convenience of the animals and plants they are studying, so hours may vary considerably.

EMPLOYMENT STATISTICS AND MAJOR EMPLOYERS

More than 82,000 biological scientists are employed in nonacademic jobs in the United States, and an additional 25,000 work in academia. About 25 percent of all biologists are employed by the federal, state, and local governments. In the federal government, biologists found employment at the Department of Agriculture working for the U.S. Forest Service and Extension Service. At the Department of the Interior, biologists work for the U.S. Fish and Wildlife Service, the National Park Service, and the Bureau of Land Management. Other agencies and institutes hiring biologists are the U.S. Public Health Service and the National Institutes of Health. Those wishing to work internationally can contact the Peace Corps or the International AID program in the Department of Agriculture. Refer to Chapter 2 for a full description of most of these government departments and agencies.

About 30 percent of all biologists work in the private sector. Biologists are employed primarily in the pharmaceutical industry, agribusiness, hospitals, offices of physicians, or research and testing laboratories. The continuing advances in biotechnology should greatly expand employment opportunities in basic research as companies compete to patent new discoveries and genetic alterations.

Biologists are employed in colleges and universities across the nation as researchers, teachers, and tenured faculty members. The majority of medium to large schools offer classes in biology or biology degree programs. Biologists, particularly those possessing Ph.D.'s, often conduct their own independent research and teach the topics that most interest them.

The remaining biologists work for nonprofit organizations or are self-employed. The Nature Conservancy, which runs more than 1,400 nature preserves throughout the United States, Canada, and Latin America, hires a good number of biologists. The World Wildlife Fund (WWF) also employs some wildlife biologists. At present, a large share of its resources are being used in Latin America where the WWF has helped create and monitor a number of national parks and wildlife preserves. Other organizations that employ biologists are the Wilderness Society, the Sierra Club, and the National Wildlife Federation.

SALARY STATISTICS

According to the U.S. Department of Labor, median annual earnings for biological and life scientists were about $36,300 in 1996. About half of those surveyed earned between $28,400 and $50,900, while about 10 percent earned more than $66,000. In a 1997 salary survey by the National Association of Colleges and Employers, beginning salaries in private industry for biology and life science students with bachelor's degrees averaged $25,400 per year. In the federal government in 1997, biological scientists earned an average salary of $52,100. The average salary for an assistant biology professor is $46,000, while full professors earn $74,000 on average.

SOURCES OF FURTHER INFORMATION

American Institute of Biological Sciences
Office of Career Services
1444 I St. NW
Washington, DC 20000
Internet address: www.aibs.org

The Ecological Society of America
1707 H St. NW
Suite 400
Washington, DC 20006

Federation of American Societies for Experimental Biology
9650 Rockville Pike
Bethesda, MD 20814
Internet address: www.faseb.org

Society of Systematic Zoology
Information Officer
Smithsonian Institution
Washington, DC 20560
Internet address: www.si.edu

The Nature Conservancy
4245 North Fairfax Drive
Arlington, VA 22208

World Wildlife Fund
1250 24th St. NW
Washington, DC 20037
Internet address: www.wwf.org

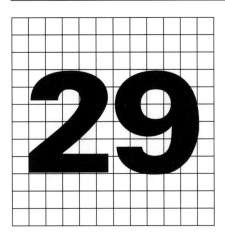

WILDLIFE MANAGER/ WILDLIFE BIOLOGIST

Wildlife managers work to protect, conserve, and manage wildlife and their habitats. They work with a variety of game and nongame animals, including mammals, waterfowl, and fish. The overall mission of wildlife managers is to ensure the health and well-being of wildlife and their habitats, mostly on multiple-use public lands. Thus, these managers must direct their energies not only to environmental issues but also to the economic, recreational, aesthetic, and scientific issues of lands used for hunting, logging, hiking, mining, and other commercial activities. Overall, they work to protect and improve the entire surroundings or ecosystem, including trees, plants, water, and soil.

Wildlife managers work on a variety of projects, which requires a broad background in the biological and conservation sciences. When taking blood tests and examining animals, for example, these professionals must possess some of the skills of veterinarians; when working in the laboratory, they need the technical know-how of zoologists. They also work regularly with fellow biologists and natural resource managers to evaluate animal habitats. Many wildlife managers either work on wildlife refuges or work to create sanctuaries where threatened or endangered animals are protected. In protected or regulated areas, they study the overall health of animal species, appraise the effects of pollution on certain species, and conduct field and laboratory tests.

Another aspect of wildlife managers' jobs is the creation and enforcement of public land use. They may patrol protected areas to maintain the well-being of animals and their surroundings and enforce hunting regulations and quotas. Public relations is another essential aspect of their work. Wildlife managers conduct public information tours, write announcements and articles, and serve as environmental specialists to legislatures.

RELATED PROFESSIONS

Zoologist   Geneticist
Marine Biologist   Dairy Scientist

Microbiologist	Physiologist
Veterinarian	Botanist
Anatomist	Mycologist

EDUCATIONAL REQUIREMENTS

The minimum educational requirement for a career in wildlife management is a bachelor of science (B.S.) degree in wildlife biology. As is the case with other careers in the biological sciences, an advanced degree is becoming the standard criterion for the employment of wildlife managers. According to *Chronicle Guidance Publications*, less than 30 percent of recent graduates with bachelor's degrees found employment as wildlife managers, while those with master's degrees have a 60 percent to 70 percent chance of finding employment. A master's degree is the standard requirement for a career in research.

There are degree programs in wildlife management/wildlife biology throughout the country, mainly in forestry departments of large colleges and universities. Some students can substitute degrees in zoology or botany and additional courses in the life and animal sciences.

First- and second-year wildlife management students typically take courses like geometry, algebra, calculus, chemistry, physics, biology, botany, geography, English, and communications and other liberal arts courses. Advanced courses include genetics, biometrics, wildlife ecology, statistics, computer courses, and mammalogy. Students are required in many courses to conduct laboratory experiments and fieldwork. Graduate students conduct focused research under the supervision of advisors. They must usually write publishable theses on their own original research and pass oral and/or written examinations.

PROFESSIONAL CERTIFICATION

The Wildlife Society offers its members the title Certified Wildlife Biologist. Members must meet Wildlife Society standards of education, experience, and ethics. Recent entrants into the field with little experience may be eligible to become an Associate Wildlife Biologist. Contact the Wildlife Society, listed at the end of this chapter, for further details on these certification programs.

SETTINGS

Wildlife managers divide their time between administrative duties and laboratory and outdoor work. Wildlife managers need to be in good physical condition; their work often requires them to spend time in the backcountry with minimal amenities. They must also handle large and sometimes dangerous animals, walk great distances, and carry heavy loads. Due to the rigorous physical requirements, most employers require their wildlife managers to pass physical examinations. Much of their work takes place in public parks and forests or designated wildlife sanctuaries or refuges. An appreciation for the outdoors and willingness to work and live in a rural setting are necessary. Wildlife managers also function as wildlife spokespeople. They give public speeches, tours, and presentations; interact with the media; and occasionally testify before legislative bodies.

Working hours can vary greatly, depending mostly on location. Office and laboratory duties usually require wildlife managers to work regular forty-hour weeks. When conducting research or tagging animals in the backcountry, wildlife managers may be required to work more hours.

EMPLOYMENT STATISTICS AND MAJOR EMPLOYERS

According to the U.S. Department of Labor, the employment outlook for biological scientists, including wildlife biologists, is expected to grow slightly faster than the average for all occupations. Because most wildlife biologists work in government and government-dependent private companies, they are fairly well insulated from cyclical fluctuations in the job market.

The majority of wildlife managers work in the federal, state, and local governments. Major federal employers include the U.S. Department of Agriculture (USDA). Specific agencies employing wildlife managers in the USDA include the Forest Service, the Extension Service, the Agricultural Research Service, and the Soil Conservation Service. The U.S. Department of the Interior also employs wildlife managers in the U.S. Fish and Wildlife Service, the Park Service, and the Bureau of Land Management. Other federal agencies and commissions hiring wildlife biologists are the Environmental Protection Agency, the Council on Environmental Quality, and the National Institutes of Health. See Chapter 2 for a full description of most of these government agencies. State fish and game departments also hire a large number of wildlife managers. These managers work on state fish and game reserves, on public hunting lands, and in state parks.

A number of private, nonprofit conservation organizations also hire wildlife managers/biologists. The Nature Conservancy, which operates more than 1,400 nature preserves in the United States, Canada, and Latin America, employs many wildlife managers. The World Wildlife Fund (WWF), which is dedicated to protecting endangered wildlife and wild lands throughout the world, also employs a number of wildlife biologists. At present, a large share of its resources are being used in Latin America where the WWF has helped create and monitor a number of national parks and wildlife preserves. Other organizations that employ wildlife managers are the Wilderness Society, the Sierra Club, and the National Wildlife Federation.

Wildlife managers find employment in such commercial industries as timber, ranching, and mining. Employment opportunities also exist in private wildlife sanctuaries, game preserves, and zoos as well as in biological laboratories and consulting firms.

SALARY STATISTICS

According to the National Association of Colleges and Employers, the average starting salary for biological scientists with bachelor's degrees was $25,400 in 1997. The average salary of those with master's degrees was $26,900, and for Ph.D. holders it was about $52,400.

In the federal government, the average salary for biological scientists was about $52,100 in 1997.

SOURCES OF FURTHER INFORMATION

The Ecological Society of America
2010 Massachusetts Ave. NW
Suite 400
Washington, DC 20036

National Wildlife Federation
1412 Sixteenth St. NW
Washington, DC 20026
Internet address: www.nwf.org

Nature Conservancy Headquarters
4245 North Fairfax Drive
Arlington, VA 22208

The Wildlife Society
5410 Grosvenor Lane
Suite 200
Bethesda, MD 20814
Internet address: www.wildlife.org

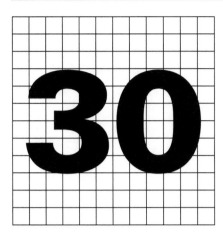

OCEANOGRAPHER

including
Marine Biologist
Limnologist
Marine Geologist

Using the principles and techniques of the biological sciences, mathematics, and engineering, oceanographers and aquatic biologists study the movements and physical properties of plant and animal life and the geologic structure of the oceans. Most oceanographers specialize in one branch of the science. *Oceanography* technically means the study of the physical characteristics of oceans and the ocean floor. Marine geologists study underwater mountain ranges, rocks, and sediments of the oceans to locate regions where minerals, oil, and gas may be found. Aquatic biologists include marine biologists and limnologists. Marine biologists study plants and animals living in saltwater; limnologists concentrate on the study of freshwater environments.

Probably the most famous marine biologist, Jacques Cousteau, brought the important study of this field to millions of people through his long-running television appearances. Marine biologists collect, measure, and identify marine specimens in order to assess the overall health of the marine environment. These biologists are very concerned with the effects of pollution on the seas. Years of pumping untreated chemicals, sewage, and airborne pollutants into the marine environment has had a serious impact. The graphic depictions of oil-drenched wildlife and shores in Valdez, Alaska, and Northern Scotland are sharp examples of two relatively minor abuses of the seas.

Oceanographers and aquatic biologists ask many questions and use modern scientific research methods in their aquatic studies. They examine living coral reefs in tropical seas, fish school populations in the North Atlantic, deep ocean trenches, cold marine environments under the polar ice caps, and complex freshwater ecosystems. Some concentrate their studies on large and endangered animals like whales, sea turtles, and dolphins to learn more about their behavior, feeding habits, population, and reproduction. Others study ocean floors, plants, and microscopic organisms to find new sources of food and medicine and to learn more about the origins of life on the planet. In the laboratory, either on land or on vessels, these scientists use the latest research technology to create complex computer models to run experiments. Because the seas and, to a much lesser extent, freshwater bodies cover more than two-thirds of the earth's surface and harbor most of its organic life, the work of these biologists is very useful and holds important discoveries for humanity.

RELATED PROFESSIONS

Marine Chemist	Microbiologist
Geologist	Biophysicist
Geographer	Physiologist
Meteorologist	Chemist

EDUCATIONAL REQUIREMENTS

The minimum educational requirement for a career in this field is a bachelor of science (B.S.) degree in marine biology or geology. Seventy-six universities and colleges offer bachelor's degrees in marine biology. Some notable programs are at the University of Miami, the University of California at San Diego Scripps Marine Research Department, and the University of Arizona. There are also a good number of schools with programs in marine geology. Like other marine-oriented programs, most marine biology programs are offered in coastal states. Programs in limnology are limited, and most can be found in the Great Lakes states.

As is the case in most other biology and physical science professions, a master's degree is becoming the standard criterion for employment. For those who wish to conduct research or teach, a Ph.D. is most often required. Many of the schools offering an undergraduate degree also have graduate programs in oceanography.

First- and second-year courses in marine biology often include algebra, geometry, calculus, general biology, organic and inorganic chemistry, physics, computer science, English, and liberal arts courses. Advanced students take classes in biometrics, biochemistry, toxicology, fish biology, evolutionary ecology, and genetics. Many of the courses that students take have laboratory components.

In all graduate program subfields of oceanography, students must conduct original research in their chosen concentrations, which often gives them the opportunity to conduct field research in locations away from their universities. Graduate training in oceanography or a basic science is required for most jobs in research and teaching and for all top-level positions. Because many oceanographers work in locations far from the United States, the knowledge of at least one foreign language is important.

PROFESSIONAL CERTIFICATION

There are no special certifications or licenses for this occupation.

SETTINGS

Oceanographers work in all kinds of climates and in locations around the world. Some spend a majority of their time in the laboratory; others work extensively at sea, and some spend their time in the classroom. Working hours are also as variable. Those working on land usually perform their jobs in regular forty-hour weeks. There are, however, times when experiments or the care of animals require marine biologists to work longer hours. Work on ships or in the ocean is often conducted in rough conditions. The sea can be treacherous, especially during storms, and divers must pay close attention to equipment safety procedures and exercise particular caution in coral reef areas and in the presence of dangerous animal species.

EMPLOYMENT STATISTICS AND MAJOR EMPLOYERS

Several thousand oceanographers are working in the United States, with more people graduating from college with appropriate degrees than the field can absorb. This has occurred mainly because the U.S. government, the major employer of oceanographers, is hiring fewer marine biologists and marine geologists than it has in the past. In addition, there has been no increase in demand from the private sector. This trend may reverse itself with the growing concern for marine environments and the expansion of the fields of marine biotechnology and particularly aquaculture (the cultivation of fish in hatcheries). There has been an increased demand for oceanographers with advanced technical and research skills, particularly at government marine research stations and universities.

The federal government hires oceanographers in the Environmental Protection Agency, the Fish and Wildlife Service, the National Oceanic and Atmospheric Administration (NOAA), and the U.S. Geological Survey (USGS). There are NOAA research facilities in La Jolla, California, Woods Hole, Massachusetts, and Washington, D.C., and USGS offices located throughout the country. Almost one-half of all oceanographers work in California, Maryland, and Virginia, with additional concentrations in Florida, Hawaii, and the Pacific Northwest. Oceanographers also work for state governments, particularly those located in coastal areas or near large freshwater bodies.

Colleges and universities are also major employers. Some institutions of higher learning, like the Scripps Institute at the University of California, San Diego, and Miami University in Florida, maintain sizable research laboratories and hire a good number of research oceanographers. In the private sector, oceanographers work for research laboratories, mapping companies, research foundations, and the fishing industry.

SALARY STATISTICS

According to the National Association of Colleges and Employers, the average starting salary in private industry for biological scientists who have earned bachelor's degrees was $25,400 in 1997. The average salary for those with master's degrees was $26,900, and for Ph.D. holders it was $52,400.

In the federal government, the average salary for oceanographers was $62,700 in 1997, higher than the average of $52,100 for general biological scientists.

SOURCES OF FURTHER INFORMATION

American Fisheries Society
5410 Grosvenor Lane
Suite 110
Bethesda, MD 20814
Internet address: www.fisheries.org

American Institute of Biological Sciences
1444 I St. NW
Washington, DC 20005
Internet address: www.aibs.org

American Society of Limnology and Oceanography
Attention: Susan C. Weiler
200 Boyer Ave.
Whitman College
Walla Walla, WA 99362
Internet address: www.aslo.org

International Oceanographic Foundation
4600 Rickenbacker Causeway
Virginia Key
Miami, FL 33149

Society for Marine Mammology
Department of Biology
EMS Building
University of California—Santa Cruz
Santa Cruz, CA 95064

Center for Marine Conservation
1725 DeSales St. NW
Suite 600
Washington, DC 20036

Marine Technology Society
1828 L St. NW
Suite 906
Washington, DC 20036
The Marine Technology Society provides a free list of education and training programs in oceanography and related fields.

Scripps Institution of Oceanography
University of California—San Diego
La Jolla, CA 92093
Internet address: www.sio.ucsd.edu

Woods Hole Oceanographic Institution
193 Oyster Pond Road
MS #2
Woods Hole, MA 02543-1525
Internet address: www.whoi.edu

Also consult *Opportunities in Marine and Maritime Careers* (1998), by William Ray Heitzmann, published by VGM Career Horizons, NTC/Contemporary Publishing Group.

CHEMIST

including
Organic Chemist
Analytical Chemist
Physical Chemist
Biochemist

Chemistry is the study of the basic structure of matter: what substances are made of, what their properties are, how they act, and how they interact. Although chemicals are often thought of as artificial or toxic substances, all physical things are composed of chemicals. Chemists are scientists who work closely with scientists from many other fields, such as physicists, biologists, medical doctors, environmental scientists, and agronomists, to solve complex problems. Chemists are, first and foremost, problem solvers who use their intimate knowledge of the composition of all living and nonliving matter to provide the basis for advances in medicine, agriculture, and other areas. They help look for cures to arrest diseases such as AIDS; devise ways to prepare, preserve, and improve our food, air, and water; and work to answer such questions as "How old is the earth?" and "What is happening to the ozone layer?" Most recently, chemists have been working with superconductivity, providing novel materials that carry electricity with minimal energy loss.

Most chemists are involved in either research and development (R&D) or production. In basic research, chemists investigate the properties, compositions, and structure of matter and the laws that govern the elements and reactions of substances. In applied research and development, they create new products or improve existing ones, often using knowledge gained from basic research. In the environmental sciences, chemists provide vital knowledge that can be applied to virtually any investigation.

Chemists often specialize in a specific subfield. In fact, the field of chemistry has more than twenty-four branches and subbranches. In the environmental sciences, the following specializations are particularly important. Organic chemists study the chemistry of the vast number of carbon compounds. Many commercial products, such as drugs, plastics, and fertilizers, were developed by organic chemists. Analytical chemists determine the structure, composition, and nature of substances and develop analytical techniques. They also identify the presence of chemical pollutants in air, water, and soil. Physical chemists study the physical characteristics of atoms and molecules and investigate how chemical reactions work. Their research often results in new and better energy sources. Biochemists study the chemical composition of living things. They try to understand the complex chemical combinations and reactions involved in metabolism, reproduction, growth, and heredity. Biochemists are on the leading edge of the new and swiftly growing field of biotechnology. In this field, biologists are able to recombine genetic material of animals or plants, making organisms more productive or disease resistant. The first application of this technology has been in the medical and pharmaceutical area. For example, the human gene that codes for the production of insulin has been inserted into bacteria, causing them to produce human insulin. This insulin, used by diabetics, is much purer than insulin from animals, the only previous source. In the field of agriculture, biochemists routinely alter the genetic characteristics of food seeds to make fruits and vegetables resistant to insects, more uniform in size and color, and better tasting.

RELATED PROFESSIONS

Chemical Engineer	Biologist
Environmental Engineer	Geophysicist
Agronomist	Toxicologist
Entomologist	Oceanographer

EDUCATIONAL REQUIREMENTS

The minimum educational requirement for a career in chemistry is a bachelor of science (B.S.) degree in chemistry or a closely related discipline. According to the American Chemical Society (ACS), there are 620 ACS-certified bachelor-degree programs in chemistry in the United States, approximately 320 master's programs, and about 190 doctoral programs.

Students planning careers as chemists should enjoy studying science and mathematics and should like working with their hands, building scientific apparatus, and performing experiments. Perseverance, curiosity, and the abilities to concentrate on detail and work independently are essential. Students are required to complete the general academic requirements, including mathematics, English, physics, biology, and humanities courses. Typical required courses in chemistry programs are analytical, inorganic, organic, and physical chemistry. Computer courses are also important; chemists are increasingly using computers as tools in their everyday work. Due to the diversity of career avenues open to undergraduate-level chemistry students, most programs stress flexibility instead of specialization. Many employers supply their entry-level chemists with additional training for specific job needs.

Graduate students typically specialize in a subfield of chemistry, such as analytical chemistry, polymer chemistry, organic chemistry, inorganic chemistry, physical chemistry, or biochemistry. At the master's and Ph.D. levels, students are required to conduct original research in their subfield and write a thesis or dissertation on their work. Many students work with chemistry faculty members on projects that give them laboratory research training and recognition for published work. Many chemists continue to study throughout their careers to keep up with new developments.

SPECIAL CERTIFICATION

The American Institute of Chemists (AIC) offers the title Certified Professional Chemist to chemists and others in related professions. The AIC does not administer an examination but requires applicants to have ample work and continuing education experience. Experience is based upon four criteria: continuing education, publications, reports, and presentations. Those who do not meet the requirements for certification may receive a Certificate-in-Training designation. Contact the AIC, listed at the end of this chapter, for further information on certification.

SETTINGS

Many chemists work in research and development (R&D); much of their work is performed in the laboratory. There is a wide variation in the quality of laboratory facilities; some resemble bare-bones high school chemistry labs, while others, particularly corporate R&D and federal labs, are large and well-equipped facilities. Chemists routinely handle dangerous and toxic chemicals, but accidents and injuries are rare because of strict safety regulations. Some R&D chemists work primarily in offices conducting theoretical research and writing reports. Other chemists work in production plants and are required to monitor and make reports on production activities. Still others work outdoors when, for example, gathering samples of pollutants or other compounds. Others work in academic settings where classroom teaching and routine academic duties are required.

Chemists typically work regular forty-hour weeks. They must occasionally work more when experiments that require constant monitoring are in progress. Some chemists working in production facilities may be required to work nights or weekend shifts.

EMPLOYMENT STATISTICS AND MAJOR EMPLOYERS

Chemists held about ninety-one thousand jobs in 1996. Nearly half of all chemists work in manufacturing firms, mostly in the chemical manufacturing industry, which includes firms that produce plastics and polymers, biotechnology, electronics, pharmaceuticals, and other chemical products. Chemists working in industry are heavily concentrated in New York, New Jersey, California, Pennsylvania, Ohio, and Illinois. Another 24 percent of all chemists work in academic institutions where they teach and conduct research. A doctorate degree is required to teach at four-year colleges and universities and is preferred by most two-year colleges. Nine percent of chemists are employed by government agencies. In the federal government, geochemists and environmental chemists work for the National Oceanic and Atmospheric Administration; physical, environmental, inorganic, and organic chemists work at the Environmental Protection Agency; agricultural, biochemical, environmental, and analytical chemists work at the Department of Agriculture. Other agencies hiring chemists are the Food and Drug Administration, the Department of Justice, the Department of Energy, and the National Science Foundation. The remaining chemists work in marketing, sales, computer firms, law offices, and libraries.

According to the U.S. Department of Labor, chemists are expected to have very good employment opportunities through the year 2006 because employment is expected to grow about as fast as the average for all occupations and the number of degrees granted in chemistry is not expected to increase enough to meet future demands. Expanded research and development, especially in pharmaceutical firms, biotechnology firms, and firms producing specialty chemicals, are expected to contribute heavily to employment growth. Chemists with Ph.D.'s are in strong demand as employers are increasingly expecting their researchers to have advanced educations.

SALARY STATISTICS

According to a 1997 survey by the American Chemical Association (ACA), the median starting salary for recently graduated chemists with bachelor's degrees was about $25,000. The median salary of ACA members (with varying degrees of experience) was $49,400 for chemists with bachelor's degrees, $56,200 for chemists with master's degrees, and $71,000 for Ph.D. chemists. In 1997, chemists in the federal government earned an average salary of $60,000. An entry-level assistant professor in the physical sciences earned about $37,012, associate professors earn $43,621, and full professors earn about $62,531.

SOURCES OF FURTHER INFORMATION

American Chemical Society
Education Division
1155 16th St. NW
Washington, DC 20036
Internet address: www.acs.org
The society distributes a free pamphlet entitled *Chemistry and Your Career.* It also operates the Employment Clearing House, which is a job bank for members.

The American Institute of Chemists
National Certification Commission in Chemistry and
    Chemical Engineering
515 King St.
Suite 420
Alexandria, VA 22314
Internet address: www.theaic.org

American Institute of Chemical Engineers
3 Park Ave.
New York, NY 10016-5991
Internet address: www.aiche.org

Chemical Specialties Manufacturers Association
1913 Eye St. NW
Washington, DC 20006
Internet address: www.csma.org

Environmental Defense Fund, Inc.
Headquarters
257 Park Ave. S
New York, NY 10010
This leading environmental advocacy organization is active in a
wide range of issues, including promotion of environmental
health through reduced exposure to toxic chemicals.

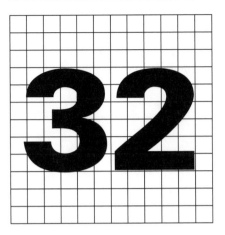

TOXICOLOGIST

Toxicologists combine the studies of biology and chemistry with many other disciplines to understand the potential harmful effects of chemicals on living organisms. They provide information on the hazards of chemical substances to the federal government, private businesses, and the public. Hardly a week passes without news about a chemical that may threaten our health: pesticides in our food, pollutants in the air we breathe, chemicals in the water we drink, or the threat of toxic dump sites near our homes. Toxicologists are concerned with answering whether substances are in fact dangerous by defining, among other things, the amount of exposure it takes to cause bodily damage. They provide data on carcinogens (cancer-causing agents) and the potential for damage to the human nervous system and birth defects.

According to the Society of Toxicology, toxicologists are responsible for the following tasks:

- Develop new and better ways to determine the potential harmful effects of chemical and physical agents and the amount (dosage) that causes such effects. An essential part of this task is developing an understanding of the basic molecular, biochemical, and cellular processes responsible for diseases caused by exposure to chemical or physical substances.

- Design and carry out carefully controlled studies of specific chemicals of social and economic importance to determine the conditions under which they can be used safely, having little or no impact on human health or the environment.

- Assess the probability or likelihood that particular chemicals, processes, or situations present a significant risk to human health and/or the environment and assist in the establishment of rules and regulations aimed at protecting and preserving human health and the environment.

With the growing use of pharmaceuticals and chemicals in this nation, the study of their potential impacts on human health and the environment has become increasingly important. The job of toxicologists in identifying levels of toxins, finding antidotes, and discovering less-dangerous alternatives will become paramount as new approaches are tried to combat air, water, and hazardous and toxic waste pollution problems.

RELATED PROFESSIONS

Chemist	Physiologist
Geneticist	Physician
Biologist	Industrial Hygienist
Risk Manager/Assessor	Health Engineer
Sanitary Engineer	Safety Engineer

EDUCATIONAL REQUIREMENTS

The minimum degree requirement for a career in toxicology is a bachelor of science (B.S.) degree in biology, chemistry, or pharmacology. With a bachelor's degree, career options in toxicology are limited, and most of these degree holders work as laboratory technicians. Advanced training is essential for a career in toxicology, which is evidenced by the fact that there are no undergraduate degree programs in toxicology. There are, however, sixty-nine graduate programs leading to a master's or doctorate degree. Toxicologists holding master's degrees work as assistant laboratory researchers or project managers, while doctorate holders conduct independent research in colleges and universities, become academic administrators, or find employment as senior staff specialists in government or private industry.

Coursework for undergraduate students majoring in toxicology preparatory degree programs should include mathematics (including mathematical modeling), chemistry, biology, biochemistry, anatomy, pathology, statistics, computer courses, and research methods. Verbal and written communication skills are essential, so courses such as English and communication should be approached seriously. Graduate students should expect a rigorous test of their academic abilities. While course work is dependent on the area of study, graduate students are generally required to take such courses as molecular biology, environmental toxicology, biostatistics, biochemistry, and epidemiology. Students who have completed the doctorate degree can enter the field by becoming postdoctoral fellows in toxicology laboratories for two to three years. The National Institute of Environmental Health Sciences offers numerous grants to postdoctoral fellows.

PROFESSIONAL CERTIFICATION

Two professional organizations certify toxicologists. The American Board of Toxicologists (ABT) certifies a toxicologist only after successful completion of a two-day examination and possession of the proper level of educational and work experience. The Academy of Toxicological Sciences (ATS) certifies toxicologists based on their educational and work experience. Contact the ABT or the ATS for further information on testing procedures and requirements.

SETTINGS

Many toxicologists work in basic research or applied research laboratories in private industry, academia, or government. These facilities are typically well funded and contain modern research equipment. Most laboratories are well lit, clean, and comfortable work environments. While toxicologists handle many dangerous chemicals and other agents, they have very low risk of injury because they carefully follow explicit and strict safety procedures. Toxicologists are sometimes required to give expert testimony in court or before legislative bodies on health, safety, and environment issues. Other toxicologists work primarily in office settings or in the classroom.

EMPLOYMENT STATISTICS AND MAJOR EMPLOYERS

The employment outlook for toxicologists is strong, particularly as the use of chemicals and concerns for health and environmental safety rise. According to the Society of Toxicology, toxicologists are heavily concentrated in the mid-Atlantic states, particularly near Washington, D.C. Many toxicologists are also found in the north central and western states.

Thirty-seven percent of toxicologists are employed in the pharmaceutical and chemical industries where they develop products, evaluate product safety, and monitor regulatory compliance. Graduates with bachelor's, master's, and doctorates are all well represented in private industry. Academic institutions employ 33 percent of all toxicologists. Most are employed by large universities with schools of medicine or public health. Some toxicologists teach biology, chemistry, and engineering in smaller colleges. Most toxicologists working in academia possess doctorate degrees. The federal and state governments employ 15 percent of toxicologists, primarily in four regulatory agencies—the Environmental Protection Agency, the Food and Drug Administration, the Occupational Safety and Health Administration, and the National Center for Toxicology—and at the many National Institutes of Health laboratories. Toxicologists with all levels of education work in government. Eight percent of toxicologists are employed by consulting firms, which primarily analyze data and make recommendations to government agencies. Many entry-level toxicologists with bachelor's and master's degrees are finding employment with these firms. Finally, 7 percent of toxicologists are employed by public and private research foundations. Toxicologists with all levels of education find employment with foundations.

SALARY STATISTICS

According to a 1998 salary survey by the Society of Toxicology, entry-level salaries for those with doctoral degrees often exceed $50,000, with rapid advancement potential. Mid-range professionals with ten years of experience can expect to earn between $70,000 and $85,000 per year, while most executive positions in toxicology exceed $100,000 per year. Entry-level technicians with bachelor's degrees can expect to earn around $25,000 per year, while those with master's degrees earn between $35,000 and $50,000 per year.

SOURCES OF FURTHER INFORMATION

American College of Toxicology
9650 Rockville Pike
Bethesda, MD 20814
Internet address: www.actox.org

Chemical Industry Institute of Toxicology
6 Davis Drive
Box 12137
Research Triangle Park, NC 27709-2137
Internet address: www.ciit.org

Committee on Toxicology
Board on Environmental Studies and Toxicology
National Research Council
2101 Constitution Ave. NW
Washington, DC 20418

National Institute of Environmental Health Science (NIEHS)
Division of Extramural Research and Training
P.O. Box 12233
Research Triangle Park, NC 27709
Internet address: www.niehs.nih.gov
The NIEHS provides ninety postdoctoral fellowships to thirty-three different academic institutions for postdoctoral training in environmental toxicology and/or environmental pathology. It is also the base of the National Toxicology Program. Write the NIEHS for a list of programs that receive NIEHS funding.

Society of Environmental Toxicology and Chemistry
1010 North 12th Ave.
Pensacola, FL 32501-3367
Internet address: www.setac.org

Society of Toxicologic Pathologists
19 Mantua Road
Mount Royal, NJ 08061
Internet address: www.toxpath.org

Society of Toxicology
1767 Business Center Drive
Suite 302
Reston, VA 20190-5332
Internet address: www.toxicology.org

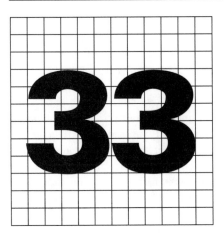

SCIENCE TECHNICIAN

including
Biological Technician
Chemical Technician
Ocean Technician

Science technicians use the principles and theories of science and mathematics to solve problems in all types of research and development and in the development of marketable products. They are highly skilled workers who are responsible for a large share of the actual work carried out in laboratories. Science technicians use a wide variety of laboratory instruments and procedures in their work and, thus, must have a broad knowledge of science. In recent years, scientific technology has become much more complex; it requires highly trained workers, which in turn raises the job prospects for well-educated technicians. With the aid of robotics, technicians have been freed from conducting rudimentary laboratory tasks and now make extensive use of computers and other high-technology equipment to perform their work.

Technicians set up, operate, and maintain laboratory instruments; monitor experiments; calculate and record results; and often develop conclusions. Those working in production test products for proper proportions of ingredients or for strength and durability. Employers are increasingly depending on science technicians to formulate, conduct, and draw conclusions in the laboratory, a task that has traditionally been reserved for personnel with higher levels of education.

Two science technicians—biological technicians and chemical technicians—play particularly important roles in the environmental sciences. Biological technicians work with biologists studying living organisms and their relationship to the environment. For every biological scientist there are several biological technicians conducting research and experiments and developing products. These technicians are presently conducting important research in medicine, helping to find cures for cancer and AIDS, working to discover new and improved medicines, and analyzing organic substances such as blood, food, and drugs to learn more about human biological processes and the effects of pesticides, toxins, and other potentially dangerous substances. Increasingly, biological technicians are working in biotechnology labs, using the knowledge, products, and techniques gained from basic research by scientists, including gene splicing and the preparation of recombinant DNA for product development. Some environmental projects presently being conducted include the creation of petroleum-digesting bacteria for large oil spills, genetically altered food seeds that are insect resistant, food production for deep space travel, and alternative organic energy sources.

Chemical technicians work with chemists and chemical engineers, developing and using chemicals for research and production. Most do research and development, testing, or other laboratory work. For example, they might test packaging for design, materials, and environmental acceptability; assemble and operate new equipment to develop new products; improve product quality; or develop new production techniques. Some chemical technicians collect and analyze samples of air and water to monitor pollution levels. Those who focus on basic research might produce compounds through complex organic synthesis. Chemical technicians work in every facet of the environmental sciences, particularly in the areas of air, soil, and water pollution, hazardous waste management, and the development of alternative energy sources.

Ocean technicians assist oceanographers in studying the physical and biological properties of the oceans and bodies of freshwater around the world. They assist in the search for precious minerals, oil, and gas; conduct research on ocean pollution and the effects of currents on weather; and help map underwater environs. Most ocean technicians work in the coastal regions of the Pacific and Atlantic oceans, but some work in the Great Lakes and other large freshwater bodies. They operate and maintain the equipment and instruments used to study marine environments. They may assist in collecting data and drafting maps of the ocean floors and collect navigational information using charts and surveying instruments. Some ocean technicians assist scientists with the study of the chemical properties of ocean water and test for chemicals, minerals, dissolved gases, and evidence of pollution.

RELATED OCCUPATIONS

Forestry Technician	Engineering Technician
Agricultural Technician	Soil Conservation Technician
Health Technologist	Wildlife Technician

EDUCATIONAL REQUIREMENTS

There are several ways to qualify for a job as a science technician. The minimum educational requirement for this occupation is a two-year associate's degree from a junior or community college or a technical institute. There are, however, many science technicians who hold bachelor's degrees in science. Most employers prefer applicants who have at least two years of specialized training. Many junior and community colleges offer associate's degrees in a specific technology or a more general education in science and mathematics. In addition, many two-year programs provide students with the opportunity to transfer to a four-year college if desired. Technical institutes generally offer technician training but provide less theory and general education than do junior and community colleges. Some of these schools offer cooperative education programs, allowing students the opportunity to work at local companies while attending school part-time or in alternate terms. Many of these programs provide students with jobs after the completion of their programs. Many biological technicians hold bachelor's degrees in the biological or life sciences. Some employers require four-year degrees, but more often bachelor-degree holders working as technicians are unable to immediately find jobs as professional scientists. This was particularly true during the economic downturn in the late 1980s and early 1990s. Some employers could not find technicians with less education who were properly trained.

Most community and junior colleges offer programs in general science and math, and many have specific programs in biological technology. Students should have a solid high school background in math and science courses. Science courses taken in college should be laboratory oriented, with an emphasis on operating and maintaining high-technology equipment. Technicians also need strong communication skills because they write reports and often work as part of teams. Because computers and computer-interfaced equipment are increasingly being used in research and development laboratories, computer skills are invaluable.

SPECIAL CERTIFICATION

There are no special certifications for this occupation.

SETTINGS

Science technicians work under a variety of conditions. Most work indoors in well-equipped and comfortable laboratories. These technicians usually work forty-hour weeks but, in some cases, such as when there is the need to continually monitor an experiment, they may be required to work longer. Some biological technicians may be required to work outdoors collecting and monitoring data. They may be required to travel far from home, sometimes to remote places where living and weather conditions are unpredictable. Chemical technicians sometimes work with toxic or hazardous chemicals. While there is a chance of injury, the risk is usually slight if proper safety procedures are followed.

EMPLOYMENT STATISTICS AND MAJOR EMPLOYERS

Science technicians held about 228,000 jobs in 1996. According to the U.S. Department of Labor, science technicians should experience very good employment opportunities through the year 2006. Employment is expected to increase about as fast as the average for all occupations through the year 2006 due to an expected growth in scientific research and development and the output of technical products. Because of the growth in biotechnology, employment of biological technicians is expected to grow faster than employment of most other science technicians. Job opportunities for chemists are also expected to be very good. Those technicians who have above-average technical and communication skills should experience the brightest job market.

Science technicians are primarily employed in private industry at research and development and product laboratories. Biotechnology laboratories are employing many biological technicians, and the number of facilities and job openings is expected to grow. Chemical technicians are employed primarily in the private sector by chemical and petroleum refining and development firms. Many biological and chemical technicians are employed in the pharmaceutical industry. Academic institutions are the other major employer of science technicians. Nearly half of all biological technicians are employed at colleges and universities. The federal and state governments also employ science technicians. In the federal government, these technicians work primarily at the departments of Agriculture, the Interior, Commerce, and Defense. State departments of environmental protection and agriculture are the primary magnets for technicians. Due to the large number of recent military base closures and hazardous and toxic waste cleanup programs, biological and chemical technicians may find a growing job market with government agencies overseeing these projects and the private companies contracted to do the actual environmental remediation work. See Part Seven for more information on these types of technical science careers.

SALARY STATISTICS

According to the U.S. Department of Labor, the median annual earnings for all science technicians, including biological and chemical technicians, was about $27,000 in 1997. The middle 50 percent earned between $19,800 and $37,100 per year. Ten percent earned less than $15,500, and 10 percent earned more than $49,500. Starting salaries in the federal government are on par with private industry. Entry-level technicians with two-year degrees can expect to earn between $15,500 and $19,500, depending upon experience. The average annual salary for science technicians working for the federal government in 1997 was $28,500.

SOURCES OF FURTHER INFORMATION

American Chemical Society
Education Division
1155 16th St. NW
Washington, DC 20036
Internet address: www.acs.org
The society distributes free of charge a pamphlet entitled *Chemistry and Your Career.* It also operates the Employment Clearing House, which is a job bank for members.

American Institute of Biochemistry and Molecular Biology
9650 Rockville Pike
Bethesda, MD 20814-3996

American Institute of Biological Sciences
1444 I St. NW
Suite 200
Washington, DC 20005
Internet address: www.aibs.org

The American Institute of Chemists
National Certification Commission in Chemistry and Chemical
    Engineering
515 King St.
Suite 420
Alexandria, VA 22314
Internet address: www.theaic.org

Chemical Specialties Manufacturers Association
1913 Eye St. NW
Washington, DC 20006
Internet address: www.csma.org

The Ecological Society of America
2010 Massachusetts Ave.
Suite 400
Washington, DC 20036

Part Six
Agricultural and Animal Sciences

OVERVIEW

Total Employment
230,000

Employment Breakdown by Job Sector

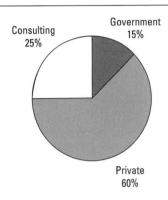

Consulting
25%

Government
15%

Private
60%

Projected Growth

Employment opportunities for agricultural and animal scientists are expected to increase about as fast as the average for all occupations through the year 2006. According to the U.S. Department of Labor, there is a projected 20 percent increase in employment for agricultural scientists up to the year 2006. While the agricultural field as a whole is expected to continue declining in terms of the number of independent farmers, employment for scientists, particularly those with advanced degrees, and highly skilled technicians is expected to be very good.

Salary Range

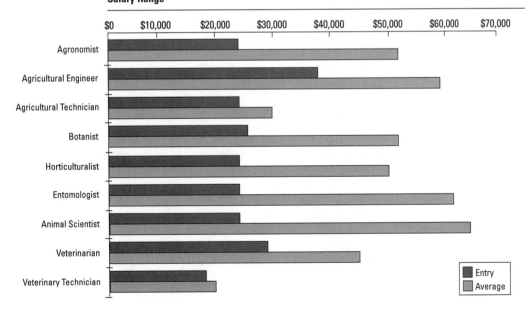

INTRODUCTION

Agriculture is a relatively new endeavor for the human race. Begun some nine thousand to seven thousand years ago, probably quite accidentally, the purposeful planting and harvesting of edible crops and the herding of livestock allowed humans to permanently settle land that they had roamed for thousands of years. Agriculture, in fact, is the cornerstone of all of the human history that followed. Without agriculture the first great city-states of Babylon, Ur, Troy, and Machu Picchu would not have existed, for it would have been impossible for large populations to gather without ample and surplus food supplies. Without agriculture the great early thinkers Lao-tse and Plato would have had no one to hear or pass on their great thoughts. Without agriculture there would be no information superhighway as it exists today. In fact, without agriculture we would, instead of reading this book, be wandering about the landscape in small groups, hunting and gathering only enough to keep us alive from day to day!

With the advent of agriculture, humans were able to develop commerce, make technological advances, and spread and intermingle their varied cultures across the globe. As humans learned more efficient ways to farm and raise livestock, they began to produce surplus crop; this allowed some members of the group to practice trades other than farming. Masonry, carpentry, pottery, and weaving became the occupations of some group members; this in turn led to trade among groups. Through this contact with other groups, agricultural practices, seeds, and animals were traded, which led to the spread of agriculture throughout the world. While the type of agriculture practiced in different parts of the world depends on the landscape, climate, and local culture, today almost all groups and societies practice some form of agriculture. And nowhere in the world is agriculture practiced more efficiently than here in the United States.

The biggest challenge for professionals in the agricultural and animal sciences is finding ways to produce more food for a swelling global population. When agriculture was first discovered, there were a mere five million humans on the face of the earth. Today, there are 5.5 billion global citizens, and food-producing capabilities are being strained in many areas, as evidenced by mass disease and famine, particularly in Africa. Population pressures will certainly continue because the global population is expected to exceed ten billion in a mere forty years!

PROFESSIONS RELATED TO AGRICULTURE AND ANIMAL SCIENCE

Animal Breeder	Silviculturist
Dairy Scientist	Agricultural Economist
Soil Scientist	Agricultural Inspector
Forester	Zookeeper
Arborist	Farm Equipment Mechanic
Environmental Scientist	Chemist
Biologist	Chemical Technician
Genetic Engineer	Pest Exterminator

HISTORY OF AGRICULTURE IN THE UNITED STATES

Indigenous Americans had been farming for several thousand years when in the 1700s and 1800s, the arrival of Europeans, with their machinery and technology from the industrial revolution, created the conditions necessary for America to become a major world producer of agricultural products. The United States offered settlers vast lands on which to practice their agrarian trades. Farming immigrants from Germany, France, Holland, and Eastern Europe migrated westward to the central region of the nation and created what is now called "America's bread-basket." By the early 1900s the basic structure of the American agricultural land-scape was in place. The Northeast has primarily small crop and dairy farms; the South is dominated by single-crop plantations growing primarily tobacco and cotton; in the Midwest, the nation's wheat basket, grain and livestock production reign, while in the great northern plain states of Iowa, Illinois, Wisconsin, Minnesota, Michigan, and the Dakotas, dairy farming, livestock, corn, and wheat dominate. In the West, the great valley of California produces a wide variety of fruit and vegetables, including most of the citrus fruits, nuts, and deciduous fruits consumed in the United States. It is also home to the world-renowned wine vineyards of the Napa Valley. In the Northwest, fruits, particularly apples, are the main crops.

The percent of farmers in the U.S. population has dropped substantially during the past several decades, from around 50 percent to just under 5 percent today. In 1950, there were 5.6 million farms, a number that dropped to 4 million in 1960 and to approximately 1.5 million today. In contrast, the total amount of farmland has dropped only slightly, which means there are now far fewer but much larger farms. In addition, agriculture has become a highly mechanized and specialized field. The average output of U.S. farms is among the highest in the world, due primarily to advances in farm machinery and technology, such as modern irrigation systems, the combine, highly efficient transportation systems, the use of powerful pesticides, and most recently the introduction of predator insect populations to control crop loss.

This nation is truly a global superpower in terms of total agricultural output. Agriculture (including forestry) produces two-thirds of the raw materials in the United States, and crops such as wheat, corn, and soybeans account for a substantial proportion of our national exports. Overall, the United States contributes 25 percent of global beef production and 15 percent of the grain produced each year.

MAJOR EMPLOYERS

Agriculture, or *agribusiness*, today is a field that encompasses not only farming but a host of related businesses. While only 5 percent of Americans are farmers, more than 20 percent are engaged in other activities related to agribusiness. These activities include food processing, packaging, storing, distributing, and retailing. Professionals and technicians are employed not only on the farm but also in such diverse industries as tractor manufacturing, fertilizer production, seed distribution, food wholesaling and retailing, insurance and banking, marketing and advertising, transportation, and real estate. In addition, most veterinarians work in private practice or at animal health centers, serving pet owners and agricultural livestock.

There are also a number of careers in federal and state government agencies. The U.S. Department of Agriculture and individual state departments of agriculture hire people with diverse agricultural backgrounds. Career opportunities also exist in research and teaching. Each state supports an agricultural land grant university where professors and instructors teach agricultural and animal science courses. In addition, a federal agricultural research station is located at each land grant university, and cutting-edge agricultural research is conducted there.

PROJECTED GROWTH AND EMPLOYMENT TRENDS

Overall, employment opportunities in the agricultural and animal sciences will grow at about the same rate as the average for all environmental science jobs. There will be substantial variation in career trends for this large career field because in some areas the growth outlook is quite bright, while in others there is expected to be substantial decline. Of the approximately twenty-one million people working in the agricultural field, only about two million are employed on farms, while the remaining nineteen million work in other parts of agribusiness. Individually owned farms are expected to shrink as costs of operation and fluctuating commodity prices make farm operations competitive for only larger operations. In addition, mechanization has substantially reduced the number of farmhands needed. According to the American Farm Bureau, only 1.9 percent of Americans now live on farms. The U.S. Bureau of Labor Statistics reports that farming has experienced one of the largest job declines in history, as increasing numbers of small family farmers have left the business, to be replaced by agribusiness concerns.

The off-farm segment of agribusiness is expected to expand, particularly in areas of applied technology. In order to keep up with rapidly changing agricultural techniques and mechanical systems, professionals and technicians will need more technical and university training. During the past few years, those entering the agricultural field have received higher levels of education than their immediate predecessors. This trend is expected to continue well into the foreseeable future.

Overall, career opportunities in agricultural and animal sciences will remain healthy through the year 2006. As the U.S. and world populations continue to grow, agribusiness must expand in order to keep up with food sustenance needs. Career-minded people will find ample opportunities, particularly in those areas described in the following pages. The career outlook in veterinary medicine is also very good. There is increasing demand for both small animal (domestic pet) and large animal (livestock) physicians and technicians throughout the country.

SOURCES OF FURTHER INFORMATION

American Farm Bureau Federation
225 Touhy Ave.
Park Ridge, IL 60068
Internet address: www.fb.com

Also consult the following publications:

The Occupational Outlook Handbook (annual), compiled by the U.S. Department of Labor, published by VGM Career Horizons, NTC/Contemporary Publishing Group. Lists and describes many agriculture and related careers using Department of Labor data and statistics.

Careers for Nature Lovers and Other Outdoor Types (1993), by Louise Miller, published by VGM Career Horizons, NTC/Contemporary Publishing Group. Contains a chapter entitled "Careers in the Agricultural Sciences."

Opportunities in Farming and Agriculture Careers (1996), by William C. White, Donald N. Collins, and Adrian A. Paradis, published by VGM Career Horizons, NTC/Contemporary Publishing Group.

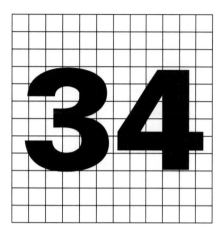

AGRONOMIST

including
Crop Scientist
Soil Scientist

Agronomy is the study of plants and soil and their surrounding agricultural environment. It represents the disciplines of crop and soil science. Agronomists are mainly concerned with efforts to increase the supply of high-quality food, fiber crops, and feed while preventing erosion and protecting and preserving the environment. A growing number of agronomists are studying the effects of pesticides on plants and soils and are looking for more environmentally friendly ways to protect crops from insects. While agronomists were considered simple farmers for centuries, their work is now highly specialized and very technical. Agronomists work closely with chemists, mathematicians, entomologists, biologists, and geologists to improve the quality and quantity of food output. Agronomists have helped make the United States the leading exporter of food fiber and livestock in the world. More importantly, crop production methods and technology developed by agronomists in the United States are used in Third World countries where population pressures have strained traditional food production methods and contributed to malnutrition and famine. Because one thousand children worldwide die of malnutrition each hour, the search for better and more reliable sources of food is a priority that agronomists are pursuing with vigor.

Agronomists concentrate in one of two areas of specialization: crop science and soil science. Crop scientists study plants and soil to increase the production of food, feed, and fiber. They also study ways to improve the nutritional value of crops and the quality of seed. Many crop scientists study the breeding, physiology, and management of crops and use genetic engineering to develop crops that are resistant to drought and insects. Soil scientists study the chemical, physical, mineralogical, and biological composition of soils as they relate to plant or crop growth. Many soil scientists investigate soil fertility, soil mineralogy, soil chemistry, soil physics, and soil management. They study the responses of various soil types to fertilizers, crop rotation, and tillage practices and advise farmers on land-use practices and ways to avoid or correct erosion problems.

RELATED PROFESSIONS

Biologist   Horticulturist
Agricultural Scientist   Plant Pathologist
Agricultural Engineer   Genetic Engineer
Botanist   Arborist
Chemist

EDUCATIONAL REQUIREMENTS

The minimum educational requirement for a career in agronomy is a bachelor of science (B.S.) degree; however, many students entering the field today have completed master's or Ph.D. degree programs. Each state supports a public land grant university whose focus is agricultural and forestry studies, and most of these schools offer advanced degrees in agronomy. Farming-dependent states, particularly those in the South, Midwest, and far West have the best agricultural science programs; however, not all schools provide specialized concentrations in agronomy. Contact your school of interest to find out if it offers a specialization that interests you.

Students are required to complete the core science requirements, including chemistry, biochemistry, biology, and botany in addition to the general school requirements of math, economics, humanities, and business courses. Within each program, students can specialize in a variety of areas. Specific crop and soil science courses may include plant pathology, plant physiology, entomology, genetics, soil chemistry, meteorology, and microbiology. Students spend a substantial portion of their classroom hours in the laboratory or conducting field studies. Many schools require students to complete field projects or technical theses. Advanced students must often conduct innovative field research and write publishable reports based on their work.

SPECIAL CERTIFICATION

The American Society of Agronomy offers the American Registry of Certified Professionals in Agronomy, Crops, and Soils. This registry establishes standards for the practice of agronomy and holds members to a code of ethics. To qualify, members must have a certain combination of work and educational experience. Contact the society, listed at the end of this chapter, for information on testing procedures and personal requirements.

SETTINGS

Because agronomists work primarily with farmers, ranchers, and agricultural researchers, they are located where these activities take place. Agronomists are well represented in every state of the nation but tend to concentrate in more agriculturally intensive areas. In the Midwest, agronomists work mainly with grains;

in the Southeast, they are involved with textile fibers like cotton and a variety of fruits and vegetables in agriculturally rich Florida; and in the arid West, agronomists are concerned with grains and associated ranching activities. In California and the Northwest, agronomists work with all types of crops and soil conditions. Agronomists spend a majority of their time in the field and laboratory studying and testing crops and soils. They also work at government and private research laboratories throughout the nation conducting cutting-edge agricultural research.

EMPLOYMENT STATISTICS AND MAJOR EMPLOYERS

The U.S. Department of Labor estimates that in 1996 about twenty-seven thousand agricultural scientists were working in the United States. In addition, several thousand people with advanced degrees held faculty research and teaching positions at colleges and universities. In 1997 about 30 percent of all agronomists worked for the federal, state, and local governments. One of five agronomists works for the federal government, primarily for the U.S. Department of Agriculture. At the state and local levels they work for state agricultural facilities and extension services.

In private industry agronomists work for agricultural service companies, seed companies, pharmaceutical companies, food and wholesale distributing companies, farm credit institutions, and commercial research and development laboratories, and they work as private farmers and ranchers. Some major agricultural companies are DeKalb Genetic Corp., Fresh International Corp., and Hudson Foods, Inc. For those with the itch to travel, there are universities, government agencies, foundations, and private firms with interests in foreign nations.

Employment opportunities in the agricultural sciences are expected to grow about as fast as the average for all occupations. This growth is expected primarily in the private sector. Plant scientists with backgrounds in genetics, biotechnology, molecular biology, or microbiology, and soil scientists with expertise in pesticide controls and other environmental issues will experience the best job opportunities. In addition, jobs will be more plentiful for college graduates because fewer students are entering agricultural programs; this minimizes entry-level job competition. Professionals with advanced degrees will face the brightest job market. Job growth in government will be slow, primarily due to budget constraints, but yearly worker turnover will create a healthy number of job openings.

SALARY STATISTICS

According to the National Association of Colleges and Employers, the average starting salaries for agronomy students graduating with bachelor's degrees in 1997 was $24,000. The average starting salary for an entry-level assistant professor in the agricultural sciences is about $35,092, and for a full professor it is $54,209. Earnings in academia should escalate much faster than in government or industry. According to the U.S. Department of Labor, the average federal salary for agronomists is $52,000.

SOURCES OF FURTHER INFORMATION

American Farmland Trust
1200 18th St. NW
Suite 800
Washington, DC 20036
Internet address: www.farmland.org

American Society of Agronomy, Crop Science Society of
    America, Soil Science Society of America
677 S. Segoe Road
Madison, WI 53711-1086
Internet address: www.agronomy.org
The society publishes free of charge *Exploring Careers in
Agronomy, Crops, and Soils.*

Food and Agricultural Careers for Tomorrow
Purdue University
1140 Agriculture Administration Building
West Lafayette, IN 47907-1140

Future Farmers of America
National FFA Organization
P.O. Box 15160
National FFA Center
Alexandria, VA 22309
Internet address: www.ffa.org
This is a national organization of high school agriculture
students.

National Association of State Departments of Agriculture
1156 15th St. NW
Suite 1020
Washington, DC 20005

National Coalition Against the Misuse of Pesticides
701 E St. SE
Suite 200
Washington, DC 20003
Internet address: www.ncamp.org

National Farmers Union
11900 E. Cornell Ave.
Aurora, CO 80014-3194

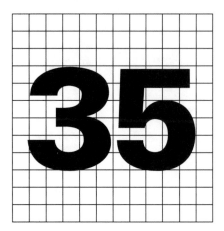

AGRICULTURAL ENGINEER

Agricultural engineers are an integral part of the agricultural sciences. They use their training in the applied sciences to adapt rapidly changing technology to the farming industry. Agricultural engineers are involved in every aspect of agriculture: from food production and processing to marketing and distribution. Their work with agricultural systems, materials, and products helps provide high-quality and affordable food and fiber to the nation and entire world. A career in agricultural engineering is for those who are oriented toward math and science and who enjoy solving complex mathematical and design problems. Overall, agricultural engineers develop and refine scientific concepts and theories into a framework of workable mechanical designs and agricultural processes.

Agricultural engineers primarily focus on four main areas: product design, process engineering, systems engineering, and resource engineering. Product design engineers develop machinery and mechanical structures, such as systems for energy-efficient tilling, planting, harvesting, and grain storage and retrieval. Agricultural process engineers work primarily with crop and food processing; they test for more efficient ways to package, transport, and store grain, livestock, and ocean products. Agricultural systems engineers are concerned with a wide array of agricultural practices including irrigation, microprocessor controls, and safety. Finally, agricultural resource engineers are concerned with most environmental aspects of farming, including water quality and soil and groundwater management.

RELATED PROFESSIONS

Agricultural Scientist	Manufacturing Engineer
Biological Engineer	Safety Engineer
Forest Engineer	Mechanical Engineer
Food and Process Engineer	Electrical Engineer

EDUCATIONAL REQUIREMENTS

Agricultural engineers must hold at least a bachelor of science degree from an accredited four-year college or university. According to the American Society of Agricultural Engineers, fifty-seven college and university degree programs offer a bachelor's degree in agricultural engineering. As is the case for other agricultural degree areas, there is a heavy concentration of agricultural engineering programs in the midwestern farming states; however, each state in the Union has at least one agricultural engineering program.

In a typical curriculum, the first two years are spent in the study of basic sciences, such as physics, chemistry, and mathematics; introductory engineering; and liberal arts courses. The remaining two years are devoted to specialized engineering courses. A master's degree is required for many teaching and research assignments and also for many management positions. In addition, many agricultural engineers are obtaining degrees in business management (M.B.A.s) to advance into mid-level and upper-level management positions.

PROFESSIONAL CERTIFICATION

Some states may require agricultural engineers to obtain the Professional Engineer (PE) certification. Generally, the registration laws for professional engineers require graduation from an accredited engineering curriculum followed by approximately four years of engineering experience and the successful completion of a written exam. The requirements for each state may vary. For more information on state requirements and accredited curriculum programs, contact the National Society of Professional Engineers or the National Council of Examiners for Engineering and Surveying, which are listed at the end of this chapter.

SETTINGS

Agricultural engineers work in laboratories, in offices, at design tables, on farms, in greenhouses, and in fields. They investigate farm operations and systems of work, survey land use, and test new equipment and machinery in order to improve agricultural output. Many agricultural engineers work at manufacturing facilities developing and testing new farm machinery. They may spend a substantial amount of time conducting research, using computers to design and test projects, and writing reports. These engineers also work extensively with other engineers because complex projects often require the services of many engineers, each working on a small part of the job. After several years of work experience, some agricultural engineers are promoted to managerial and executive positions. In this role, they work in office environments to oversee daily operations and chart company goals.

Many engineers work standard forty-hour weeks. At times, deadlines or design standards may bring extra work pressure to the job. When this happens, engineers may work long hours and experience considerable stress.

EMPLOYMENT STATISTICS AND MAJOR EMPLOYERS

More than 15,000 agricultural engineers are employed in the United States and many thousand more in Canada. The employment outlook for agricultural engineers is expected to be better than average due to several factors: the growing mechanization of the agricultural field, the need to produce more food for a growing population, the demand for the conservation of resources such as water and soil, and the drop in the number of engineering graduates during the past decade.

The majority of agricultural engineers are employed in agribusiness by seed and pesticide manufacturers, manufacturers of farm equipment and heavy machinery, private design and research companies, and corporate and family farmers and as private consultants. The federal government employs agricultural engineers for soil and water management projects and as cooperative extension agents, mostly in the Department of Agriculture. State departments of agriculture also hire a number of engineers. Agricultural engineers also teach and conduct research in colleges and universities across the nation. A master's degree or Ph.D. is usually required for employment in academia.

SALARY STATISTICS

According to the Bureau of Labor Statistics, the average starting salary for agricultural engineering graduates in 1997 was around $38,500, while graduates with master's degrees earned $45,400, and those with Ph.D.'s earned an average starting salary of $59,200. Starting salaries for agricultural engineers employed by the federal government are lower than in private industry, but engineers obtain parity after several years of employment due to more incremental pay raises.

The average starting salary for an engineering professor is around $45,753, while the average salary for a tenured professor is $77,721.

SOURCES OF FURTHER INFORMATION

American Society of Agricultural Engineers
2950 Niles Road
St. Joseph, MI 49085-9659
Internet address: www.asae.org

Accreditation Board for Engineering and Technology, Inc.
111 Market Place
Suite 1050
Baltimore, MD 21202-4012
Internet address: www.abet.org

National Council of Examiners for Engineering and Surveying
P.O. Box 1868
Clemson, SC 29633
Internet address: www.ncees.org

National Society of Professional Engineers
1420 King St.
Alexandria, VA 22314-2794
Internet address: www.nspe.org

American Society for Engineering Education
1818 N St. NW
Washington, DC 20036-2479
Internet address: www.asee.org

Society of Women Engineers
1120 Wall St.
Eleventh floor
New York, NY 10005-3902
Internet address: www.swe.org

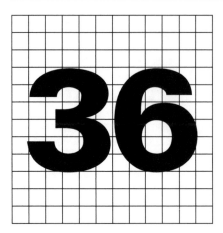

AGRICULTURAL TECHNICIAN

Agricultural technicians work with agricultural scientists in food and fiber research, production, and processing. They assist farmers in the planning, planting, cultivating, harvesting, and marketing of field crops. Some conduct tests and experiments to improve the yield and quality of crops or to increase the resistance of plants and animals to disease, insects, or other hazards. Other agricultural technicians do animal breeding and nutritional work.

Because of the highly technical nature of modern agribusiness, many of these technicians perform specialized tasks that require a high degree of skill and knowledge. Thus, a solid understanding of applied mathematics and science is becoming essential in this field. Technicians must be able to apply the appropriate scientific principles to their work in the laboratory or on the farm. In addition, good communication skills are necessary because most agricultural technicians work as part of a team or supervise other technicians and work crews.

Technicians in the field of agriculture have many opportunities for advancement. Those working on farms or related business may become farm managers or owners, managers of cooperatives, or sales managers. Technicians working in government can advance to inspector or supervisory positions, while those working in the laboratory can receive additional academic training and become professional agronomists.

RELATED OCCUPATIONS

Agronomist
Soil Conservation Technician
Biological Technician
Farm Crop Production Technician
Farm Sales Representative
Agricultural Equipment Technician

Seed Production Field Supervisor
Disease and Insect Control Field
   Inspector
Plant Propagator
Agricultural Inspector

EDUCATIONAL REQUIREMENTS

A career as an agricultural technician requires a two-year technical or community college program in agriculture. There are many such programs throughout the country, especially in farming areas, that offer a specific degree in agricultural technology. Students should have a good high school background in mathematics and science and possess the desire to learn many of the technical aspects of the agricultural field. It is also helpful and quite typical for students to have prior experience working on farms or in other agricultural capacities.

A typical first-year program in agricultural technology includes courses like introduction to soil science, algebra or calculus, introduction to chemistry, animal husbandry, English, entomology, and introduction to computers. Second-year programs include such courses as agricultural economics, plant pathology, math, science, advanced soil science, and computer applications. Many community and technical colleges encourage or place students in summer internship programs for hands-on experience. Check with your school for job placement programs after graduation.

SPECIAL CERTIFICATION

There are no special certifications for this occupation.

SETTINGS

Like agronomists, agricultural technicians work primarily in rural locations under a wide variety of conditions. In general, they should be in good physical condition and enjoy working outdoors. Farm technicians work on the planting, cultivating, and harvesting schedule, which requires them to work long hours during critical stages of crop production. Researchers work both indoors in laboratories, where working hours are regular, or in the field, where hours and weather conditions may vary considerably. Those involved in sales may spend a considerable amount of time traveling, often far from home.

EMPLOYMENT STATISTICS AND MAJOR EMPLOYERS

While the number of American farms has been decreasing for the last half of the twentieth century, the job outlook for agricultural workers with technical expertise is quite good. According to the U.S. Department of Labor, employment for agricultural technicians is expected to increase about as fast as the average for all occupations through the year 2006 due to an expected growth in scientific research and development and the continued development of highly technical agricultural systems. The largest percent of agricultural technicians work in the farm product, production, and distribution industries, and the farm servicing and supplying industries. Most research technicians work for government, colleges and universities, or private research and testing services.

SALARY STATISTICS

Salaries for agricultural technicians vary widely depending on a number of factors. Laboratory research technicians and office workers typically receive higher salaries than do technicians working on the farm. In addition, salaries vary according to the geographic area in which the technician is working. According to the U.S. Department of Labor, the median annual earnings for all science technicians, including agricultural technicians, was about $27,000 in 1996. The middle 50 percent earned between $19,800 and $37,100 per year. Ten percent earned less than $15,500, and 10 percent earned more than $49,500. Agricultural technicians working on the farm typically receive wages at the middle and lower end of the salary scale, but they often receive food and housing benefits that can be the equivalent of several thousand dollars per year.

SOURCES OF FURTHER INFORMATION

American Society of Agronomy
677 South Segoe Road
Madison, WI 53711-1086
Internet address: www.agronomy.org

Cooperative League of the U.S.A.
1828 L St. NW
Washington, DC 20036

Future Farmers of America
National FFA Organization
P.O. Box 15160
Alexandria, VA 22309
Internet address: www.ffa.org

National Grain and Feed Association
1201 New York Ave. NW
Suite 830
Washington, DC 20005-3917
Internet address: www.ngfa.org

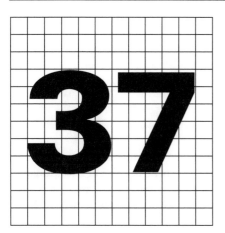

BOTANIST

Botanists study plant life to discover its structure, physiology, heredity, distribution, and economic value. Botany is the base field of plant biology, and separate disciplines such as agronomy, horticulture, and forestry have emerged as specialized subfields. Botanists study everything from microscopic algae to the giant sequoia tree. Their intimate knowledge of plant organisms is shared with other conservation scientists who apply it in their own fields.

Botanists face difficult challenges as the world population grows, increasing the need for better food output, as environmental concerns such as soil and water pollution problems adversely affect crop production, and as the destruction of the forests decreases biological diversity, which limits important medical discoveries. The loss of wild foodstuff species such as potatoes, rice, and corn raises serious concerns about the safety of our genetically engineered domestic food plants. It is the work of botanists to identify new plant species, test chemical properties of plants for human use, and protect the natural biological diversity of our plant life.

There are many interrelated specialty areas within the field of botany. The diversity of interests provide many career concentrations for people with differing backgrounds and aptitudes. Those interested in outdoor activities may be suited for careers in ecology or taxonomy, traveling the world identifying new plant species. For mathematical types, systems ecology, genetics, and biophysics are exciting quantitative fields. Chemistry affectionados might find exciting careers in plant physiology, plant biochemistry, chemotaxonomistry, or molecular biology. For those with global food concerns, careers in plant pathology (plant diseases) and plant breeding will satisfy a need to help the world's undernourished. Those enamored with microscopic organisms often choose to study microbiology, phycology (the study of algae), or mycology (the study of fungi).

RELATED PROFESSIONS

Agronomist	Range Scientist
Horticulturist	Entomologist
Forester	Chemist
Soil Scientist	Agricultural Economist

EDUCATIONAL REQUIREMENTS

A four-year bachelor of science degree is the minimum requirement for a career in botany. At this level, laboratory, garden, and park technician and academic research assistant positions are available. More advanced degrees are required for professional careers in botany. Because the majority of botanists work in colleges and universities, a master's degree is required and a Ph.D. is preferred.

Botany students are required to take a host of biological science courses. Therefore, students should have completed high school courses in chemistry, biology, earth science, and advanced mathematics. A typical college curriculum includes science classes in chemistry, zoology, biochemistry, and physics and several specialized courses in botany. Because the career track is heavily oriented toward college teaching, students are encouraged to take additional courses in English, communication, the arts, and the social sciences. A number of U.S. schools offer majors in botany or a combination of botany and zoology. Each state maintains a public land grant university that concentrates in the agricultural sciences, and a good number of these offer degree programs in botany.

For career development, students can participate in research and internship programs. Students are often encouraged or required to conduct undergraduate research projects. Working with a professor in a specialty area gives students insights into the area or areas of botany of greatest interest to them. There are opportunities for summer internships in government agencies, with private companies, at agricultural experiment stations, and in college and university research laboratories, which are a wonderful source of field training and can lead to job offers.

PROFESSIONAL CERTIFICATION

There are no special certifications or licensing requirements for this occupation.

SETTINGS

The setting in which botanists work is heavily dependent upon their areas of specialization. In general, most botanists work for colleges and universities or are affiliated with such institutions. Botanists conduct research in laboratories, greenhouses, agricultural areas, and open forests around the world. They spend many hours analyzing plant specimens and conducting experiments that can go on for several days. Therefore, botanists should enjoy delicate work with their hands and have an appreciation for the outdoors. Botanists also spend part of their time teaching and conducting other routine academic duties.

EMPLOYMENT STATISTICS AND MAJOR EMPLOYERS

Botanists are primarily employed by colleges and universities, government agencies, and private companies. The best employment opportunities exist for those who have earned advanced degrees. Holders of Ph.D.'s can expect the greatest employment opportunities, particularly at colleges and universities, where most professional botanists find employment. Community and state colleges are oriented primarily toward teaching and offer few research opportunities. For both Ph.D. and master's degree holders who enjoy teaching, the state and community college setting can be highly rewarding. In addition, universities and colleges employ botanists in research positions or administrative posts.

Federal and state agencies also employ a good number of botanists. In the U.S. Department of Agriculture, botanists work at the Medical Plant Resources Laboratory, the Germ Plasma Resources Laboratory, the Animal and Plant Health Inspection Service, the U.S. Forest Service, and the National Arboretum. At the Department of the Interior, botanists are employed by the National Park Service and the U.S. Geological Survey. Botanists are employed by several other agencies, including the Smithsonian Institution, the Environmental Protection Agency, the Public Health Service, and the National Aeronautics and Space Administration. See Chapter 2 for a full description of many of these agencies. Botanists are also employed in agricultural agencies in each of the fifty states and territories.

Botanists can also find employment opportunities in private industry. Sectors of the economy in which botanists are employed include the pharmaceutical and petrochemical industries, the lumber and paper industries, food companies, fruit growers, seed and nursery growers, biotechnology firms, and fermentation industries.

The employment outlook for botanists is above average. Population pressures on food sources, the potential of genetically engineered plants, the need to discover new sources of medicine from exotic plants, and the urgent need to protect plant biodiversity all contribute to a strong job market for botanists. In some specialized fields like plant genetics and biochemistry, botanists will be in even greater demand.

SALARY STATISTICS

According to the American Association of University Professors, the average starting salary for a botany professor is around $35,092. The average salary for a tenured professor is around $54,209, while part-time instructors earn about $27,000.

Entry-level botanists working for the federal government with bachelor's degrees can expect to earn around $25,000. The holders of master's degrees will earn around $26,900, while those with Ph.D.'s can expect salaries of around $52,400. Starting salaries for those in private industry are commensurate with government salaries; state employees earn slightly less.

SOURCES OF FURTHER INFORMATION

American Society of Plant Physiologists
15501 Monona Drive
Rockville, MD 20855-2768
Internet address: www.aspp.org

Botanical Society of America
Department of Botany
Ohio State University
1735 Neil Ave.
Columbus, OH 43210

The Ecological Society of America
2010 Massachusetts Ave. NW
Suite 400
Washington, DC 20036

Phycological Society of America
P.O. Box 1897
Lawrence, KS 66044-8897
Publishes a free information sheet on careers involving algae.

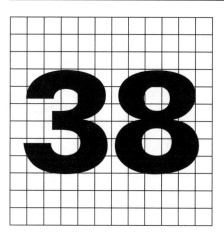

HORTICULTURIST

Horticulturists study and cultivate vegetables, fruits, nuts, berries, and flowers in order to discover better growing and harvesting methods. They develop higher-yielding and better-quality food plants, and after growth, they also develop better storage, shipment, and marketing techniques. Thus, horticulturists are involved with all stages of plant production. In general, horticulturists are involved with plants destined for food markets or ornamental plants like flowers and shrubs. The term *horticulture* is derived from the Latin roots *hortus,* meaning "garden," and *culture,* meaning "cultivate." Unlike agronomists or plant scientists who work with vast tracts of relatively few plant species, horticulturists study and cultivate many plant species but on a very small scale.

Horticulturists work with chemists, plant pathologists, and entomologists to perfect pesticide-free bug-resistant plants for large-scale agriculture. They introduce other predator bugs that eat harmful pests but have no appetite for the host plant. With increasing consumer concerns about harmful pesticides in food, horticulturists must look for more ways to grow pesticide-free foods. Horticulturists have genetically altered fruits and vegetables, such as sweet corn, peaches, oranges, and broccoli, for better taste, longer shelf life, and better transport. They specialize in lawn maintenance and turf production and work to improve the grasses and other flora of public parks and roadways and on private properties such as golf courses and cemeteries. Horticulturists also work to enhance the livability of urban areas. They work with city planners to design aesthetically pleasing public areas and maintain bastions of nature, such as arboretums or botanical gardens, within the concrete confines of urban areas.

RELATED PROFESSIONS

Agronomist	Plant Pathologist
Botanist	Soil Scientist
Forest Ecologist	Wood Technologist
Silviculturalist	Range Manager

EDUCATIONAL REQUIREMENTS

While there are no minimum educational requirements for a career in horticulture, most private employers prefer that prospective workers have associate's or bachelor of science degrees in horticulture. According to the American Horticultural Society, there are 198 certificate- or degree-granting two-year colleges and 102 colleges and universities offering degree programs in horticulture. Many of the four-year schools also offer advanced degrees in horticulture. Horticultural technicians should pursue associate's degrees, and those interested in professional careers should hold at least a bachelor's degree.

In order to succeed in a horticultural program, students should be well prepared with solid backgrounds in math and science. Students are required to take courses in chemistry, physics, botany, statistics, and business. Some of the more common core courses for a horticulture degree are plant propagation, plant materials, plant taxonomy, floral design, plant toxicology, and landscape techniques. Students can pursue either a *scientific direction*, which readies them for a career in food production, plant physiology, and plant engineering, or a horticultural design program leading to a career in ornamental design and landscape planning.

Students preparing for a career should find employment in work-study programs in college laboratories and greenhouses or with private florists, nurseries, and garden businesses. This type of hands-on fieldwork augments the classroom learning experience.

PROFESSIONAL CERTIFICATION

The American Association of Botanical Gardens and Arboreta (AABGA) offers the North American Certificate in Horticulture. This certificate verifies that the holder has attained the practical, hands-on skills in horticulture that most students receive only after completing a college program and gaining work experience. The certificate is considered equivalent in education and experience to a two-year degree or a botanical garden internship. Contact the AABGA for information on testing procedures and personal requirements.

SETTINGS

Most horticulturists work with plants in green and healthy surroundings. They work in greenhouses, gardens, laboratories, fields, parks, and forests. A majority of their time is spent tending to flora, but they may also be required to work in office settings or with the public. Horticulturists work throughout the country in cities, suburbs, and rural areas, but they tend to be clustered in more populated areas. Horticulturists working for government or private research firms may travel year round to provide information and services throughout the country. In temperate zones like southern California and the deep South, horticulturists work outdoors all year; while in the North, they work indoors during the winter months. Their busiest months are during harvest seasons and around holidays.

EMPLOYMENT STATISTICS AND MAJOR EMPLOYERS

In 1998, more than thirty-five thousand professional horticulturists were working in the United States. Most horticulturists are employed in the private sector in such businesses as pharmaceutical and chemical firms, landscape design firms, and food-processing plants. These horticulturists conduct experiments and research to improve food quality and retain the nutritive value of foods through processing; they engineer foods for more uniform growth and shelf life; and they discover new life-saving drugs that can be derived from plants. Some are marketers and sales executives in the food industry. Many horticulturists own and manage their own garden centers, nurseries, landscape firms, and florist shops. Many homeowners and companies are turning to horticulturists to find environmentally balanced ways to maintain lawns and gardens. Horticulturists work in the lawn and turf care industry as grounds supervisors, golf course superintendents, and sod production managers. They work for large companies and corporations to landscape and plant grounds and brighten office environments.

Horticulturists also work in all levels of government. The U.S. Department of Agriculture employs a number of horticulturists, and many others work for state and local agricultural departments conducting research at experimental stations and public information campaigns. Municipal and city departments hire horticulturists to landscape and plant zoos and parks and manage botanical gardens and arboretums.

Employment opportunities for horticulturists are expected to grow substantially. According to the U.S. Department of Labor, employment opportunities will grow faster than average for all occupations through the year 2006. This growth will primarily take place in the private sector, where horticulture is already a multi-billion-dollar business. Horticulturists with specific technical know-how in areas like plant genetics will be in great demand. Also look for large growth in the lawn and turf care industry, where environmental concerns are particularly focused.

SALARY STATISTICS

According to the National Association of Colleges and Employers salary survey, in 1997 the average starting salary for an entry-level horticulturist with a bachelor's degree was $24,000. In the federal government, horticulturists earn an average annual salary of $50,400.

Starting salaries in the private sector are comparable to government pay. However, salary level depends heavily upon the region of the country and population density. The success of small business owners is dependent upon many factors, including the state of the economy and their own business savvy.

SOURCES OF FURTHER INFORMATION

American Association of Nurserymen
1250 Eye St. NW
Suite 500
Washington, DC 20005

American Horticulture Society
P.O. Box 0105
Mount Vernon, VA 22121
Internet address: www.ahs.org
The society publishes the *American Gardener*, and its website
provides a source of in-depth information as well as helpful hints.

American Society for Horticultural Science
600 Cameron St.
Alexandria, VA 22314-2562
Internet address: www.ashs.org
The society distributes information on schools, careers, and job
openings to society members.

Botanical Society of America
1735 Neil Ave.
Columbus, OH 43210-1293

Society of American Florists
1601 Duke St.
Alexandria, VA 22314

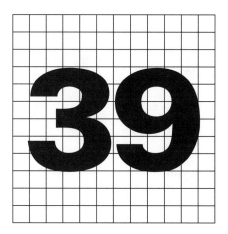

ENTOMOLOGIST

Entomologists are scientists who study insects, particularly pests and bugs, that inflict disease upon and kill crops and animals. Insects are the most widespread animal species on earth, and entomologists have already identified one million species, which is believed to be just a fraction of the total insect population. In most cases insects are beneficial to humans and the ecosystem. Bees, for example, pollinate plants and are an intricate part of their life cycle. Earthworms aerate and churn topsoil so that plants can root and grow more easily. Spiders help keep insect populations in balance by consuming other species, and many microscopic insects help fungi and bacteria break down organic matter into rich topsoil. However, some insects damage and destroy billions of dollars of crops in the United States and spread disease among animals and humans. In the 1970s, the entire corn crop in the United States was almost wiped out by a single insect species. Insects damage crops in Third World countries and ecologically sensitive areas; this destruction has caused mass famine and widespread disease. It is the job of entomologists to protect plants and animals from these harmful effects.

Entomologists work both in the field and in the laboratory. They are mainly concerned with the life cycles of insects, their body processes, and group behavior. Recently, entomologists have been working on insect control methods that require only a minimal use of toxic pesticides. Instead of using deadly poisons, they sterilize and trap insects before they can harm crops and livestock. They have also been successful in introducing predator insects that eat the plant-threatening pests but have no interest in the host crop. They are also helping agronomists and plant scientists develop crops that are more insect resistant. Entomologists often work closely with other agricultural scientists, such as botanists, veterinarians, and plant pathologists, to help produce higher-yielding crops and healthier livestock.

RELATED PROFESSIONS

Agronomist	Chemist
Botanist	Microbiologist
Plant Pathologist	Pest Control Specialist
Horticulturist	Pest Exterminator

EDUCATIONAL REQUIREMENTS

The pursuit of a career in entomology requires an advanced degree. Students holding a bachelor of science degree in entomology, zoology, or biology can work as agricultural pest control specialists, pest exterminators, or entomology assistants. Those interested in pursuing careers as professional entomologists must hold master's or Ph.D. degrees because most entomologists work as applied researchers and teachers in academic settings where advanced degrees are required. Core courses at the undergraduate level include biology, botany, chemistry, zoology, and physics. There are several universities offering advanced degrees in entomology.

PROFESSIONAL CERTIFICATION

There are no special certifications for this profession.

SETTINGS

Most entomologists are affiliated with colleges or universities so they spend most of their time on laboratory work, administrative duties, and teaching. Working hours are flexible and depend mostly on the nature of the research and teaching schedule, but like most academics, entomologists can expect to put in more than forty hours per week. Entomologists should enjoy working outdoors in all types of climates and weather conditions. Research interests often permit entomologists to travel throughout the world. Many entomologists conduct field research in the rain forests of South America, Africa, and Indonesia, where the majority of insect species are located. They must also travel to agricultural areas where experiments with pest-resistant plant strains and predator insects are taking place. Other entomologists involved in pest control spend a substantial amount of time outdoors working with chemicals and other potentially dangerous substances.

EMPLOYMENT STATISTICS AND MAJOR EMPLOYERS

Colleges and universities employ the majority of professional entomologists, although there are also job opportunities with the federal and state governments and private industry. In the federal government, entomologists work for the U.S. Department of Agriculture, the Department of the Interior, and the Centers for Disease Control and Prevention. Entomologists also work in every state agricultural agency. In private industry, entomologists work for seed companies and pharmaceutical firms and as agricultural consultants. Some entomologists form their own research and pest control companies.

With bachelor's degrees, entomologists can find employment as food inspectors, biological technicians, and agricultural sales representatives. In order to conduct research and teach, an advanced degree with specialized training is required. Entomologists work in botany, zoology, and agricultural science departments of colleges and universities throughout the country as well as direct research in government agencies and private industry. The best employment opportunities in academia are in large universities, particularly at state land grant institutions, where substantial funds support research and purchase modern laboratory equipment.

The employment outlook for entomologists is very good because many problems with insect control are still unresolved. Only a small number of entomologists enter the field each year, so job opportunities, particularly in government agencies and private industry, are quite good. There is always sharp competition for academic positions, and the recent funding cuts in higher education will probably shrink the already limited number of available tenured professorships.

SALARY STATISTICS

Entomologists entering the field with bachelor's degrees can expect to earn around $24,000 per year as pest control or biological technicians. Entry-level entomologists in the federal government holding bachelor's degrees can expect to earn around $24,900. The average salary for an entomologist working for the federal government was $62,200 in 1997. The average starting salary for an agribusiness professor is $35,092. The average salary for a tenured professor at a public institution is $60,909, while part-time instructors earn about $27,000.

SOURCES OF FURTHER INFORMATION

Entomological Society of America
9301 Annapolis Road
Lanham, MD 20706

American Institute of Biological Sciences
1444 I St. NW
Suite 200
Washington, DC 20005
Internet address: www.aibs.org

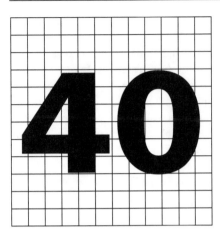

ANIMAL SCIENTIST

Animal scientists strive to develop healthier and more efficient ways of producing and processing meat, poultry, eggs, and milk. They are concerned with the breeding and production of domesticated livestock. Their primary goal is to produce livestock that is profitable and that is safe for human consumption. Animal scientists are also concerned with the humane living conditions of animals. Those who are employed as production managers study animal housing structures for safety and efficiency, monitor sanitary conditions for the presence of parasites and disease, prepare production reports, and find ways to make production more time- and cost-effective.

Other animal scientists conduct research to improve the breeds, diet, care, and environment of livestock. In reaction to negative reports of animal treatment and pressure from animal rights groups, animal scientists have increasingly been researching ways to improve animal living conditions. Scientists studying livestock behavior have found that animals that are treated better are the best meat producers and are much less susceptible to disease. Breeding pens, milking stations, feed quality, and housing conditions are being improved to give livestock more space and better food. Breeding methods that produce genetically superior animals are also being developed. Larger cows producing more milk, sheep with thicker wool coats, and larger chickens are some of the advances already made. Animal scientists are now breeding steer and pigs that have smaller percentages of body fat, supplying consumers with leaner and healthier meats.

RELATED PROFESSIONS

Animal Breeder
Animal Trainer
Dairy Scientist
Poultry Scientist
Zookeeper
Zoologist
Veterinarian
Range Manager

EDUCATIONAL REQUIREMENTS

The minimum educational requirement for an animal scientist is a bachelor of science degree. Animal scientists working as managers and technicians in the livestock industry most often have bachelor's degrees. Those interested in research and teaching should hold master's or Ph.D. degrees. Most animal scientists have degrees in animal science, animal husbandry, poultry science, dairy science, or agribusiness. More than one hundred colleges and universities in the United States offer degrees in these areas. Each state supports a public land grant university that has an animal science or related major.

Students interested in animal science should have strong science backgrounds. Most colleges offering degrees in animal science offer a core of science classes, including chemistry, biology, physiology, anatomy, genetics, and physics. Specific courses in animal science include animal behavior, reproductive physiology, food science, molecular biology, animal management, and animal morphology.

Most students are required to do fieldwork on college farms where they learn about the daily operations of a livestock farm. Students should also find summer employment with private ranchers, dairy farmers, stockyards, or feedlots. There are also a number of internship opportunities with the U.S. Department of Agriculture and state agricultural agencies. See Chapter 2 for a full description of these agencies.

PROFESSIONAL CERTIFICATION

There is no special certification or licensing for this occupation.

SETTINGS

Animal scientists work in laboratories, stockyards, feedlots, offices, and research stations around the country. Most work settings are production oriented, so the atmosphere is often fast paced and geared toward shipping deadlines. Because this type of work is hands-on, animal scientists should be in good physical condition and enjoy working outdoors with animals. The majority of animal scientists work in rural settings where most livestock operations are located. Some who work in research facilities or private laboratories find themselves in urban areas, but this situation is much less common.

EMPLOYMENT STATISTICS AND MAJOR EMPLOYERS

The U.S. Department of Labor estimates that in 1996 agricultural scientists held about twenty-four thousand jobs in the United States. Several thousand of these workers were animal scientists. A number of animal scientists teach and conduct research at colleges and universities. In addition, animal scientists work in all levels of government as extension agents or consultants advising agricultural producers on a variety of production and animal care issues.

In the private sector, animal scientists are employed by companies in a variety of industries, including livestock producers, livestock transport firms, packing companies, animal feed companies, pharmaceutical companies, veterinary suppliers, farm equipment firms, and food product companies. Animal scientists work as laboratory scientists and technicians, sales and service representatives, managers, marketers, and consultants.

Animal scientists working in government hold jobs at the U.S. Department of Agriculture as agricultural and meat inspectors and at state agricultural agencies as extension workers and agricultural agents. They also conduct research and monitor sanitation and health conditions at the Food and Drug Administration, U.S. Public Health Service, Consumer Product Safety Commission, and National Institutes of Health. State universities hire researchers and community education professionals to work at agricultural research stations and in farming communities.

The job outlook for animal scientists, particularly those with advanced degrees, is expected to be very good up to the year 2005. The role of biotechnology in animal growth and production will require more specially trained animal scientists in the coming years. Job openings will exceed the number of qualified applicants because enrollment in agricultural science curricula has dropped considerably during the past few years. Job growth in government will be slower due to budget constraints, but ample opportunities exist due to yearly employee turnover.

SALARY STATISTICS

According to the National Association of Colleges and Employers, beginning salary offers in 1997 for graduates with bachelor's degrees in animal science averaged $24,900 per year. Animal scientists in the federal government earned an average annual salary of about $65,500. According to the American Association of University Professors, the average starting salary for agribusiness professors is around $35,092. The average salary for tenured professors at a public institution is $60,909, while part-time instructors earn about $27,000. The average salary for a federal employee working as an animal scientist is around $50,000. See Chapter 2 for a complete description of federal salaries and benefits.

SOURCES OF FURTHER INFORMATION

American Farm Bureau Federation
225 Touhy Ave.
Park Ridge, IL 60068
Internet address: www.fb.com

American Society of Animal Science
1111 N. Dunlap Ave.
Savoy, IL 61874
Internet address: www.asas.org

Food and Agriculture Careers for Tomorrow
Purdue University
1140 Agricultural Administration Building
West Lafayette, IN 47907-1140

Institute of Food Technologists
221 North LaSalle St.
Suite 300
Chicago, IL 60601

Also consult the following publications:

Opportunities in Agriculture (1988), by William C. White and Donald N.
Collins, published by VGM Career Horizons, NTC/Contemporary
Publishing Group.

Opportunities in Biological Science Careers (1990), by C. A. Winger,
published by VGM Career Horizons, NTC/Contemporary Publishing
Group.

VETERINARIAN

Veterinarians, or doctors of veterinary medicine (D.V.M.), are responsible for maintaining the health of the millions of animals kept as pets and livestock in the United States as well as those animals in zoos and sporting and research facilities. They inoculate animals, perform surgery, treat diseased and injured animals with medications, and give advice on care and breeding. They perform research and look for ways to cure animal diseases. Veterinarians work wherever there is an animal population. Some of the more common places are rural areas where veterinarians care for farm animals, cities and suburbs where domestic pets need medical attention, government agencies that oversee public health issues, and the biomedical research industry.

Because there are thousands of species of domesticated animals and many types of medical procedures, veterinarians must choose between several areas of specialization. Veterinarians most often select one of two general areas of animal medicine, which can most easily be distinguished by the size of the animals treated. More than one-half of all veterinarians treat small animals, such as cats, dogs, hamsters, birds, snakes, rabbits, and other common household pets. Many of these professionals also specialize further, treating mainly canine and feline species. In most communities in the country one can find a local veterinarian to treat a favorite pet. Another 10 percent of veterinarians concentrate on large animals, which include farm livestock such as horses, cows, cattle, pigs, sheep, and goats. These doctors maintain the health of herds and other livestock by providing vaccinations against disease, performing surgery, performing birthing and impregnation techniques such as artificial insemination and embryo transplants, and monitoring sanitation, health, and feeding conditions. Other veterinarians have more narrow specializations, such as in anesthesiology, radiology, pathology, neurology, microbiology, or cardiology. Some serve as laboratory researchers, using animals to search for ways to control illness and disease in both humans and animals.

RELATED PROFESSIONS

Veterinary Technician   Toxicologist
Laboratory Animal Technician   Veterinary Meat Inspector
Livestock Inspector   Poultry Veterinarian
Bacteriologist

EDUCATIONAL REQUIREMENTS

In order to become a veterinarian, a student must complete the requirements for
the degree of doctor of veterinary medicine (D.V.M. or V.M.D.). To receive this
degree, a candidate need first complete a four-year bachelor's degree that includes
preparatory courses to qualify the student for a four-year veterinary school. Some
colleges offer preveterinary degrees, while others offer undergraduate majors
such as animal science, biology, health science, and agricultural science, which
prepare students for veterinary school. Students should have very strong backgrounds in math and science and take courses such as algebra, calculus, statistics, chemistry, biology, and animal anatomy. Students should also take as many
courses as possible that offer laboratory training.

Presently, twenty-seven colleges in twenty-six states offer doctor of veterinary
medicine degrees. These schools are highly competitive and scattered throughout
the nation. During the first two years of veterinary school, students are required
to take the basic animal medicine courses, like anatomy, immunology, microbiology, pathology, biochemistry, and pharmacology. Third- and fourth-year students
receive applied medical training in courses such as animal surgery, radiation biology, pathology, and applied anatomy. Veterinarians, unlike physicians, are not normally required to complete two-year medical internships before beginning
practice, although some states may require it.

PROFESSIONAL CERTIFICATION

In addition to having a medical degree, all veterinarians must have a license to
engage in private practice. Students who have completed all the scholastic requirements for the doctor of veterinary medicine degree must then pass state and
national licensing examinations in order to practice. These exams are both written and oral. Some states will issue a license to a veterinarian already certified in
another state. Federal and state agencies that hire veterinarians may also require
applicants to pass an examination. Check with the federal government, state, or
state agency on specific licensing requirements.

The American Veterinary Medical Association (AVMA), listed at the end of
this chapter, is the major professional society that certifies all twenty-seven university veterinary programs and works with federal and state agencies to ensure
standard licensing procedures. The AVMA also supports student chapters throughout the country.

SETTINGS

Most veterinarians are small animal specialists who work in their own private practices or at animal clinics or hospitals. These are usually pleasant and comfortable facilities. Veterinarians are scattered throughout the country in urban, suburban, and rural settings, although rural veterinarians tend to have general practices. Many veterinarians return to their hometowns to practice. They also work long hours, often well over forty hours per week, because they are often on call day and night. The working conditions for those going into research are similar to those of private practitioners, although research veterinarians tend to work fewer hours.

Large animal veterinarians most often work in rural areas near farms and other agricultural centers. Their work occurs mostly outside or in unheated barns and stables. Large animal veterinarians also must own their own trucks or other heavy-duty vehicles because they haul medical equipment and animals. These veterinarians work long hours, averaging more than fifty hours per week, and are exposed to possible injuries from large animals, diseases, and hazardous substances.

EMPLOYMENT STATISTICS AND MAJOR EMPLOYERS

About fifty-eight thousand veterinarians were employed in the United States in 1996. Of these professionals, more than 80 percent were in private practice as either large or small animal specialists. About two thousand veterinarians worked for the federal government, chiefly in the U.S. Department of Agriculture. About five hundred military veterinarians worked for the U.S. Army and U.S. Air Force, and several hundred more were employed with state governments during this same time period. Others involved in applied research work for pharmaceutical companies, medical research laboratories, food manufacturers, public health agencies, and international health agencies. A small number are employed as professors at colleges and universities around the country.

The employment outlook for veterinarians is generally quite good. While there has been a large increase in the number of students enrolling in veterinary schools, there has also been a corresponding increase in the demand for animal health care. Thus, the supply of veterinarians is currently in stride with demand. The employment outlook for veterinarians specializing in animal research is even better. The trend in the agricultural sciences toward high technology and biomedical research has put laboratory research specialists in high demand. Those with advanced academic degrees and postgraduate research experience have the brightest job prospects.

SALARY STATISTICS

Veterinarians spend a substantial amount of money on veterinary school, but unlike their physician counterparts, they rarely earn in the six-figure range. According to the American Veterinary Medical Association, entry-level veterinarians entering a private practice earned about $29,000 per year. Those with established practices may earn from $40,000 to $75,000 per year, depending on the kind of practice and whether it focuses on large or small animal care. In the federal government, veterinarians start at around $35,800. According to the American Association of University Professors, the average salary for an assistant professor in the health sciences is around $46,149, and for a full professor it is $73,058.

SOURCES OF FURTHER INFORMATION

Association of American Veterinary Medical Colleges
1101 Vermont Ave. NW
Washington, DC 20005
Internet address: www.aavmc.org

American Veterinary Medical Association
1931 North Meacham Road
Schaumburg, IL 60173-4360
Internet address: www.avma.org

Also consult *Opportunities in Veterinary Medicine Careers* (1993), by Robert E. Swope V.M.D., published by VGM Career Horizons, NTC/Contemporary Publishing Group.

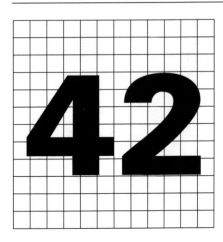

VETERINARIAN TECHNICIAN

including
Animal Health Technician
Laboratory Animal Technologist

Veterinarian technicians, also known as animal health technicians, do everything that a veterinarian does except diagnose ailments, prescribe medication, and perform surgery. They keep records, take specimens, perform laboratory tests, prepare animals and instruments for surgery, take and develop radiographs, dress wounds, and assist veterinarians with examinations and surgery. They may also manage a hospital's drug dispensary and in smaller hospitals conduct routine office work such as making appointments and greeting pet and livestock owners. Veterinarian technicians work primarily in animal hospitals or for farms, breeding kennels, pharmaceutical companies, and zoos. These workers should not be confused with animal caretakers, who only do routine activities such as feeding animals and cleaning cages.

Veterinarian technicians also work in laboratories conducting research, where they are known as laboratory animal technologists or laboratory animal technicians. Animal research is conducted to improve livestock output, study disease and infections, improve animal health, perfect new surgical procedures, and test drugs for human use. With the proliferation of the animal rights movement, there has been serious scrutiny of the use of animals in many medical testing procedures. Thus, the work of laboratory animal technicians has become more important because now they more closely supervise the daily care and maintenance of animals, and they also may assist in surgical care and conduct other health maintenance procedures.

RELATED OCCUPATIONS

Veterinarian	Poultry Veterinarian
Gamekeeper	Poultry Breeder
Livestock Inspector	Artificial Breeding Technician
Zookeeper	Zoo Veterinarian

EDUCATIONAL REQUIREMENTS

A career as a veterinarian technician or a laboratory animal technician requires completion of a two-year degree program from a community or technical college in veterinary technology. According to the American Veterinary Medical Association (AVMA), there are seventy associate programs and five bachelor degree programs certified by the AVMA. Laboratory animal technologists must possess four-year degrees in the life sciences.

Students should have strong high school science backgrounds. Typical first-year general college courses include chemistry, math, biology, anatomy, humanities, and communication. Specific second-year courses approved by the AVMA may include animal pharmacology, veterinary physiology, animal care and management, radiography, anesthetic nursing and monitoring, and animal husbandry. Students also receive training in clinical practice with live animals at the school and field experience working in a veterinary practice or other animal health care facility.

SPECIAL CERTIFICATION

In about forty states, veterinary technicians are licensed, registered, or certified. Licensure requirements in most states include graduation from an AVMA-accredited animal technology program, successful completion of a state certification examination, and at least one year of full-time work experience. Contact the American Veterinary Medical Association, listed at the end of this chapter, for more information on testing procedures and requirements.

Laboratory animal technologists and technicians may receive voluntary certification from the American Association for Laboratory Animal Science (AALS). Laboratory animal technologists must have six years of training, four of which may be college-level courses in the life sciences, and at least two years of laboratory experience. Laboratory animal technicians must have three years of laboratory experience. They may substitute two years of education in college-level life sciences for two years of lab experience. Contact the AALS for more information on the requirements for certification.

SETTINGS

The first job for about 85 percent of veterinary technicians is in private practice, with companion animal practice leading the list. Veterinary technicians work primarily in veterinary offices or animal care facilities throughout the nation. These facilities are much like hospitals: They are clean and comfortable and have waiting rooms, reception rooms, treatment rooms, examination rooms, surgery rooms, and pharmacies. Working conditions are sometimes noisy, and all veterinary personnel run the risk of being bitten and kicked by nervous animals. Most veterinarians and veterinary technicians work regular forty-hour weeks, but some offices are on call twenty-four hours a day or offer home visitation services, which make working hours more irregular. Those working in rural areas may work at small offices and in mobile care services that take them frequently to farms and other livestock facilities.

Laboratory animal technologists and technicians also work in clean and well-maintained research facilities. They work regular forty-hour weeks and are rarely required to conduct field research. Laboratory facilities are located throughout the nation but tend to be clustered in agricultural regions such as the South and Midwest.

EMPLOYMENT STATISTICS AND MAJOR EMPLOYERS

According to the U.S. Department of Labor, employment for veterinary technicians and laboratory animal technologists and technicians is expected to grow much faster than the average for all occupations through the year 2005 as the population and economy expand. The number of domestic dogs and cats has increased significantly during the last ten years, and more veterinarians and technicians are needed to care for these pets. Also, as concern for animal welfare increases, so will the need for certified personnel in laboratories.

The vast majority of veterinary technicians work in the private animal medical industry, but some work for federal and state agricultural agencies and at college and university research facilities. This distribution is also similar for laboratory animal technicians and technologists, except slightly more of them work in government and university research facilities.

SALARY STATISTICS

According to the Bureau of Labor Statistics, veterinary technicians earned an average of $19,300 in 1997. In some states, such as California and New York, veterinary technicians earned $26,000 or more. Starting salaries for laboratory animal technologists with four-year college degrees are typically higher. Benefit packages, such as health insurance, sick and vacation days, and retirement programs, vary widely, but larger employers are usually able to provide more generous benefits. Technicians and technologists working for government or universities can expect similar starting salaries but higher average salaries after a few years of experience.

SOURCES OF FURTHER INFORMATION

American Veterinary Medical Association
1931 North Meacham Road
Schaumburg, IL 60173-4360
Internet address: www.avma.org
The society distributes free of charge *Your Career in Veterinary Technology,* which gives detailed education and job descriptions for aspiring veterinary technicians. They also publish *Programs for Educating Veterinary Technicians,* a list of institutions

offering AVMA-accredited programs in veterinary technology; to receive this list, send a self-addressed, stamped envelope.

North American Veterinary Technician Association
P.O. Box 224
Battle Ground, IN 47920
Internet address: www.amva.org/navta

Also consult *Opportunities in Animal and Pet Care* (1993), by Mary Price Lee and Richard S. Lee, published by VGM Career Horizons, NTC/Contemporary Publishing Group.

Part Seven
Waste Management and Environmental Assessment

OVERVIEW

**Total Employment
500,000**

Employment Breakdown by Job Sector

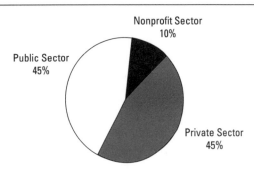

Public Sector
45%

Nonprofit Sector
10%

Private Sector
45%

Projected Growth

Employment is expected to increase faster than the average for all occupations through the year 2006. Growth is expected to be exceptionally strong due to the number of hazardous waste sites, the need to reduce solid waste, the complexity of environmental remediation programs, and federal, state, and local regulations.

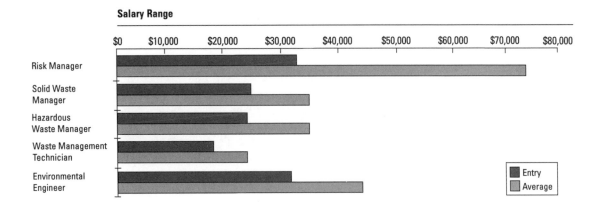

Salary Range

	$0	$10,000	$20,000	$30,000	$40,000	$50,000	$60,000	$70,000	$80,000

Risk Manager

Solid Waste
Manager

Hazardous
Waste Manager

Waste Management
Technician

Environmental
Engineer

■ Entry
□ Average

HISTORY OF WASTE MANAGEMENT AND SITE ASSESSMENT

When people think of waste, they generally conjure images of large manufacturing and chemical companies spewing thick, black smoke and producing dangerous solid chemicals. While industry is the largest producer of hazardous waste, churning out nearly 400 million tons per year, the average citizen also produces a fair share of refuse. The typical U.S. family produces an astounding 6,500 pounds of garbage each year, and a portion of this is considered hazardous waste. Not only do we discard such common solid waste as paper, plastics, and biodegradable foodstuffs, but we also throw away dangerous materials, including paints, chemicals, and medicines. The amount of waste we produce has increased rapidly during the last thirty years—from 2.7 pounds of trash per person to almost 4 pounds daily.

While industrial output and consumption have risen steadily during the past several decades, the nation's ability to dispose of the by-products of economic growth has fallen dramatically. Of the 18,000 landfills operating in 1976, more than one-half had closed by 1990; at the present rate only 1,800 will be in operation by the year 2010. Garbage from the City of New York is being shipped as far as Illinois, while hazardous waste produced in North Carolina is being shipped to poor nations around the globe, where safe disposal methods are likely to be ignored. The waste crisis is also manifest in the careless and often illegal dumping of waste across the nation.

Up until 1976, there were only loose guidelines for the disposal of hazardous waste. The oozing of chemicals into the homes of Love Canal, New York, awakened the nation to the reckless discarding of very dangerous chemicals and compounds. Since 1980, the EPA has tracked potential hazardous waste sites to include on its Superfund priority list, and to date more than fifty thousand locations are under consideration. We are finally becoming aware of the fact that our industrial society has caused serious damage to the environment. Those employed in waste management and environmental assessment are now tackling these and many other pressing problems.

PROJECTED TRENDS AND EMPLOYMENT GROWTH

Both the solid and hazardous waste management fields are expected to experience higher than average employment growth well into the next decade. According to the Environmental Careers Organization, employment growth in solid waste management is expected to average 13 percent per year, while growth in hazardous waste management will be around 18 percent for the next several years. Likewise, the demand for environmental engineers is expected to grow faster than average. Much of the growth in this field is tied to the reduction of solid waste, the cleanup of hazardous waste sites, and the large number of oversight regulations recently mandated by federal, state, and local governments.

Of the many concerns and issues that affect employment trends in the waste management and environmental fields, here are some of the most pressing:

- **The solid waste disposal crisis.** Currently there is a shortage of industrial and municipal landfills and incinerators. Of the 18,000 facilities operating in 1976, only about 6,000 are still open today. Finding locations for landfills and incinerators is a long and difficult process due to stringent environmental regulation and the intensity of public opposition to most site proposals.

- **Landfill technology and operations.** New technologies are required to ensure that the solid waste that is buried or burned does not result in additional pollution. For example, new methods to prevent the leaching of landfill contaminants into groundwater supplies and to prevent toxic ash emissions from waste incinerator plants need to be developed and applied.

- **Hazardous waste cleanup.** The number of hazardous waste sites has increased dramatically during the past few years. Currently fifty thousand sites are being considered for the EPA Superfund list. The cleanup of just a small number of these sites will require the work of tens of thousands of environmental scientists and technicians throughout the next several decades.

- **Military base closures.** The Base Realignment and Closure Act will result in the opening of tens of thousands of acres for public and private use. The federal government prevents transferring any part of a military base to the public until the land has been certified environmentally clean by at least one branch of the military and all appropriate federal, state, and local environmental regulatory agencies. More than $2.2 billion was committed to environmental cleanup and conversion in the late 1990s, and the cleanup of military bases also provides high-paying jobs for many hazardous waste professionals and technicians.

THE RISE OF THE ENVIRONMENTAL SITE ASSESSMENT AND REMEDIATION PROFESSION

Why Site Assessment?

In January 1970, the president signed the National Environmental Policy Act (NEPA). This legislation established a national policy of balancing human needs with the preservation of the environment. The main purpose of the legislation was "to declare a national policy which will encourage productive and enjoyable harmony between man *[sic]* and his *[sic]* environment; to promote efforts which will prevent or eliminate damage to the environment and biosphere and stimulate the health and welfare of man *[sic];* to enrich the understanding of the ecological systems and natural resources important to the Nation; and to establish a Council on Environmental Quality."

Title I of NEPA sets forth the national policy on the restoration and preservation of the environment. Under this program the federal government has the responsibility to minimize adverse environmental effects and preserve and enhance the environment by implementing appropriate public plans and policies. In addition, the various federal agencies must make a full and adequate analysis of all environmental effects of proposed programs or actions. Essentially, NEPA requires a systematic scientific study of any project that may have an adverse impact on the environment. These required reports are called *environmental impact assessments* (EIAs) or *environmental impact reports* (EIRs). Thousands of EIRs are compiled each year to conform with federal, state, and local land-use regulations.

The Process of Site Assessment and Remediation (Cleanup)

Site assessment and remediation is the process of assessing the environmental damage to a site, characterizing the environmental hazards, and cleaning up the site. Generally, site assessment and remediation is done in three phases, conveniently referred to as phases I, II, and III.

Phase I reports seek to identify any potential hazardous materials on the site. Generally, a Phase I environmental assessment will involve reviewing public records to describe the prior uses of the site. Reviewing public records may also include reviewing aerial photographs of the property and surrounding areas as well as mapping the known locations of nearby contaminated sites. During the Phase I assessment, the site is inspected for obvious signs of contamination, such as the presence of asbestos, oil drums, or chemical contaminants. Items that may be on a site are storage tanks, transformers (PCBs), asbestos, formaldehyde, radon, or known hazardous materials such as solvents or cleaning solutions. Off-site issues include the location of contaminated soils, wells, and groundwater, sensitive ecological areas, mining activities, or military operations.

During the site inspection, interviews with property owners, tenants, neighbors, and government officials are conducted in order to determine if hazardous materials were used on the site. The final step is to prepare a report that outlines the work performed as well as identifies any suspected hazardous material that warrants further study.

If the Phase I study indicates the presence of hazardous materials, a Phase II study is prepared. The most common Phase II study involves the collection of samples of soil and groundwater to determine if contamination exists from on-site or off-site sources. Another common Phase II study is a detailed asbestos study.

After the Phase II study is complete, the final step (Phase III) is the actual remediation. Remediation technologies for water include chemical treatment of contaminated water, removing water, carbon absorption, and bioremediation. Soil remediation technologies include thermal destruction/incineration, chemical treatment of soil, vacuum/vapor extraction, solvent/chemical extraction, and soil flushing/washing. Asbestos abatement generally involves removing the material. Site assessment and remediation work requires both skilled professionals who are able to recognize hazardous materials and technicians who can collect samples and analyze the samples for the presence of hazardous substances.

The Rise of an Industry

Most EIRs are prepared by environmental engineering and consulting firms, real estate consulting firms, firms that specialize in planning, and various government agencies. Major federal government employers include the departments of Defense, Transportation, and Energy and the Environmental Protection Agency. The majority of remediation work is carried out by environmental and engineering firms. A few of the larger environmental consulting firms are ICF Kaiser Engineers with 2,100 employees, Bechtel Corporation with 820 employees, and Emcon with 990 employees.

During the past twenty years, this industry has experienced rapid growth. According to the *Environmental Business Journal,* approximately 60,000 firms compete in the environmental protection field. In the 1990s, this industry had revenues of between $180 billion and $250 billion. The annual growth rate for all environmental protection industries ranges from 5 percent to 35 percent. Clearly this is one of the strongest and fastest-growing sectors of the U.S. economy, with high-paying and stable jobs for a range of environmental science professionals and technicians. In addition to those professionals covered in the following chapters, chemists, geologists, geographers, planners, biologists, science technicians, and many others are represented in this emerging field.

SOURCES OF FURTHER INFORMATION

Air and Waste Management Association
One Gateway Center
Third floor
Pittsburgh, PA 15222
Internet address: www.awma.org

Keep America Beautiful, Inc.
1010 Washington Blvd.
Seventh floor
Stamford, CT 06901
This organization works to educate the public on litter prevention
and improved waste handling.

The Solid Waste Association of North America
P.O. Box 7219
Silver Spring, MD 20907-2719
Internet address: www.swana.org

Also consult *The Complete Guide to Environmental Careers in the 21st Century* (1993), by the Environmental Careers Organization, published by Island Press. Included are separate chapters on solid waste and hazardous waste management. This is an excellent companion to this book because it concentrates on the effects of federal regulations on the job market, gives tips for getting started in a career, and gives profiles and case studies of companies and employees.

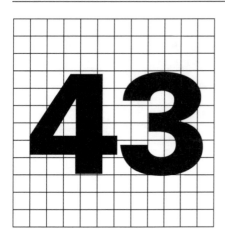

ENVIRONMENTAL RISK MANAGER/SITE ASSESSOR

Traditionally, risk management covered five areas: (1) damage to property, (2) loss of income, (3) injury to others, (4) fraud and criminal acts, and (5) death and injury to employees. The first task of a risk manager is to understand the business being assessed and identify possible risks. Risk managers are responsible for ensuring a safe workplace and that the business or organization maintains an acceptable level of risk exposure. The risk manager is also responsible for measuring and weighing risks from a cost standpoint. Risk control involves reducing the odds that any risk will become a reality. After accidents happen, the risk manager is responsible for reducing the damage. Risk management is a relatively complex field that involves a solid understanding of physics, chemistry, engineering, economics, finance, law, insurance, accounting, and environmental issues.

More and more environmental firms are hiring risk managers to oversee their environmental assessment and remediation operations. These professionals review all aspects of the reports and often determine the course of action of the remediation projects. In addition, companies are now focusing on the environmental effects of their products and manufacturing processes. Thus, risk management offers a unique career opportunity for those concerned with the environment who have strong business and science backgrounds.

RELATED PROFESSIONS

Planner	Chemical Engineer
Solid Waste Manager	Civil Engineer
Hazardous Waste Management Specialist	Environmental Engineer
Biochemist/Biologist	Safety Engineer
Chemist	Environmental Toxicologist
Hydrologist	Geologist

EDUCATIONAL REQUIREMENTS

More than eighty universities offer risk management majors. Risk managers must have a strong business backgrounds with an emphasis on management, finance, and insurance. Risk managers must also have a working knowledge of physics, chemistry, engineering, and hydrology. Some risk managers may receive undergraduate degrees in one of the traditional science or engineering fields and master's degrees in business or risk management. For those interested in preparing EIRs, fifteen colleges offer specific degree programs in environmental design that will help a student develop an understanding of the physical characteristics of a property. Several universities bring together faculty from different departments to form interdisciplinary environmental science programs. The purpose of these programs is to integrate the teachings of various disciplines and present the student with a more complete understanding of environmental issues. Interdisciplinary programs are probably best for those interested in environmental assessment and remediation work and for students with biological or physical science backgrounds.

PROFESSIONAL CERTIFICATION

There are no special certification or licensing requirements for this profession.

SETTINGS

Risk managers are employed by oil and drug companies, in the communications industry, and, most recently, by environmental firms. These professionals most often work in offices, reviewing and writing reports and meeting with other professionals to discuss projects. Risk managers work all around the country but are clustered in urban areas where most manufacturing and government activities take place. The largest cluster of environmental engineering and consulting firms is in and around Washington, D.C. Risk managers work typical forty-hour weeks, but project deadlines and a considerable workload often force them to work more hours.

EMPLOYMENT STATISTICS AND MAJOR EMPLOYERS

Employment opportunities for risk managers are considered excellent. The need for risk managers will continue to increase as life and technology become more complex, companies and government strive to produce safer products and minimize public health risks, and the number of environmental cleanup projects continues to spiral upward. During the past ten years, the number of environmental impact statements and remediation projects has risen dramatically. Risk managers with strong backgrounds in the environmental sciences will be among the most actively recruited workers in environmental science. Because this is an emerging career, no reliable labor statistics are available.

SALARY STATISTICS

In 1997 the average salary for all risk managers was about $74,000. Salaries in the private sector range from about $30,000 to $260,000 or more. Risk manager salaries for jobs with the federal government with a GS-11 rating ranged from $37,744 to $49,066 in 1997.

SOURCES OF FURTHER INFORMATION

Risk and Insurance Management Society, Inc.
655 Third Ave.
New York, NY 10017
Internet address: www.rims.org

American Institute for Chartered Property Casualty Underwriters
    and the Insurance Institute of America
720 Providence Road
Malvern, PA 19355-0716
Internet address: www.aicpcu.org

Insurance Resource Council
718 Providence Road
P.O. Box 3025
Malvern, PA 19355-0725
Internet address: www.ircweb.org

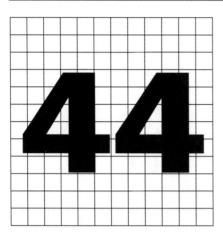

SOLID WASTE MANAGEMENT PROFESSIONAL

Solid waste professionals are responsible for overseeing the disposal of waste in ways that are environmentally sound as well as economically viable. They conduct studies on solid waste management and devise strategies for treating and containing waste. They may analyze the cost and effectiveness of various methods of disposing of solid waste. They make recommendations for ways of collecting, moving, storing, and disposing refuse. There are a variety of methods for dealing with waste problems, including reducing waste, composting, and recycling. Solid waste specialists also advise how to collect, transport, store, and destroy garbage. In addition, these professionals monitor and direct the cleanup of land, water, and air. In industry, solid waste specialists generally work in one of four areas: waste source reduction, recycling, clean waste combustion, and sanitary landfills. A growing number of solid waste professionals write environmental impact reports (EIRs) and work with the public to reduce the growing amount of residential and commercial waste.

RELATED PROFESSIONS

Environmental Assessor   Civil Engineer
Environmental Engineer   Hydrologist
Chemist   Health Inspector
Biologist   Risk Manager

EDUCATIONAL REQUIREMENTS

Currently few schools offer degrees in solid waste management; most professionals hold degrees in engineering, geology, chemistry, or related fields. High school students interested in becoming solid waste specialists should have strong math and science backgrounds, including such courses as calculus, chemistry, physics, and computer science. College courses should also be heavily oriented toward the physical sciences, including courses such as geomorphology, organic and inorganic chemistry, and physics.

Approximately 170 colleges and universities offer at least one formal credit course in solid and hazardous waste management, and 89 offer training courses for no credit. Four schools offer master's degrees in hazardous materials management: Tufts University, the New Jersey Institute of Technology, Wayne State University in Detroit, and the University of San Francisco. Hazardous waste management programs tend to be multidisciplinary and encompass such fields as civil environmental engineering, chemical engineering, public/allied health, biology, chemistry, forestry, geology, and environmental science. Most of these master's programs are offered through departments of engineering.

A growing number of universities and community colleges offer certification programs for professionals already in the field. The University of California at Berkeley, for example, offers certificate programs in environmental site assessment and remediation, hazardous materials management, integrated solid waste management, advanced environmental law and management, air quality management, and environmental health and safety auditing. Students enrolled in hazardous materials management must take courses on such topics as principles of hazardous materials management, environmental law and regulation, and health and environmental effects of hazardous materials. Elective classes include hazardous waste minimization and management, principles of toxicology, and air pollution control systems. A growing number of community colleges nationwide are also offering these programs.

PROFESSIONAL CERTIFICATION

There are no federal or state licensing requirements for solid waste specialists; however, many engineers must be certified. All fifty states and the District of Columbia require registration for engineers whose work affects life, health, or property or who offer their services to the public. The Accreditation Board for Engineering and Technology (ABET) offers the Professional Engineer (PE) license. Attainment of the license is based upon the acquisition of an engineering degree from an ABET-approved institution, successful completion of the Engineering-in-Training examination, four years of relevant work experience, and successful completion of a state examination. Licenses are generally transferable among states. Contact ABET, listed at the end of this chapter, for further information.

SETTINGS

With landfills and Superfund sites scattered across the nation, professionals can find jobs in both urban and rural areas in every state. Solid waste professionals may work in a variety of environments, including laboratories that are generally clean and comfortable, in offices primarily writing EIRs, and in the field conducting tests. They may also work in manufacturing plants and other production facilities in management, inspection, and control positions. Most of these professionals work eight hours a day, five days per week.

EMPLOYMENT STATISTICS AND MAJOR EMPLOYERS

Employment opportunities for solid waste professionals are divided evenly between the public and private sectors, with a relatively small percentage of people employed in the nonprofit sector. Within the public sector, local and state government agencies are the largest employers, and the federal government employs the fewest workers. Often, recycling programs and other innovative solid waste programs are initiated at the state level because the state has more resources than do local governments. Generally, local governments are responsible for collection and recycling programs. Currently, more than thirty states have recycling programs that deal with more than 23.5 million tons of material per year. In addition, there are approximately one thousand composting projects nationwide. As the number of recycling and compost projects increases, the demand for solid waste specialists increases.

While government agencies are responsible for solid waste management, much of the actual work is contracted out to private firms. The largest private employers are waste management companies and consulting firms. The National Solid Waste Management Association (NSWMA) estimates that approximately 75 percent of the nation's total waste is moved by private companies. The trend in the late 1990s was toward the consolidation of smaller companies, with fewer and fewer companies competing.

Nonprofit organizations employ relatively few people. Nonprofit groups include advocacy and lobbying groups, planners, scientists, and other professionals who work to solve problems related to solid waste management.

SALARY STATISTICS

Salaries in this field vary depending on the job, sector, years of experience, and education. The private sector generally pays the most, followed by the public and nonprofit sectors. Within the public sector, the federal government generally pays the most, followed by state and local agencies. The starting pay for solid waste specialists averages about $25,000 per year. With three to five years of experience, solid waste professionals generally earn between $35,000 and $40,000. Engineers and people with master's degrees can earn substantially more.

The average starting salary for an engineer with a bachelor's degree is expected to be around $32,000, master's degree holders earn an average starting salary of around $38,000, and professionals with doctoral degrees generally earn more than $50,000.

SOURCES OF FURTHER INFORMATION

Accreditation Board for Engineering and Technology
111 Market Place
Suite 1050
Baltimore, MD 21202-4012
Internet address: www.abet.org

The board publishes a list of accredited schools of engineering throughout the country.

Air and Waste Management Association
One Gateway Center
Third floor
Pittsburgh, PA 15222
Internet address: www.awma.org

Association of State and Territorial Solid Waste Management
    Officials (ASTSWMO)
444 North Capitol St. NW
Suite 315
Washington, DC 20001-1512
Internet address: www.astswmo.org

The Solid Waste Association of North America
P.O. Box 7219
Silver Spring, MD 20907-7219
Internet address: www.swana.org

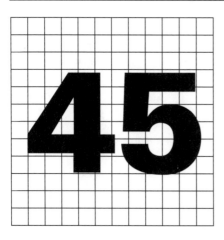

HAZARDOUS WASTE MANAGEMENT PROFESSIONAL

Dealing with the hazardous waste generated by military, industrial, medical, and other producers is a critically important job in the protection of the environment. Hazardous waste professionals conduct studies on hazardous waste problems and work to devise strategies for the treatment and containment of waste. Hazardous waste professionals analyze the cost and effectiveness of various methods of disposing of hazardous wastes. They make recommendations for various ways of collecting, moving, storing, and disposing of hazardous materials. A variety of methods is used to deal with hazardous waste, including reducing the waste, recycling, and treatment. Three promising areas of treatment include thermal treatment (incineration), which involves burning at high temperatures to destroy toxic materials; chemical treatment, which involves using a chemical process to reduce the hazard; and biological treatment, which employs microorganisms that consume the waste material. As landfill space becomes more limited and concerns about the safety of communities around these facilities arises, new approaches to hazardous waste management must be found. At present, the United States produces around 400 million tons of hazardous waste annually, much of which, by law, cannot be placed in landfills. Because of these immediate problems, hazardous waste management is one of the fastest-growing fields in the environmental sciences.

RELATED PROFESSIONS

Environmental Assessment
Environmental Engineer
Chemical Engineer
Chemist
Biologist
Risk Manager

Civil Engineer
Hydrologist
Geologist
Health Inspector
Solid Waste Specialist

EDUCATIONAL REQUIREMENTS

Currently few schools offer degrees in hazardous waste management; most professionals hold degrees in engineering, chemistry, geology, or related fields. High school students interested in becoming solid waste specialists should have strong backgrounds in math and science.

Approximately 170 colleges and universities offer at least one formal credit course in solid and hazardous waste management, while 89 schools offer training courses for no credit. Four schools offer master's degrees in hazardous materials management: Tufts University, the New Jersey Institute of Technology, Wayne State University in Detroit, and the University of San Francisco. Hazardous waste management programs tend to be multidisciplinary in nature, encompassing such fields as civil/environmental engineering, chemical engineering, public/allied health, biology, chemistry, forestry, geology, and environmental science. Most of these master's programs are offered through departments of engineering.

A growing number of universities and community colleges offer certification programs for professionals already employed or interested in the field. The University of California at Berkeley, for example, offers certificate programs in environmental site assessment and remediation, hazardous materials management, integrated solid waste management, advanced environmental law and management, air quality management, and environmental health and safety auditing. Students enrolled in hazardous materials management must take courses on such topics as principles of hazardous materials management, environmental law and regulation, and health and environmental effects of hazardous materials. Elective classes include hazardous waste minimization and management, principles of toxicology, and air pollution control systems. A growing number of community colleges also offer similar programs.

PROFESSIONAL CERTIFICATION

There are no federal or state licensing requirements for solid waste specialists; however, many engineers must be certified. All fifty states and the District of Columbia require registration for engineers whose work affects life, health, or property or who offer their services to the public. The Accreditation Board for Engineering and Technology (ABET) offers the Professional Engineer (PE) license. Attainment of the license is based upon the acquisition of an engineering degree from an ABET-approved institution, successful completion of the Engineering-in-Training examination, four years of relevant work experience, and successful completion of a state examination. Licenses are generally transferable among states. Contact ABET, listed at the end of this chapter, for further information.

SETTINGS

Professionals may work in laboratories that are clean and comfortable, in offices primarily writing reports and analyzing data, or in the field conducting experiments and monitoring disposal practices. Most professionals work eight hours a day, five days per week. In an emergency, such as a chemical spill, they may work overtime or on weekends. The materials with which these people work can be dangerous. Some emit toxic fumes; others burn skin and eyes; many are poisonous; some produce radiation or cause cancer. Few accidents occur because safety procedures are followed carefully.

EMPLOYMENT STATISTICS AND MAJOR EMPLOYERS

Most hazardous waste specialists work for the federal government. State and local governments also employ hazardous waste specialists. Within the federal government, the EPA is one of the largest employers. The EPA is in charge of overseeing the Superfund program and offers employment opportunities in every state. With thousands of hazardous waste disposal and cleanup sites across the United States, employment opportunities are available in urban, suburban, and rural areas in every state.

In the private sector, the largest employers are consulting firms that specialize in hazardous waste management. Consulting firms include planners, engineering firms, and companies that develop waste-processing equipment. Many of these companies prepare environmental impact reports (EIRs) and conduct the actual remediation work.

SALARY STATISTICS

Salaries in this field vary depending on the job, sector, years of experience, and education. The private sector generally pays the most, followed by the public and nonprofit sectors. Within the public sector, the federal government generally pays the most, followed by state and local agencies. The starting pay for hazardous waste specialists is about $24,000 per year. With three to five years of experience, specialists generally earn between $30,000 and $40,000. Engineers and people with master's degrees can earn substantially more.

The average starting salary for an engineer with a bachelor's degree is expected to be around $33,000, while the starting salary for master's degree holders is expected to be around $45,000, and for Ph.D. holders it is $50,000. Engineers with advanced degrees can expect to earn 10 percent to 15 percent more than entry-level bachelor-degree holders.

SOURCES OF FURTHER INFORMATION

Accreditation Board for Engineering and Technology
111 Market Place
Suite 1050
Baltimore, MD 21202-4012
Internet address: www.abet.org
The board publishes a list of accredited schools of engineering throughout the country.

Air and Waste Management Association
One Gateway Center
Third floor
Pittsburgh, PA 15222
Internet address: www.awma.org

The Solid Waste Association of North America
P.O. Box 7219
Silver Spring, MD 20907-7219
Internet address: www.swana.org

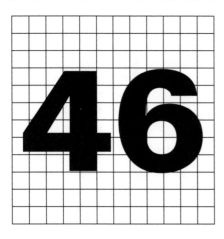

WASTE MANAGEMENT TECHNICIAN

including
Sanitary Landfill Operator
Hazardous Waste Technician

Waste management technicians help determine sources of hazardous waste and methods of removing hazardous waste from a property. Solid waste technicians are concerned with waste reduction, recycling, clean waste combustion, and sanitary landfills. Hazardous waste technicians primarily focus on the treatment and removal of hazardous materials. The demand for solid and hazardous waste technicians has grown substantially since 1976 when the Resource Conservation and Recovery Act (RCRA) was passed. This law stopped the open and uncontrolled dumping of solid waste and created strict guidelines for landfill disposal. Hazardous waste includes materials that corrode other materials, react strongly with water, are flammable or unstable with heat, or release toxic chemicals when mixed with mildly acidic solutions. Common hazardous materials are paint, batteries, medicine, and household cleaners. In 1991, RCRA established new requirements for the construction and operations of landfills. The new landfills must include liners and leachate collection systems, be covered, include wells to monitor the groundwater, and include ventilation systems. These new regulations have increased the demand for both solid and hazardous waste technicians. In addition, the ever-increasing piles of garbage, new innovative recycling programs, and increased amounts of hazardous materials ensure that these technicians will be in heavy demand for years to come.

Most solid waste technicians work as sanitary landfill operators, who construct landfills and operate these facilities, and as hazardous waste technicians, who remove harmful pollution from contaminated sites. Solid waste technicians are responsible for distributing wastes, compacting the materials from trucks, and covering the trash with soil. They drive earth-moving equipment including bulldozers and large steel-wheeled compactors. Sanitary landfill operators also inspect incoming trucks for hazardous waste.

Hazardous waste technicians provide information on how to collect, transport, handle, and dispose of dangerous materials. They are responsible for establishing procedures for preventing accidents and for cleaning contaminated sites.

RELATED OCCUPATIONS

Boiler Operator   Wastewater Treatment Technician
Gas-Compressor Operator   Chemical Plant Operator
Power Plant Operator   Petroleum Plant Operator
Chemical Technician   Biological Technician
Agricultural Pest Control Specialist   Soil Conservation Technician

EDUCATIONAL REQUIREMENTS

There are no minimum education requirements for a landfill operator. Because of the hands-on nature of the work, most operators are trained on the job. However, prospective employers look for some skills and knowledge, including mathematical and mechanical skills. According to the National Solid Waste Management Association (NSWMA), vocational and technical training can include specialized driver training for refuse collection trucks and mechanical training for a wide range of equipment—such as trucks, compactors, bulldozers, and balers—used in the collection, recycling, treatment, and disposal of material.

Only a few community colleges currently offer specific hazardous waste management programs, but the number of schools offering these degrees is expected to increase in the near future. Students are encouraged to call their local community colleges to find out if programs are available. Hazardous waste technicians should attend two-year community or technical colleges. Students can receive degrees or certificates in environment control, ecology, environmental sciences, and similar programs.

While in high school, students should take algebra; science classes including chemistry, biology, and physics; machine shop; blueprint reading; and English. Because of the increasing use of computers, technicians should have either taken high school computer courses or have an understanding of the operation of these machines. While enrolled in community colleges or technical schools, students should take radiation physics, mathematics, electricity and electronics, organic and inorganic chemistry, and blueprint reading.

SPECIAL CERTIFICATION

There are no federal or state licensing requirements for waste technicians.

SETTINGS

Landfills and hazardous waste sites are in every part of the country in both urban and rural areas. Landfill workers spend most of their day outdoors in all kinds of weather. They may work in rain and snow, but most drivers are protected from the elements. Sanitary landfill operators work forty or more hours a week. Because many landfills are open on Saturday, they may also be required to work on weekends.

Hazardous waste technicians usually assist hazardous waste professionals but generally spend more time out of doors than do their professional colleagues. Technicians also work in laboratories that are generally clean and comfortable. Technicians typically work regular forty-hour weeks but may occasionally be required to work overtime. The materials with which these people work can be dangerous. Some emit toxic fumes; others burn skin and eyes; many are poisonous; and others produce radiation or cause cancer. Hazardous waste technicians wear protective clothing and devices to protect their eyes, lungs, and skin. As safety standards are strictly enforced, relatively few technicians are seriously injured.

EMPLOYMENT STATISTICS AND MAJOR EMPLOYERS

Solid and hazardous waste technicians held approximately one hundred thousand jobs in the late 1990s. According to NSWMA, approximately eight thousand municipalities and private trash haulers pick up our nation's garbage. In addition, there are approximately one thousand composting projects nationwide. As the number of recycling and compost projects increases, the demand for solid waste specialists will also increase. They are employed around the nation, primarily in larger towns and cities where the populations are greatest. Employment of solid and hazardous waste technicians is expected to grow faster than the average for all occupations through the year 2006. As Americans produce more garbage and hazardous waste, the demand for technicians is expected to increase. In addition, the environment cleanup projects that will be conducted on former military bases and Superfund sites will increase the demand for solid and hazardous waste technicians.

While local governments are responsible for solid waste management, much of the actual work is contracted out to private firms. The largest private-sector firms are waste management companies and environmental engineering firms. These firms hire the majority of hazardous waste technicians.

SALARY STATISTICS

In the late 1990s, annual salaries for solid waste technicians averaged about $24,000, compared to around $30,000 for hazardous waste technicians. Entry-level hazardous waste technicians earn between $18,000 and $24,000. The salaries for hazardous waste technicians increase to between $30,000 and $35,000 after three to five years of employment. Given the relatively low educational requirements, salaries for these technicians are high compared to those of most other science technicians. Fringe benefits can be generous because many of these technicians are city or municipal employees. They usually receive generous health plans, sick time, and vacation time.

SOURCES OF FURTHER INFORMATION

The Solid Waste Association of North America
P.O. Box 7219
Silver Spring, MD 20907-7219
Internet address: swana.org

Air and Waste Management Association
One Gateway Center
Third floor
Pittsburgh, PA 15222
Internet address: www.awma.org

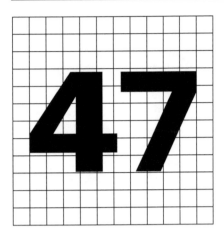

ENVIRONMENTAL ENGINEER

The career usually known as environmental engineering encompasses a very broad category of jobs. The majority of people called *environmental engineers*, however, are scientists and engineers. Environmental engineers use their training in both the physical (mechanical) and biological (ecological) sciences to solve complex problems. These engineers use their expertise to solve environmental problems in such diverse areas as design and planning, manufacturing, product development, computer programming, research and development, public policy, and management. Their major areas of work are air pollution control, industrial hygiene, radiation protection, hazardous waste management, toxic materials control, wastewater disposal, solid waste disposal, environmental remediation, and land management.

Environmental engineers design and build wastewater treatment facilities, monitor treatment processing, devise strategies to deliver water during droughts, and work internationally building sanitation facilities in impoverished countries and refugee camps. They design and build treatment processes to control air pollution, work with industries to comply with air pollution laws, and use computer simulations to help solve metropolitan air pollution problems. These engineers also work with government agencies responsible for maintaining clean air and water standards. Environmental engineering is one of the fastest-growing subfields in the engineering sciences, and a large number of these engineers are being called upon to help solve some of the nation's most pressing environmental problems.

Environmental engineers often use computers to solve mathematical equations to determine how a structure or system operates. They also use computer-aided design systems (CAD) to produce and analyze designs.

RELATED PROFESSIONS

Biologist
Waste Manager
Civil Engineer

Biochemist
Agricultural Engineer
Petroleum Engineer

Geotechnical Engineer	Sanitary Engineer
Hydrologist	Air Quality Engineer
Chemical Engineer	Radioactive Waste Engineer
Risk Manager	Toxicologist
Hydrologist	

EDUCATIONAL REQUIREMENTS

The minimum requirement for a career in environmental engineering is a bachelor of science (B.S.) degree in environmental engineering, civil engineering, or a related engineering field. Presently more than 320 schools offer engineering degree programs that are accredited by the Accreditation Board for Engineering and Technology (ABET). A large number of these institutions offer a specialty degree in civil engineering, and more than twenty-five schools offer specific degrees in environmental engineering. In addition, five universities offer graduate degrees in environmental engineering. High school students interested in becoming environmental engineers should take mathematics, chemistry, physics, computer sciences, and English.

In a typical four-year curriculum, students spend the first two years studying the basics, such as mathematics, physics, chemistry, introduction to engineering, English, the social sciences, and humanities. During the last two years, students take courses in the environmental engineering concentration. Some schools offer a general engineering curriculum in which students are not able to choose a concentration until reaching graduate school. In addition, some institutions offer five-year master's degree programs.

Graduate training is essential for engineering faculty positions but is not required for the majority of entry-level engineering positions. Many engineers do obtain master's degrees to learn new technologies, to broaden their education, or to enhance promotion opportunities. Many engineers are obtaining M.B.A. degrees to advance to management and sales positions.

PROFESSIONAL CERTIFICATION

All fifty states and the District of Columbia require registration for engineers whose work affects life, health, or property or who offer their services to the public. ABET offers the Professional Engineer (PE) license. Attainment of the license is based upon the acquisition of a engineering degree from an ABET-approved institution, successful completion of the Engineering-in-Training examination, four years of relevant work experience, and successful completion of a state examination. Licenses are generally transferable among states. Contact ABET, listed at the end of this chapter, for further information.

The American Academy of Environmental Engineers (AAEE) has established the designation Diplomat Environmental Engineer (DEE) to establish criteria for those who have excelled in environmental engineering. A number of criteria must be met before taking a qualifying examination. All candidates must possess AAEE-recognized bachelor's degrees in engineering or a closely related field; candidates must already hold a valid PE license; they must have eight years of experience prior to taking the acceptance exam; and they must be of high moral character. Applicants must then take an examination that concentrates on one of the following eight areas: air pollution, water supply and wastewater, general environmental engineering, solid waste management, hazardous waste management, industrial hygiene, radiation protection, or sanitary engineering. Contact the AAEE, listed at the end of this chapter, for further information.

SETTINGS

While members of many branches of engineering spend all or most of their time indoors working in laboratories, industrial plants, or offices, environmental engineers often spend a good amount of time outdoors at construction or work sites. However, a good number of environmental engineers work almost exclusively in offices. Many engineers work standard forty-hour weeks, but at times deadlines or design standards may bring extra pressure to the job. When this happens, engineers may be required to work long hours and sometimes experience considerable job stress.

EMPLOYMENT STATISTICS AND MAJOR EMPLOYERS

In 1996, of the more than 1.3 million engineers employed in the United States 196,000 were civil engineers. There has been a steady drop in the number of engineers graduating from colleges and universities during the past decade. According to the U.S. Department of Labor, employment opportunities in all branches of engineering are expected to be good through the year 2006 because employment is expected to increase faster than the average for all occupations, while the number of degrees granted in engineering is not expected to increase much above present levels. In addition, opportunities for environmental engineers are expected to remain strong for several decades, given the number and complexity of the environmental issues facing the world today.

Approximately 40 percent of environmental engineers work for federal, state, and local government agencies. In the federal government, environmental engineers work for the departments of Transportation, Defense, the Interior, and Energy and in the National Aeronautics and Space Administration. In state and local government agencies, many engineers are employed in departments of water resources and transportation.

In private industry, environmental engineers work for engineering firms specializing in environmental issues. Many federal agencies contract out much of their actual work to engineering consulting firms in and around Washington, D.C., and around the country. Environmental engineers work in every large and medium-sized urban area, and in many rural communities around the nation. In addition, many engineers teach and conduct research at colleges and universities around the nation.

SALARY STATISTICS

According to the American Academy of Environmental Engineers, in the late 1990s the average starting salary for an environmental engineer with a bachelor's degree was between $30,000 and $34,000, while the starting salary for master's degree holders was between $32,000 and $36,000, and for Ph.D. holders it was between $36,000 and $45,000. A typical environmental engineer with a bachelor's degree can expect to earn $40,000 to $45,000 annually after five years in the field. Like most engineering disciplines, the salary versus time curve for environmental engineers is characterized by rapid, significant increases early in the career.

In academia, assistant engineering professors earn an average salary of $45,753. Associate professors have an average income of $52,896, while full professors earn $77,721 per year. Part-time engineering instructors earn an average of $27,000 per year.

SOURCES OF FURTHER INFORMATION

Accreditation Board for Engineering and Technology, Inc.
111 Market Place
Suite 1050
Baltimore, MD 21202-4012
Internet address: www.abet.org

American Academy of Environmental Engineers
130 Holiday Court
Suite 100
Annapolis, MD 21401
Internet address: www.aaee.org

American Society of Civil Engineers
1801 Alexander Bell Drive
Reston, VA 20191-4400
Internet address: www.asce.org

Junior Engineering Technical Society
JETS—Guidance Project
1420 King St.
Suite 405
Alexandria, VA 22314-2794
Internet address: www.asee.org/jets
The society describes careers for many different engineering concentrations. For further information on a certain area of engineering or a list of accredited programs, send a stamped, self-addressed envelope to JETS.

National Society of Professional Engineers
Education Foundation
1420 King St.
Alexandria, VA 22314-2794
Internet address: www.nspe.org